MIGRATION AND NEW MEDIA

'An exemplary and groundbreaking study, with contributions to theory and our understanding of polymedia in everyday life, this stands out as an extraordinary read on the technology of relationships.' – Zizi Papacharissi, *University of Illinois-Chicago, USA*

'This fascinating, richly detailed book investigates the role that fluency across multiple digital platforms plays in enabling mothering and caring to be sustained at a distance. A genuine breakthrough.' – Nick Couldry, *Goldmiths, University of London, UK*

How do parents and children care for each other when they are separated because of migration? The way in which transnational families maintain long-distance relationships has been revolutionised by the emergence of new media such as email, instant messaging, social networking sites, webcam and texting. A migrant mother can now call and text her left-behind children several times a day, peruse social networking sites and leave the webcam on for 12 hours, achieving a sense of co-presence.

Drawing on a long-term ethnographic study of prolonged separation between migrant mothers and their children who remain in the Philippines, this book develops groundbreaking theory for understanding both new media and the nature of mediated relationships. It brings together the perspectives of both the mothers and children and shows how the very nature of family relationships is changing. New media, understood as an emerging environment of polymedia, have become integral to the way family relationships are enacted and experienced. The theory of polymedia extends beyond the poignant case study and is developed as a major contribution for understanding the interconnections between digital media and interpersonal relationships.

Mirca Madianou is Senior Lecturer in Media and Communication at the University of Leicester, UK. She is the author of *Mediating the Nation* and several articles on the social consequences of the media.

Daniel Miller is Professor of Material Culture at the Department of Anthropology, University College London, UK. His most recent books include *Tales from Facebook* and *Digital Anthropology* (edited with Heather Horst).

Anthropology/Media

MIGRATION AND NEW MEDIA

Transnational families and polymedia

Mirca Madianou and Daniel Miller

Routledge
Taylor & Francis Group

LONDON AND NEW YORK

First published 2012
by Routledge
2 Park Square, Milton Park, Abingdon, Oxon OX14 4RN

Simultaneously published in the USA and Canada
by Routledge
711 Third Avenue, New York, NY 10017

Routledge is an imprint of the Taylor & Francis Group, an informa business

British Library Cataloguing in Publication Data
A catalogue record for this book is available from the British Library

Library of Congress Cataloging in Publication Data
Madianou, Mirca.
Migration and new media : transnational families and polymedia / Mirca Madianou and
Daniel Miller.
    p. cm.
  Includes bibliographical references and index.
  1. Foreign workers, Philippine–Family relationships–Great Britain. 2. Women foreign
workers–Family relationships–Great Britain. 3. Children of foreign workers–Family
relationships–Philippines. 4. Communication in families–Philippines. 5. Interpersonal
communication–Technological innovations–Social aspects–Philippines. 6. Communication,
International–Technological innovations–Social aspects–Philippines. I. Miller, Daniel, 1954–
II. Title.
  HD8398.F55.M33 2011
  331.40941–dc23

                                                                                    2011022759

ISBN: 978–0–415–67928–2 (hbk)
ISBN: 978–0–415–67929–9 (pbk)
ISBN: 978–0–203–15423–6 (ebk)

Typeset in 10/12.5pt Bembo
by Graphicraft Limited, Hong Kong

CONTENTS

ACKNOWLEDGEMENTS

As is always sadly the case in ethnographic work, we cannot acknowledge any of our participants individually, since our whole project was based on a promise of anonymity. But it will be obvious from every page of this book how much we owe to them all. They have provided not merely the gift of time and information. When mothers gradually revealed their long history as migrants, often punctuated by considerable suffering including abuse, or poignantly conveyed the emotional traumas of their long-term separation from their children, and in turn these same children bared their souls with regard to their own feelings, we realised the privilege of any researcher who has been granted this intimacy and confidence. We hope this book goes some way to a deeper appreciation of those lives and their futures.

We can, however, happily acknowledge the assistance given to us by Cora Castle and all her staff at the Centre for Filipinos in London. The Centre proved very sympathetic to the aims of our research and allowed us to hang out as much as we liked with both the staff and those who came to use their facilities and advice, typically on Sunday mornings, the only free time many of the domestic workers were actually given. We are also very much obliged to Jonathan Corpus Ong for working as our research assistant and providing accommodation during our stay in Manila. We are grateful to Anna and Raul Pertierra, Dierdre McKay, and the anonymous readers provided by Routledge for comments on our draft texts. In Manila we enjoyed the hospitality of Raul Pertierra and conversations with many academics at the University of the Philippines, Ateneo de Manila and Miriam College, including Jun Aguilar, Maruja Asis, Oiye de Dios, Lourdes Gordolan, Lulu Ignacio and Emma Porio. The Department of Media and Communications at Ateneo also kindly organised a symposium for us to explain our project. We would like to acknowledge the help of Lidia Pola, who hosted Danny and allowed him to participate in her surveys of the use of new media by school children in a town south of Manila. We are deeply grateful to our respective spouses, John and Rickie, for their generous support and tolerance, especially of our absences during fieldwork both in the Philippines and later in Trinidad. Mirca would like to thank Alex Thompson for being a tremendous research assistant during the Philippine fieldwork at the age of 15–18 months. She would also like to thank her own mother, Dimitra Gefou-Madianou for transnational grandparenting and for uncomplainingly giving up much of her time to make our fieldwork possible. Finally, Mirca would like to express her gratitude to the Fellows of Lucy Cavendish College, University of Cambridge for their support and for granting her the necessary study leave which was essential for carrying out the research.

The research was funded by the ESRC as part of the award on 'Migration, ICTs and the transformation of transnational family life' (RES-000-22-2266), with an additional grant from British Telecom specifically to cover the cost of interview transcriptions.

1

INTRODUCTION

Within the past few years a revolution has been taking place, one with huge consequences, but so far subject to only limited systematic research. While there are many studies of globalisation and migrant transnationalism, few have addressed the consequence that probably matters most to those involved, which is the separation of families. Specifically, how do parents and children care and look after each other when they live in different countries for many years separated because of migration? Although transnational families are not new, they are becoming increasingly common. Furthermore this type of separation now often involves mothers and their children as a consequence of the feminisation of migration, partly fuelled by the insatiable demand for care and domestic workers in the developed world. The dramatic change which has revolutionised the way in which families maintain long-distance communication, is the emergence of a plethora of internet- and mobile phone-based platforms such as email, instant messaging (IM), social networking sites (SNS) and webcam via voice over internet protocol (VOIP). These new media have engendered the emergence of a new communicative environment, which we will call 'polymedia'. This book is dedicated to the understanding of this new type of 'connected transnational family' which is the result of the convergence of these two phenomena: migrant transnationalism and the explosion of communicative opportunities afforded by new media.

This book makes both a substantive and theoretical contribution to the understanding of these profound, parallel developments of family separation and transnational communication that are shaping our contemporary worlds. We believe that to understand these transformations we cannot and should not separate them as, on the one hand, a study of the media, and on the other hand, an enquiry into what it means to be a migrant, or a mother. Our understanding will be much enhanced if we study media situated in the context of what it means to be a transnational mother in this environment of polymedia. As a result, this book contains not just a theory of polymedia, but also a theory of mediation in which we consider in general terms how relationships and media are mutually shaped. We do so by drawing on a long-term ethnographic study of prolonged separation between transnational Filipino migrant mothers based in London and Cambridge and their (now adult) left-behind children in the Philippines. No other country exemplifies the phenomenon of 'distant mothering' as clearly as the Philippines with over 10 per cent of its population working overseas, the majority of whom are women with children left behind. The Philippines is also at the forefront of globalisation in terms of its appropriation of new media platforms, notably mobile phones, the consequences of which have already been documented, especially with regard to the public sphere (Castells *et al.*, 2006; Pertierra *et al.*, 2002; Rafael, 2003). More than 10 million Filipino children are officially estimated to be left-behind, most of whom see their migrant parents only once every two years. Given that such visits are even less frequent for families of undocumented migrants, it is evident that such parent–child relationships have become increasingly dependent on the available communication media. We argue that focusing on this case of prolonged separation and intense mediation helps to bring to light and crystallise aspects of both parts of this equation: a better understanding of the consequences of new media, and an insight into the very nature of parent–child relationships. Starting from this case of accentuated separation and mediation, we then move on to develop a new theory of polymedia and of mediated relationships which, we argue, can have a wider applicability. The book is equally driven by the aim to make an original contribution to the migration literature as well as to develop a theoretical understanding of digital media, distant love and the nature of mediated relationships. It also follows Stafford (2000) in arguing that understanding separation is a route towards understanding the basis of human relatedness, autonomy and dependence and thereby the very nature of relationships.

One of the book's arguments is that although information and communication technologies (ICTs) do not solve the problems of separation within families, they do contribute to the transformation of the whole experience of migration and parenting. For example, it is telling that the opportunities for cheap and instant communication feature strongly in migrant mothers' justifications regarding their decisions to migrate and to settle. However, the fact that ICTs can potentially contribute, even if indirectly, to the shaping of migration patterns is not to say that the communication is necessarily successful. In fact, we will show how the perpetual contact they engender can often increase rupture and conflict between parents and children. The only way this becomes clear is through our transnational approach to research, which involved working with both the migrant mothers and subsequently the left-behind children of these same mothers whom we interviewed back in the Philippines. In the book we both demonstrate and interpret a discrepancy between the mothers' and children's accounts. While for the mothers new communication technologies represent welcome opportunities to perform intensive mothering at a distance and to 'feel like mothers again', for their young adult children such frequent communication can be experienced as intrusive and unwanted, although this often depends on specific issues such as the age of the children at the time the mothers left and the nature of the media available to them.

In addition, this book aims to make a wider theoretical contribution by developing a theory of polymedia and a theory of mediated relationships. The theory of polymedia emerged through our need to develop a framework for understanding the rapidly developing and proliferating media environment and its appropriation by users. Although our analysis of communication technologies begins by investigating the affordances (Hutchby, 2001) and limitations of each particular medium, technology or platform, our discussion of the emergence of a new environment of proliferating communicative opportunities that is polymedia shifts the attention from the individual technical propensities of any particular medium to an acknowledgement that most people use a constellation of different media as an integrated environment in which each medium finds its niche in relation to the others. We will also argue that, as media become affordable and once media literacy[1] is established and continues to develop, the situation of polymedia amounts to a re-socialising of media itself, in which the responsibility for which medium is used is increasingly seen to depend on social and moral questions rather than technical or economic parameters.

If the term 'polymedia' recognises the importance of the human context for media use, this leads the way to our final chapter where we are able to bring this theory into alignment with the theorisation of relationships to create a theory of mediated relationships, which builds upon prior theories of mediation in media studies (Couldry, 2008; Livingstone, 2009b; Silverstone, 2005), but is here combined with debates about kinship, religion and mediation in anthropology (e.g. Eisenlohr, 2011; Engelke, 2010). In this final theoretical chapter we demonstrate that the key to understanding mediated relationships is not to envisage them as simply a case of how the media mediates relationships. Rather we start from our theory of relationships which demonstrates that all relationships are intrinsically mediated and that we can understand the impact of the media only if we first acknowledge this property of the relationship.

This book exemplifies the benefits of giving equal weight to relationships, media, ethnography and theory. But it is also sensitive to the context of its own case study, to the stories of suffering, separation, loss and also empowerment and love that make this more than just grounds for delineating such academic terrain. We have focused this volume just as much on the need to convey these stories and the background in the political economy of global labour and its impact especially on migrant women and their left-behind children.

The rest of this chapter will review the three key literatures which underpin this study, namely, global migration and transnational families; new media, consumption and transnational communication, and finally motherhood. We will end the chapter by providing an overview of the whole book.

Global migration and transnational families

Families whose members are temporally and spatially separated because of work are nothing new. Thomas and Znaniecki's classic *The Polish Peasant in Europe and*

America (1996) is a riveting account of the early twentieth-century migration to the US partly told through the letters that sustained these long-distance relationships between separated family members. The recent intensification of global migration and, crucially, the increasing feminisation of migration, have brought about a new type of transnational family where women seek employment in the global north, leaving their children behind. Transnational motherhood (Hondagneu-Sotelo and Avila, 1997), precisely because it challenges entrenched and often ideological views about the role of mothers and the value of children (see also Zelizer, 1994), has largely been seen as one of the hidden injuries of globalisation: the high social cost the developing world must pay for the increased income through remittances which keep the economies of the global south afloat.

The impact on left-behind families and the relationship people maintain to their countries of origin have been a relatively recent focus of attention, perhaps because for so long the migration literature focused on questions of assimilation and integration in the host societies (Vertovec, 2009: 13). An influential approach for understanding transnational families has been the 'care chains' approach (Hochschild, 2000; Parreñas, 2001) and the related notion of 'care drain' affecting developing countries which experience a 'care deficit' by exporting their mothers and care workers (Hochschild, 2000; Widding Isaksen *et al.*, 2008). The work of Parreñas (2001) on Philippine migration has acquired paradigmatic status in exemplifying the connections between different people across the world based on paid or unpaid relationships of care. The concept of a global care chain has particular poignancy because of the way this is refracted in the impact upon left-behind children. The paradigmatic case is where a Filipina woman from Manila spends much of her life looking after a child in London, using part of her wages to employ a Filipina from a village to look after her children in Manila. This woman in turn uses part of her urban wages to pay someone else in her village to look after her own children. These images of a global care chain are powerful representations of the larger inequalities of contemporary political economy.

There exists a corresponding debate at a popular level within the Philippines itself with regard to the impact of migration upon parent–child relationships. Critical to our fieldwork was a film called *Anak* (the word in Tagalog for 'child') which portrays the extreme example of a mother who feels she has sacrificed herself for her children by taking on domestic work in Hong Kong. But during her absence, her son drops school grades and loses his scholarship, and her daughter falls into a life of assorted vices including smoking, drinking, drugs and abusive boyfriends leading to an abortion. The film is dominated by the relationship between the mother and the sullen and resentful daughter who blames all her woes on being abandoned by her mother. This was a hugely popular film in the Philippines. It was directed by R. Quintos and starred Vilma Santos, a well-known actress and politician, now the mayor of a major town. We often started our discussion with the children by asking for their reaction to the film, which was easier to broach than immediately discussing their own childhood. So in addition to any academic debates, we also have to be aware of the way these issues are constantly appraised within the Philippines itself.

In the academic literature, gender has been understood as being key to under-standing dynamics in transnational families. Parreñas (2005a) in her study of Filipino left-behind children noted that when mothers migrate they are expected to perform the caring and emotional work typically associated with their mater-nal role, but also to take on the traditional male breadwinning role. Globalisation and female migration have not reversed, nor even challenged traditional gender roles and hierarchies. This finding is also shared by Hondagneu-Sotelo and Avila (1997) in their study of Latina transnational mothers in California as well as Fresnoza-Flot (2009) in her research with Filipina migrants in Paris. Hondagneu-Sotelo and Avila (1997: 562) argue that female migration has not replaced caregiving with breadwinning definitions of motherhood, but rather has expanded 'definitions of motherhood to encompass caregiving from a distance and through separation'. For Pessar (1999), any advances by women's breadwinning capacity are cancelled by the fact that female migrants are overwhelmingly employed in the care and domestic sector, thus preserving patriarchal ideologies. However, McKay (2007) and Pingol (2001) observed a different gendered division of domestic work in the Philippine region of Northern Luzon.

based on economy

The political economy of care and the feminist critique on which the care chains approach is based have made significant contributions to the literature on migra-tion, with their emphasis upon the economic motivations for emigration. However, the focus of the care chains approach on structural factors does not acknowledge the empowering potential of migration for women and does not grant much agency to migrants themselves in determining their own trajectory (McKay, 2007; Silvey, 2006; Yeates, 2004). The care chains approach also assumes a normative and uni-versal perspective of biological motherhood which should be performed in a situation of co-presence (actually living together in the same household). What the more ethnographically based studies such as McKay (2007) and Aguilar *et al.* (2009) demonstrate is that both the global feminist discourse employed by Parreñas (2001), and also globalised ideas about women's responsibilities (which are found in the Hollywood-style melodrama that clearly influenced the film *Anak*) have to be complemented by grounded study within the Philippines, which may reveal very different and more nuanced expectations about mother–child relationships.

Mothers themselves are subject to competing discourses about the moralities of their own actions. In such circumstances it seemed vital to recognise the migrant women's own perspective, particularly when the research agenda concerns sensi-tive and emotive issues such as family separation. In our research we have adopted an ethnographic approach which recognises migrants as reflexive subjects, albeit ones positioned in structures of power. For example, crucial for understanding the relationships and communication between mothers and left-behind children is the analysis of the context of migration, including the reasons why women migrate in the first place. The bottom-up ethnographic perspective followed here can uncover the contradictory and perhaps less socially acceptable motivations for migration and cast light on the processes through which women negotiate their various roles, identities and relationships. This is an approach followed by

Constable (1999) in her work with Filipina migrant workers in Hong Kong, where she focused on the ambivalent narratives of return amongst her participants. Such accounts of the motivations for migration and settlement often highlight personal reasons which are not captured by more top-down perspectives such as that of the care chains with its emphasis on the role of the state and the political economy of care.

In Chapter 3 we build upon Parreñas (2001: 27) who developed an intermediate level analysis combining a bottom-up perspective with the macrostructural approach of political economy of labour migration (Sassen, 1988). This allowed Parreñas to identify a range of 'hidden motivations for migration' which extend beyond the well-rehearsed and socially accepted reasons, which are usually economic. For example, Parreñas observed that personal reasons including the breakdown of a relationship, domestic abuse and extramarital affairs, constitute a significant motivation for women's migration (2001: 62–69), often in conjunction with other well-documented economic and political reasons. However, our work suggests that migrants do not always articulate the contradictions (what Parreñas calls the 'dislocations of migration' [2001: 23]) in their narratives. Rather, often the discrepancy between their own accounts (which often draw on well-rehearsed public discourses about what constitutes good mothering and a good reason to go abroad) and their actual practices, points to the contradictions and ambivalence that is part of the project of migration. To unearth such discrepancies one needs the long-term and in-depth involvement of ethnography. Migrant women occupy simultaneously different and often contradictory subject positions: breadwinners and caregivers; devoted mothers and national heroines; global consumers and exploited workers. Our ethnographic perspective documents how they negotiate these conflicting identities both discursively and through practices.

Although, as we noted earlier in this section, research on transnational families is part of the transnational turn within migration studies, it is perhaps ironic that one still encounters a degree of 'methodological nationalism' (Wimmer and Glick-Schiller, 2002) within such scholarship. It is as if researchers cannot escape the 'assumption that the nation/state/society is the natural social and political form of the modern world' (Wimmer and Glick-Schiller, 2002: 301). Although it would be foolish to entirely repudiate the relevance of the nation-state in the analysis of migrant transnationalism, it seems that one way of overcoming the straightjacket of methodological nationalism is to actually conduct research transnationally. Our research has benefited from this comparative, multi-sited perspective. By focusing on the relationships between migrant mothers based in the UK *and* their left-behind children in the Philippines we have 'followed the thing' through a multi-sited ethnography (Marcus, 1995). The comparisons – and contradictions – between the mothers and the children's perspectives lie at the heart of this book. We came to recognise that we would have written an entirely different book if we had concentrated on migrant mothers only, or on their children. Transnationalism is all about relationships, and following them (rather than assuming them) is one way of dealing with the perils of methodological nationalism.

Transnational communication and new media

For transnational families who are reunited on average every two years,[2] new media are essential for keeping in touch. Dependence on new media is exacerbated in the case of irregular migrants who often do not see their families for longer periods (in our sample the longest period without a visit was 13 years; for similar observations see also Fresnoza-Flot, 2009). In such cases new communication technologies become the only means through which migrant mothers can maintain a relationship with their children. Given this almost extreme dependency, it is perhaps surprising that new media have not received much attention in the literature of migrant transnationalism, although studies have highlighted the more general importance of the mobile phone as a social resource in the lives of migrants (see Thompson, 2009). Most academic writing on new media and migration has looked at the important questions of identity and integration (Gillespie *et al.*, 2010) and the political implications for diasporic and national populations (Brinkerhoff, 2009; for a review see Siapera, 2010). Although this literature has been very useful and influential, it does not address the urgent question of sociality and intimacy in a transnational context (although see Horst, 2006; Miller and Slater, 2000; and Wilding, 2006), while the focus on the rather bounded concept of identity does not always capture the dynamic nature of transnational processes (Glick-Schiller *et al.*, 1992; Madianou, 2011).

In the context of Philippine migration, Parreñas observed that among separated Filipino families mobile phones actually tie migrant women to their traditional gender roles (Parreñas, 2005b), echoing North American studies about mobile phone use and the spillover of the domestic into the professional sphere (Chesley, 2005; Rakow and Navarro, 1993). Apart from gender inequalities, Parreñas also argues that the political economic conditions of communication determine the quality of transnational intimacy and family life (Parreñas, 2005b), as families without access to the internet or even a landline are deprived of care and emotional support. In the next chapter we shall acknowledge these stark asymmetries both between the communications infrastructure of the Philippines and the UK and within the Philippines. But although a political economic analysis has to inform our understanding of transnational family communication, it cannot fully account for the dependency of such families on digital media and the mutual shaping of technologies and relationships.

The greatest challenge of studying new media in the context of transnational family relationships is that the technologies themselves are constantly changing and research often seems to be chasing a moving target of technological developments and innovative appropriations on the part of the users. Each new mode of communication seems to become what Vertovec (2004) described for cheap international cards, that is 'the social glue of transnationalism', with examples provided by Wilding (2006) on email, or Uy-Tioco on texting (2007). This is reflected in our own studies. When we began our fieldwork three years ago, transnational family communication was often mainly centred upon one medium such as telephone calls or email, each with its own affordances and limitations. It was often possible to see the consequences of that particular type of communication on the relationships in question. However, gradually, and certainly over the past couple of years, we noticed a shift towards a situation of multiple media. Relationships, increasingly, do not depend on one particular technology, but on a plurality of media which supplement each other and can help overcome the shortcomings of a particular medium. People can also take advantage of these different communicative opportunities in order to control the relationship. So, for example, if they want to avoid confrontation they do not call but send an email. This is what led us to consider polymedia with a focus on the social and emotional consequences of choosing between a plurality of media rather than simply examining the particular features and affordances of each particular medium (see also Baym, 2010; Gershon, 2010).

Although we recognise that this new environment of communicative opportunities is not yet a reality for everyone in the Philippines or even in the UK, it already represents a qualitative shift in the way technologies mediate relationships. This is why we felt the need for this new term to allow us to describe the situation. Although the term 'media ecology' could be an alternative, it is concerned with the wider systems of communication such as transport, or issues of usage such as politics and health (Slater and Tacchi, 2004), while we wanted a term that will highlight the unprecedented plurality and proliferation of media. 'Multimedia', on the other hand, is now an established term with a very different meaning (a situation where several different forms of media are being used simultaneously and in direct relationship to each other, for instance using instant messaging on social networking sites) and it would therefore be confusing to use that term. 'Multichannel', or 'multi-platform' might be closer to what we wish to describe, although choosing either term would force us to prioritise either the terms 'platform' or 'channel' when in fact our findings suggest that such technological hierarchies are not particularly meaningful to users. This is why we chose 'polymedia' as a new term to describe the new emerging environment of proliferating communicative opportunities.

It may seem that the term 'polymedia' merely acknowledges the plethora of different media that are now available, but the point we wish to make is both more profound and closer to the heart of social science. Our argument will be that this growth of diverse media is crucially linked to changes in their pricing structure as well as in users' media literacy (Livingstone, 2004), and it is the combination of these factors that transforms the relationship between people and media. Previously people would assume that the choice of media was dictated by issues of availability of technology or price, and were constrained from extending their inferences from the choices other people made. But the word 'polymedia' will be used to consider much more generally how media are socialised, which is why it then leads on to a subsequent theory of mediation. Both draw upon a number of theoretical developments such as the rich tradition of consumption and domestication of ICTs (Berker *et al.*, 2006; Miller and Slater, 2000; Silverstone and Hirsch, 1992) and the theory of mediation (Chouliaraki, 2006; Couldry, 2008 and 2012; Eisenlohr, 2011; Livingstone, 2009b; Madianou, 2005 and 2012b; Miller, in press; Silverstone, 2005).

Historically, mediated interaction was understood as being inferior compared to the golden standard of face-to-face. This was mainly due to the reduced amount of symbolic cues (for example, lack of visual cues in a letter, or telephone communication) which gave rise to ambiguities and potential misunderstandings (Baym, 2010: 51–54; Thompson, 1995: 84). Also problematic was the perceived lack of norms to regulate mediated interaction which also had the potential to amplify conflict (through the case of 'flaming') (Baym, 2010: 55). Recent studies on the social shaping of technologies (MacKenzie and Wajcman, 1999; Wajcman *et al.*, 2008), domestication (Berker *et al.*, 2006; Miller and Slater, 2000) and mediation (Couldry, 2008; Livingstone, 2009b; Madianou, 2005; Silverstone, 2005) have shown that mediated interactions are more complex than that and that society and relationships are mutually constitutive. Similarly, polymedia aims to contribute to this academic discussion by showing how users can overcome the limitations of any particular medium by choosing an alternative in order achieve their communicative intents and to assume control over their relationships. We should stress, however, that we are not implying that media power is becoming redundant in a situation of polymedia. On the contrary, power is a recurrent theme in this volume and will be analysed as being present in both the social and family contexts (family relationships are asymmetrical) and the political and economic contexts of migration and telecommunications.

All of these are brought together in our final chapter, which culminates in a theory of mediation which can be traced back to the early days of media and communications research when Lazarsfeld and Merton wrote in 1948 that research ought to try to understand the effects of the sheer presence of media institutions on society. Silverstone developed this notion of mediation as:

> a fundamentally dialectical notion which requires us to understand how processes of communication change the social and cultural environments that support them as well as the relationships that participants, both individual and institutional, have to that environment and to each other. At the same time it requires a consideration of the social as in turn a mediator: institutions and technologies as well as the meanings that are delivered by them are mediated in the social processes of reception and consumption (Silverstone, 2005: 3).

In this volume the term 'mediation' applies just as much to the question of what is a social relationship as to the question of what is a medium. The situation of transnational mothering raises huge issues of what the very terms 'mother' and 'child' mean. When we come to the analysis of our research material it will become clear that this extreme case actually throws light on the question of what is a mother as it applies to any situation including that of co-presence because a social relationship is already a form of mediation. A mother is both a normative concept – the ideal as to what a mother should be – and the experience of actually being, or having, a mother. As this book unfolds it will show why any further development of a theory of mediation as applied to media is best achieved through equal attention to the theory of mediation as to the relationship. This point leads directly to our third discussion of the literature, which starts to open up this question of what we mean when we use the term 'mother'.

[handwritten marginalia: *bad mother*]

Transnational motherhood: normativity and ambivalence

The last section suggests that in order to assess the impact of ICTs on the relationships between transnational mothers and their left-behind children, we need to pay just as much attention to the issue of motherhood as to an appreciation of the media. In the next chapter we will provide a discussion of the Filipino idioms of family, motherhood and childhood. The present discussion is a more general reflection on motherhood which we argue is indispensable to the understanding of mother–child relationships and their mediation. One of the reasons such a clarification of terms and theoretical baggage is crucial is because motherhood is a constant trope in ideological debate. Moral panics regularly erupt about what constitutes good, or 'good-enough' mothering (Winnicott, 1971), feeding into questions and often translated into policy regarding mothers' employment and identities (Riley, 1983; Rutter, 1981; Smart and Neale, 1999). Even though there is an increasing recognition of the changing nature of family and the plurality of parenting arrangements (Golombok, 2000) – from single mothers and working mothers to stay-at-home mothers and from heterosexual mothers to lesbian mothers and so on – there is widespread assertion, even among feminists, that parenting needs to take place in a situation of co-presence. This is nothwithstanding anthropological accounts of many regions, such as the Caribbean, where the nuclear co-present family has never been the norm (for a classic account see Clarke, 1957). In this climate mothers leaving their children to pursue their own ambitions are quickly branded 'bad mothers' (Jackson, 1994; for a discussion of the Philippine case see Parreñas, 2008: 22–39). Transnational mothering disrupts this normative notion of co-present parenting. This is the dominant discourse that we now see reflected in the film *Anak* discussed earlier. Our purpose in the next few paragraphs is to clarify our analytical tools that will help us understand the changing nature of mother–child relationships in the context of separation and mediation.

Being a mother is defined by being in a particular relationship. As Miller (1997) has shown in his paper 'How infants grow mothers in North London', the development of the child as a new being is equally reflected in the process, much more commonly taken for granted, by which a female becomes a mother. This disrupts the dominant literature which is driven by a concern to examine the impact of maternal behaviour on children's development. Feminist critique has for a long time identified such one-sided emphasis in psychoanalysis and developmental psychology (Hollway and Featherstone, 1997; Parker, 2005: 15–18). Even

Winnicott's (1975) essay 'Hate in the countertransference', which is now considered a classic text on maternal ambivalence, is concerned with its impact on the baby's development. To simply see the mother from the point of view of her child's needs would be tantamount to her infant's own narcissism: seeing the mother as merely an extension of the infant's needs. Parker (2005: 18) refers to 'maternal development' to contest the one-sided emphasis on child development, thus acknowledging that mothers, just like their children, are changing also as part of the challenges of the experience of motherhood. This is part of Parker's efforts to theorise mothers, rather than treat them as empty vessels to be filled with their children's needs and desires. Our research contextualises motherhood in the wider lives of these Filipina women, subjects with multiple identities and needs, that can become manifest as ambivalence. Although most writing on ambivalence is located within psychoanalysis (Hollway and Featherstone, 1997; Parker, 2005), we feel it is essential to recognise these same issues within an ethnographic encounter that can equally expose what Hays (1997) terms the 'cultural contradictions of motherhood'.

Our evidence will show that ambivalence is particularly relevant to the experience of migration. For mothers with left-behind children, migration as deterritorialisation can exacerbate such maternal ambivalence. We regard ambivalence as a normal state for many mothers (Hays, 1997), who must negotiate contradictory roles as workers and mothers, but equally the ideal freedoms posed by feminism contradicted by the constraints and re-gendering created by motherhood (Miller, 1997). For migrant mothers such negotiation is more challenging because work (in the UK) and mothering (in a transnational space) are spread across different countries and continents, leading to a situation of 'accentuated ambivalence' (Madianou, 2012a). In Chapters 3 and 5, which aim to illustrate the contours of transnational mothering from the bottom up, we will explore the ways in which mothers negotiate this ambivalence and the role that ICTs play in this process.

This insistence upon acknowledging the perspective of mothers need not be opposed to the perspective of their children, which for us would be an abnegation of our understanding of the constitution of both mother and child as a relationship. According to Hollway (2001) the literature on motherhood and child development seems to have been marked by a certain dualism between those perspectives which see mothers as objects of their babies' and their families' needs (rather than people in their own right) and the feminist critique which sees women as subjects and active agents. Hollway (2001) proposes an alternative perspective of intersubjectivity as part of the attempt to examine mothers' and children's needs *in tandem*. Accordingly, here we directly juxtapose the points of view of both mothers and children. We were able to accomplish this because methodologically we sought to interview not only the mothers in the UK, but then with their permission their left-behind children – now young adults – in the Philippines. In total we were able to pair 20 mothers and children, but our wider sample contains many more mothers and children who were not 'paired up' (see Appendix for a detailed discussion of our sample and overall method).

Overview of the book

Having provided an overview of the literatures that inform our analysis and an outline of our own approach, we will now provide a synopsis of the rest of the book. In Chapter 2 we show that the more abstract issues raised here are particularly well exemplified in the case of the Philippines. An intensely migrant country with over 10 per cent of its population working abroad, the Philippines can be seen to epitomise processes of globalisation and the asymmetries between the global south and north. The chapter provides a brief introduction to the history of Philippine migration before presenting the statistics and an account of the feminisation of migration. This is followed by a discussion of the main literature on Filipino migration and its consequences. It reveals the unusual situation where the state itself actively promotes and celebrates this phenomenon. The focus then turns to Filipino migration into the UK, which has become one of the most popular destinations for Filipino migrants in recent years, especially following the systematic recruitment of Filipino nurses by the British National Health Service between 1998 and 2005. The second part of this chapter briefly describes the Philippines as having been in the vanguard of some aspects of digital communication, such as mobile phone texting.

Chapter 3 is dedicated to unearthing the reasons why women migrate in the first place and why they often choose to prolong migration and even settle in the UK. This analysis is crucial if we are to understand the communication between migrant mothers and their children. Contrary to popular perceptions and influential approaches such as neoclassic economics and world systems theory (for a review see Castles and Miller, 2009; Massey *et al.*, 1993), our research has found that economic motivations, albeit crucial, are not the only catalysts for migration and they are even less salient in explaining the reasons why women do not return to the Philippines. This chapter details the myriad motivations for female migration in the Philippine context and argues that ambivalence is a central theme in the experience of migration. This is particularly the case for women, whose lack of employment opportunities in the Philippines coupled with other structural push and pull factors mean that their jobs (and the respect and satisfaction they derive from them) are and can only be abroad, while their children remain in the Philippines. This chapter develops a concept of 'accentuated maternal ambivalence' (Madianou, 2012a) to highlight the particularly challenging and contradictory nature of transnational mothering.

This book deliberately flows between an emphasis upon the media and a focus upon the relationships. Chapter 4 achieves two key goals that help give the book structure and narrative as a whole. Firstly it provides material on the earlier stages of separation, mostly taken from oral historical accounts, so that we have a clear sense of the underlying conditions from when mothers were initially communicating with mainly young children. But at the same time the fact that this was based largely on only two dominant media, letters and cassettes, with only the occasional phone call, means that we can introduce the other key theme of this book, which is the focus upon media themselves. In particular, the chapter systematically discusses the affordances and constraints of these old media and the ways in which they framed communication in these long-distance relationships. Even within this rather simple early media environment we see that users exploited the contrasts between these two available media in order to express their emotions and achieve their aims with regard to their relationships. In that sense in Chapter 4 we see the earliest evidence of polymedia: of media as an integrated communicative environment. Having a relatively simple distinction between two media in this chapter helps the book's movement towards the final chapters where we are faced with the proliferation of many different forms of media as part of an emergent environment of polymedia.

Chapter 5 is dedicated to the mother's perspective. It observes how the explosion of opportunities for cheap and synchronous communication through new communications technologies has allowed for 'a more complete' practice of intensive mothering at a distance. Different communicative media fulfil different aspects of mothering, allowing women to be in control of their households and children's upbringing. The digital divide within the Philippines and between the global north and south has implications for the type and cost of 'distant care', affording more opportunities to those with access to internet-based platforms. However, intensive mothering is also performed though mobile phones, which are widely available and represent a significant improvement from the past situation when communication was asynchronous and prohibitively expensive. Even though the frequency of communication through new media can often involve conflict and disappointment, for mothers it represents a more 'real experience' of mothering and an opportunity to 'feel like mothers' again. In this sense, communication technologies have implications not only for practices of mothering, but also for maternal identities. Even though there is evidence for the persistence of traditional gender roles in the transnational division of reproductive labour, transnational communication cannot simply be understood as confirmation of a negative spillover (Chesley, 2005) and asymmetrical gender relationships as the existing literature suggests (Parreñas, 2005b). We argue that new media are fundamental in the negotiation of the 'accentuated ambivalence' of migrant women by allowing them to negotiate a plurality of roles and identities across distances (see Madianou, 2012a). In that sense, new media can also be seen as a kind of solution (however imperfect) to the cultural contradictions of migration and motherhood.

If, as Chapter 5 has shown, the opportunities for cheap and instant communication are generally welcomed by the mothers, in Chapter 6, which focuses on the perspective of those left behind, we observe how transnational communication can be experienced as a burden by around half the children we worked with. We start by contrasting the mothers' perspective given in the previous chapter against the evidence that around half of the now adult left-behind children whom we met do not agree that these new technologies effectively reinstate their mothers in that role. However, this observation is not uniform. The other half of our participants feel that in some ways the combination of physical distance and control over new media made the transition through teenage life easier and even strengthened their relationships to their mothers. Three factors account for the success or failure in these mediated relationships: the age of the child when the mother left, the quality of the pre-existing relationship and the range of the available media. We end this chapter with a tentative theorisation of relationships as they have emerged in the light of this study.

In Chapter 7 we begin to extend beyond the specifics of the empirical case study by developing a systematic comparison of each of the individual media discussed in the book, ranging from older technologies such as the phone to more recent additions such as email, instant messaging, social networking sites, webcam and texting. Our comparison revolves around the following parameters: interactivity, temporality, materiality and storage, replicability, mobility, public/private, social cues and information size. Having already established how the particular relationships appropriate the communication technologies (in Chapters 5 and 6), our aim here is to identify the ways in which each medium frames communication. Thus we ask what is qualitatively different about communicating via webcam (using applications such as Skype) compared to email or telephone calls? Why is webcam perfect for helping children with homework, or simulating situations of co-presence during family meals, but not as successful an environment for expressing love? Why is email communication so prone to misunderstandings and even the amplification of conflict? And what is it about phone calls that people find so appealing in terms of gauging their loved one's true emotions? This leads to a general discussion of media affordances and propensities as evident from our substantive study.

Chapter 8 develops our theory of 'polymedia', one of the book's original concepts. After considering the affordances and limitations of each particular medium in the previous chapter, we now turn to the combination of all these different media and the way this constitutes the emergence of a new communicative environment. Polymedia thus has to be understood as more than a sum of its parts as it represents a qualitative shift in the relationship between media and its social context. A theory of polymedia shows how the existence of multiple alternatives within an integrated communicative structure leads to a different environment for relationships themselves. This recognition extends our focus to the social and emotional consequences of choosing between a plurality of media (rather than simply examining the particular features and affordances of each discrete medium). In particular, this chapter examines the impact of the situation of polymedia for the nature of sociality, for the emotional aspects of communication and for the importance of power as a context for the analysis of asymmetry in relationships.

In our final chapter we develop our theory of mediation. Having made a contribution both to the understanding of the transformation of family relationships in the context of migration and globalisation and to the understanding of the different communication technologies in the context of long-distance love, the theory of mediation brings the two together. We start by introducing a theory of the relationship as an intrinsically mediated form. We then show how the impact of media within relationships is transformed with the advent of polymedia. This allows us to create a theoretical framework that transcends the emphasis upon media in media studies, and on relationships and kinship in social science, to create a theoretical structure that can equally inform both. Although these final chapters are increasingly devoted to issues of theory, they remain constantly grounded in our ethnographic encounter combining the perspectives of migrants and their left-behind families. The struggles of these mothers and their children with regard to the relationships that matter more than almost anything else in their lives, is what ultimately reveals what is at stake in these theoretical discussions, an attempt to understand empathetically a situation which seems to be becoming ever more widespread as international migration becomes an inescapable feature of our contemporary world.

2

THE PHILIPPINES AND GLOBALISATION

Migration, mothering and communications

The processes highlighted in Chapter 1 are particularly well exemplified in the case of the Philippines. In this chapter we argue that the Philippines is at the forefront of globalisation in three interrelated areas crucial to the focus of this study: migration, family and telecommunications. It is hard to think of a more intensely migrant country than the Philippines, with over 10 per cent of the population living abroad and a million people currently being deployed every year. The fact that most of the current migrants are women who often face barriers to bringing their children has led to the phenomenon of family separation. Transnationalism for such families is not an exotic exception, but an everyday affair with implications for traditional ways of parenting and clearly also for the appropriations of new media.

Philippine migration

Behind and prior to contemporary migration from the Philippines is a complex history. The Philippines is a colonial construct comprising selected segments from a much larger South East Asian Malay region (Zialcita, 2005), with a long period of Spanish colonialism (1565–1899) and a shorter period of US colonialism ending in 1946. The boundary with Indonesia to the South is particularly unclear and remains contested. This is nicely illustrated in the early novels of Joseph Conrad in which one has a sense of an island world where a typical journey might include Palawan, now in the Philippines, along with Kalimantan, now in Indonesia, and which give no sense of where such colonial boundaries will one day crystallise. Generally the Philippines became conscious of itself as a nation only through resistance movements against colonial rule (Aguilar, 2005). Despite the degree of homogenisation that comes with nationalism, Le Espiritu (1996) makes the essential point that the Philippines is a highly diverse region internally. This is very evident in anthropological studies which stretch from Johnson (1997) in the South, to Rosaldo (1980) in the North. These also reflect continued regional differences in the respective influence of Islam in the South and Christianity elsewhere.

Some of the early migrations were clearly a product of US colonialism. This included sugarcane workers who went to Hawaii and nurses who went to the US in the early twentieth century (Choy, 2003), as well as sailors who jumped ship from the US navy, which was the harbinger of Filipino male dominance of world shipping labour (see Sampson, 2003). The colonial link and early migrations to the US resulted in a strong Filipino American diaspora (presently estimated as around 3 million although that number excludes the second and third generations [POEA, 2008]) and explains why the US remains the dream destination for contemporary Filipino migrants (Le Espiritu, 1996). The heavy recruitment in nursing by the US, UK and Canada led to an annual migration of around 15,000 nurses between the late 1960s and late 1980s (Choy, 2003: 108). A quite separate stream of migration into Japan including prostitution and bar work led to the contemporary stereotypes of the *Japayuki* (Suzuki, 2002: 178–179).

But the migration of most of the participants in our research is the result of factors which have little to do with colonialism. They followed a trend towards large-scale labour migration after the 1970s oil boom in the Middle East which led to a high demand for construction workers in that region. Migration has intensified since, with the increased demand in the global north for female labour in both the health care and domestic sectors. Today the official estimate is that more than 8.18 million[1] Filipinos work abroad (POEA, 2009) from a country of 88 million people. Official estimates provided by relevant government agencies such as the Philippine Overseas Employment Administration (POEA), the Overseas Workers Welfare Administration (OWWA) and the Commission for Filipinos Overseas (CFO), are generally regarded as underestimating the true extent of migration (Asis, 2008). Official figures tend to be based on fixed-term contract workers, commonly referred to as Overseas Filipino Workers (OFW), or Overseas Contract Workers (OCW), usually excluding those permanently settled abroad and often naturalised, as well as those who migrate on student visas but who mainly work as caregivers in nursing homes, a practice increasingly common in the UK. Finally, although the 8.2 million estimate includes 653,609 irregular migrants, there is agreement that the true figure is considerably higher. In our interviews with representatives from government agencies, advocacy groups and telecommunications companies we were told that the total number could be even 30 per cent higher, which would imply a figure more like 12 million (15 per cent of the population).

What makes the Philippine case almost unique is that the state has actively sponsored overseas migration through policies that have systematically encouraged and celebrated the phenomenon. Migration has become an official economic strategy for the Philippines (Acacio, 2008; Asis, 2008; Parreñas, 2001). This was made concrete in the 1974 presidential decree by Marcos which founded the Overseas Employment Development Board and National Seaman Board. Later came the creation of POEA in 1982 and the 1995 Migrant Workers' and Overseas Filipinos Act (Acacio, 2008). As well as economic advantages, a key factor that practically coerced the state into still greater involvement in regulating migration was what Aguilar (1996) called 'the dialectics of transnational shame and national identity' that followed the execution of Flor Contemplacion, a Filipina domestic worker in Singapore in 1995.

As part of its conception of migration as an integral aspect of economic polity, the state created a series of complex tax and other incentives to help ensure the flow of money back to the Philippines (Szanton, 1996). The steady flow of remittances is also ensured by the short nature of (often state-sponsored) employment contracts which do not allow migrants to be joined by their families (see Parreñas, 2001). Today remittances account for over 10 per cent of the country's GDP, making the Philippines one of the world's highest remittance-recipient countries (Jha et al., 2009). In 2008 remittances reached $16.5 billion (POEA, 2009), a record figure despite the global economic crisis and the slight decline in OFW numbers from previous years. It is no surprise, then, that since the 1980s OFWs have been hailed as the 'heroes and heroines' of the economy (Asis, 2005) and the state has instituted special days such as the International Migrants Day to celebrate migration.

In 2006 the Philippine government met its official target of deploying over 1 million migrants (that number includes new hires and rehires) (Asis, 2008), while in 2008 annual deployment reached 1,236,013 emigrants (equal to approximately 3,500 daily departures). More than half of these migrants are deployed on temporary fixed-term contracts, which require renewal. The Philippine government has bilateral agreements with a number of countries, mainly in the Middle East, to send workers on limited-time contracts which require migrants to return to the Philippines after a set period of time (on average two years). Although it is common to renew one's contract and thus prolong migration, the temporary status of the worker in the receiving country means that they are not able to be joined by their families, or to enjoy other benefits of permanent residency (even though residency may be effectively long-term). The recent work of Aguilar and his colleagues (2009) gives an ethnographic portrait of the consequences of all this on some areas in the Philippines where villages have become in effect the left-behind segment of an essentially transnational population.

If earlier migration was dominated by men working on construction sites in the Middle East and then for global shipping (Lamvik, 2002), recent years have seen a growth in female migration for nursing care and domestic work (POEA, 2008). Female migrants now outnumber men in annual deployments (POEA, 2008) so that if one parent remains behind, it is increasingly the father (Pingol, 2001). In 1992, 50 per cent of first-time migrants were female, rising to 72 per cent in 2006 (ILO, 2007).

Generally speaking, there are three avenues for legally recruiting migrants. The first type of recruitment is 'government to government' whereby the Philippine government agencies recruit directly to provide workers for the countries with which they have signed bilateral agreements. The second is through the hundreds of recruitment agencies which are regulated by POEA, the dedicated government organisation which processes all legal paperwork. Finally, the third option is what is called 'direct-hire', whereby a foreign employer recruits one or more individuals without the involvement of an agency. For this type of contract to be legal, all paperwork still has to be processed and approved by the government via POEA.

The processing of recruitment and the relevant paperwork can take anything from a few weeks up to several months depending on the destination and any legal obstacles. The cost of actually migrating also varies widely depending on the type of recruitment and the destination country. Although Philippine law stipulates that it is the employer who should shoulder the cost of migration, in practice it is often employees who pay for their own airfare or placement costs. Although by law no employee should pay recruitment fees exceeding the equivalent of one month's salary, in practice agencies may extract very steep payments which do not appear on the official paperwork. Representatives from recruitment agencies suggested that a contract in Taiwan typically costs about 50,000 PHP (£550) while a UK one can be up to 280,000 PHP (almost £4,000). Some of our participants were duped by scam agencies and ended up paying such sums several times over before gaining employment abroad. Given that local Filipino monthly salaries for nurses average 8,000 PHP (£88), it usually takes several years just to repay money borrowed to cover these costs, often creating debts within extended families. Remuneration abroad can greatly vary: a domestic in Brunei receives 11,500 PHP (£120) per month and a factory worker in Taiwan is paid 50,000 PHP (£550), while a fully registered nurse in the UK can expect to earn around £1,800 (180,000 PHP) per month including overtime. Even taking into account disparities in the local cost of living, these figures imply tremendous variation in the OFW experience and the potential benefits of migration, including the possibility that some migration is not justified if only economic criteria are considered.

The central role of the state in organising and regulating migration was evident from our research on the two government agencies, the POEA and the Overseas Workers Welfare Administration (OWWA) where we conducted interviews. The POEA deals with the process of migration up to the point of actual departure, while OWWA deals with the post-migration period and the subsequent welfare of migrants. The POEA identifies overseas labour demand and recruits relevant workers, oversees bilateral government agreements, regulates the recruitment process, monitors agencies, processes paperwork and checks for the legality of contracts and documentation. Finally, the POEA is the main provider of the pre-departure orientation seminars, which are mandatory for all workers prior to their departure from the Philippines. These seminars (which we attended) provide practical information about destination countries, but also a highly didactic framework of education in how the state expects overseas workers to behave when abroad.

OWWA was initially established as the 'Welfare Fund' in the early 1970s in order to provide assistance with the repatriation of Filipino migrants when encountering problems abroad. Gradually it grew into a fully fledged Administration that deals with OFW welfare and benefits. All legal migrants pay mandatory OWWA dues which make them eligible for this help. In order to support OFWs, OWWA has 35 posts/bureaus in 25 destination countries. OWWA helps with the repatriation of ill or distressed migrants and often acts as a mediator when there are disputes with employers regarding non-payment of wages, mistreatment, contract violation or passport confiscation. OWWA also deals with requests by left-behind families in locating lost or out-of-contact relatives, implying some incidences of abandonment. OWWA also provides benefits and special programmes for the families of OFWs, for example, scholarships for migrants' children, but also IT training for migrants' families who are encouraged to remain in touch. In Madianou and Miller (2011a) we note the increasing optimism amongst government agencies and policy-makers that mobile phones can alleviate some of the social costs of migration. Observations at the obligatory pre-departure seminars revealed migrants being urged to learn how to use the internet and encouraged to use their mobile phones to remain in frequent contact with families.

It is not surprising to see that the main sponsor of both POEA and OWWA is Globe, the second-largest telecommunications company which, amongst other things, sponsors one of OWWA's flagship awards: the 'Model OFW Family of the Year' which is awarded on three counts: the family's financial success; their retaining close ties despite separation and finally their positive contribution to the wider community. In 2008 the prize was considerable: 600,000 PHP (£6,600). Globe also sponsored the Pamaskong Salubong, 'Christmas Welcome' for returning OFWs, a group of whom is selected to be greeted by the President at the airport, and an 'OFW Family Day' celebrated at all OWWA regional offices across the Philippines and abroad.

The UK-based Filipino population

The official estimate for 2008 was that there were 203,497 Filipinos in the UK (POEA, 2009), making it the sixth most popular destination (POEA, 2008). However, our interviews within the telecommunications industry revealed that the incoming call traffic from the UK to the Philippines indicated a significant presence of undocumented, or other, migrants. The Philippine government has no bilateral agreement with the UK, which means that Filipino migrants come to the UK through their own social networks, or following their own employers in the case of domestic workers. In our sample, almost all domestic workers came to the UK following stints in the Middle East, Hong Kong, Taiwan or Singapore (or a combination of these), where they worked for employers who either moved, or returned to the UK, bringing their employees with them. A very significant proportion of the UK Filipino population consists of care workers following the British National Health Service's (NHS) systematic recruitment of nurses from the Philippines between late 1998 and the mid-2000s. The East Anglia NHS Trusts, which includes Cambridge, employs 3,000 to 4,000 Filipino nurses who have set up their own association (*Guardian*, 2006). Indicatively, representatives from one Manila recruitment agency which specialised in recruiting nurses for the NHS, told us in an interview that between 1999 and 2003 their agency alone would send up to 4,000 nurses per annum to the UK.

The systematic recruitment of nurses for the NHS and other national health systems prompted the establishment of hundreds of nursing and caregiving schools across the Philippines as such training was seen as a passport to work abroad. During our fieldwork we came across such colleges sometimes in the most remote areas of the country. However, as demand for care workers has dried out due to cutbacks and changes in immigration law across the EU, thousands of graduates were left stranded. According to a recent report, in 2009 about 100,000 nurses graduated from the Philippines but only 13,000 managed to get contracts abroad.[2]

Since the NHS stopped recruiting from the Philippines, Filipinos have come to the UK on student visa schemes which involve a combination of training and up to 20 hours of work per week (in 2010 reduced to 10 hours a week) in care homes for which 'students' receive the minimum wage. Given their formal status as students, these care workers do not feature in the official statistics, and they often incur very considerable migration costs in the region of £2,200–£3,000 which, as we will demonstrate in the next chapter, take a long time to repay. This is in sharp contrast to the situation of NHS recruited nurses, whose migration costs are minimal, with employers shouldering agency and travel expenses.

One of the reasons that explains the continued popularity of the UK as a destination country even after the NHS stopped recruiting is the fact that, for legal migrants, there is no maximum period of stay. In contrast to countries in the Middle East or South East Asia with which the Philippine government has signed bilateral agreements for the provision of short-term migrants, migrants see their stay in the UK as potentially long-term and many aim for naturalisation, which increases their rights as workers. The relative strength of the pound, especially before the economic crisis, was an additional significant factor. Yet, such observations should not be seen simply as evidence of migration being a rational decision made by individuals who seek to maximise their returns (as neoclassical economics would suggest, see Borjas, 1989). As we have already demonstrated, the conditions of UK-based migrants vary significantly, with nurses enjoying a range of benefits compared to migrants on student visas for whom the sheer cost of migration is particularly steep, making migration appear as a false calculation. In Chapter 3 we will illustrate the complex and often contradictory motivations for migration by focusing on the experiences of our actual participants.

Behind these institutional forces and factors that exemplify migrant trans-nationalism (Vertovec, 2009) lies quite another story. Most of our research was not within institutions, but directly with Filipina workers. For them the overriding concern was with their relationship to their families, and most especially to left-behind children. So to appreciate the specificity of Filipino migration we also need to engage with the particular idioms of motherhood and mothering and how these are undergoing transformations in a globalising context.

The cultural contradictions of Filipino motherhood

Our research recognised from the outset that motherhood cannot be reduced to some universal psychological model, but rather is embedded in social and cultural codes (see Glenn *et al.*, 1994; Scheper-Hughes, 1993), as are the meaning and social value of childhood (Zelizer, 1994). All social science research in the Philippines acknowledges the centrality of kinship and the family, but this is just as much the case with political and everyday discourse (Asis *et al.*, 2004).

The academic and popular literature on mothering and migration in the Philippines varies considerably depending both on the premises used and on the regions in which studies took place. By far the most influential account has been that of Parreñas (2001, 2005a) whose perspective comes largely from feminist and more universalist models of gender equality. Highly influential are popular and journalistic accounts which these days tend to assume that proper mothering depends on the explicit and demonstrative expression of certain emotional bonds in which love and care are made clear.

However, such explicit demonstrations of feelings may be contrary to Filipino traditional values, where both parents and children may have been expected to curb any such overt expressions of emotion and care. The extreme example of this difference may be found in nearby Bali where, as analysed by Wikan (1990), every effort is made to ensure that both mother and child suppress any overt display of emotion which is regarded as entirely uncivilised behaviour. Even the death of a loved one should not be met by tears. The Philippines is not Bali, but as McKay (2007) points out, it is not the US either. McKay analyses a concept of emotion *mailiw* that also depends precisely on not being overtly expressed. As Wolf (1997) notes, the revelation of emotional issues and problems is tightly controlled since the greatest fear is that this will lead to *hiya*, or shame.

This is highly relevant to our study because as the title of McKay's paper suggests, it is possible that for Filipinos the more appropriate way to express love and affection would be the sending of dollars rather than declaring emotional attachment. This is much closer to the understandings of parent–child relationships as dominated by idioms of reciprocal debt which were recorded by earlier anthropologists (Lynch and Guzman, 1974; Rafael, 1993). In a similar vein one can read Cannell's (1999: 29–58) highly nuanced analysis of the way marriage develops as a process, with the emphasis upon what people do for each other rather than what they say to each other. But also her evidence (*contra* Parreñas, 2001, 2005a) showed that in many respects marriage in the Philippines assumed a much more equal sharing of domestic work than that found in the West, which puts a rather different inflection upon critiques from outside (Cannell, 1999; Go, 1993: 24).

This is also true of Pingol (2001), whose work focuses upon left-behind husbands. Based on work with 50 such men in the Illocano region, she demonstrates that there are a series of often contradictory models of male behaviour, some of which reflect elements of machismo that may derive from more Spanish influences, and others which may have Malay roots which are much more compatible with men fully taking on the role of domestic labour. Furthermore, masculinity is differently expressed with respect to different areas of life, so that how a man behaves with respect to sexual relationships may be quite different from aspects of fatherhood or household work. Even working within older Illocano concepts of masculinity, there is therefore a wide range of potential reactions to this situation of men being left with primary responsibility for bringing up left-behind children. Finally there is Johnson's (1997) extraordinary and exemplary analysis of the intricacies of gender and power seen through the lens of transgendered bodies, again with a key focus upon exchange, that portrays a cosmology of gender that is clearly an altogether different world from understandings of gender elsewhere.

All these writings suggest we need to be quite circumspect when talking about expectations of mothering in the Philippines. But we also need to be careful to distinguish between studies of discourse and practice. In many ways our observations more closely accorded with the account given by Parreñas (2001, 2005a), than these alternative discussions. While we found that most people were aware of these traditional ideals, we have encountered several instances of strong emotional outbursts, quarrels and explicit demands for the overt expression of love. Part of the explanation may lie in the degree of regional diversity within the Philippines. The Philippines as a national entity is a relatively recent colonial construction (e.g. David, 2001; Zialcita, 2005) and anthropological, historical and sociological work has always suggested considerable regional differentiation. For example, McKay (2007) and Pingol (2001) draw from ethnographies in the Ifugao region of Northern Luzon. Cannell (1999) was researching in the lowlands of the Central region, while Johnson (1998) worked in the far South. By contrast, Parreñas (2001, 2005a) identified the resilience of gender inequalities despite the feminisation of migration in the provinces surrounding Manila – the same areas where we worked.

We argue that the main reason why we might expect the area around metro-Manila to differ from the rest of the Philippines is that it has for a considerable time been more exposed to international discourses. The clear evidence that Filipinos are well aware of the kind of presumptions of emotional bonding and care that are widely recognised as Western was evident from the discussion of the film *Anak* in the previous chapter, whose model of parent–child relationships are evidently as much derived from Hollywood as from any local source. Yet *Anak* was a highly successful and meaningful intervention into popular debates over the situation of left-behind children. Furthermore, we are dealing specifically with migration and it is likely that the very process of migration and the exposure this brings to models of care in places such as the UK will also favour these more international models as compared to local and regional expectations. Nevertheless we recognise that it is always problematic to talk simply in terms of 'the Filipino family' (though see Go, 1993; Medina, 2001). Rather we have to contend with an ever-expanding range of family patterns and practices, often underpinned by the experience of migration and transnationalism. In several of the succeeding chapters we shall see that the tension between competing models of motherhood is critical to the wider ambivalence we have addressed in the previous chapter, and which is itself accentuated by transnationalism. There are of course other parameters of difference. Some of our informants were from urban areas and evidently of middle-class background, while many were the children of migrant mothers whose background tended to be in low-income farming. But we did not note any systematic variation with regard to kinship and parenting norms along these lines, perhaps because of migrants' increasing exposure to international norms and increased incomes.

Migration seems to be both a catalyst contributing to such changes, but also itself a result of changes in family values. For example, while mothers commonly migrate in order to afford private education and material goods for their children, representing increasing pressures and expectations on the responsibilities of motherhood (Zelizer, 1994), these can also be related to more traditional ideas of kinship as a form of debt and obligation. Furthermore, the way traditional and more recent ideologies of both parenthood and childhood create a mixture of complementary and sometimes contradictory ideals, though this may be equally true of countries such as Germany or the UK (Beck-Gernsheim, 2002).

To the extent that it is possible to generalise about Filipino families, they may be described as extended and tightly knit, based on systems of bilateral, or cognatic kinship (Aguilar et al., 2009; Cannell, 1999; Medina, 2001), where descent is recognised equally down male and female lines. Family relationships are cemented through reciprocal exchanges which create strong bonds of debt and obligation. Individual family members are expected to promote collective family interests, and in this context the decision to migrate has often been understood as a household rather than an individual strategy (Asis et al., 2004). Within such a kinship system the bonds between siblings may be considered even stronger than the bond of marriage (Cannell, 1999). Such kinship systems tend to increase the number of people who may be considered relatives. And if that were not sufficient, the numbers can be even greater since our evidence (including the contents of *balikbayan* boxes, the cargo boxes filled with goods which are sent back as part of remittances [Szanton, 1996]) showed a tendency to incorporate some neighbours and friends as fictive kin on analogy with sibling sets (a tendency discussed in more detail with regard to seafaring families by Swift, 2010). As one participant put it, 'even if you are not a close relative you still have to help if asked'. This system of kinship is a critical factor throughout this book, since it means that the number of people who feel they can then make demands upon the income of migrants sometimes seems infinite.

Recent research (Aguilar et al., 2009; Asis et al., 2004; Tacoli, 1996) has suggested that motivations for migration are increasingly individualised although often still justified as family strategies. It is the family, rather than the state which is expected to provide basic support such as childcare given the absence of a welfare state. Because of the closeness of extended families, it is common for children to be looked after by the wider family members, in our sample typically the *lola* (grandmother), who tend to live nearby.

Even if gender remains different in each particular region of the Philippines, it is still safe to suggest that generally within Filipino societies parenting is a clearly gendered activity. Mothers are popularly referred to as 'the light of the home' (*Ilaw ng tahanan*) (Arellano-Caradang *et al.*, 2007; Asis *et al.*, 2004) and are assumed to be natural caregivers. At first glance this stress on clear-cut gender roles and the social value of the family would seem to be at odds with the state-sponsored female migration and the attendant family separation, though as noted above this is what facilitates high rates of remittances. In practice it is the closeness of family bonds which often explains why women migrate in the first place. Earning money abroad facilitates women's obligations to care and provide for their extended family and thereby fulfils their roles and related obligations as daughters, eldest sisters (*ates*) and mothers. Even when motivations to migrate are more personal, the fulfilling of one's obligations to one's family is always a ready, and widely accepted, justification for employment abroad. At the same time, many of the women who migrate are aware that their children will be looked after by their family network and are often confident (in practice, sometimes over-confident) about the quality of the care arrangements. In fact, there is a long tradition of internal migration when women from rural areas left their children behind with their own mothers or other relatives in order to seek work as domestics in urban centres (Brandewie, 1998). Domestic labour is not just the product of the transnational political economy. It is possible to argue that it is precisely because they are very close to their families, that women are able to migrate.

The co-presence in contemporary Philippines of more universal idioms of motherhood as exemplified by the film *Anak*, and basic to Parreñas (2005a), alongside more varied traditional expectations, is nothing new. Precedents would have included the successive impact of Islamic, Catholic, colonial and other hegemonic models. These are not to be regarded as simply 'Western'; for example one of the most influential forms of contemporary television are Korean soap operas. Today the influence of both education and the media contribute to the sense of dominance and normativity in these more hegemonic models, such as expressive emotional care and increasingly feminist ideals of gender equality, leading to an 'ideology of intensive mothering' (Hays, 1997) where Filipina transnational mothers 'expend a tremendous amount of time, energy and money to raise their children' (Hays, 1997: x). In practice this may apply primarily to middle-class and urban families rather than to rural Philippines who retain more local variations (see Cannell, 1999; Aguilar *et al.*, 2009), though it is precisely middle-class women who are most likely to migrate (Constable, 1999). This is because contrary to popular perceptions of migrants as coming from situations of destitute poverty, it is those who already possess the economic, social and cultural capital who can undertake the expensive project of migration (Portes and Rumbaut, 2006). Parreñas has observed that for many Filipinos migration therefore represents downward social mobility offset by an increase in financial status – what she terms 'contradictory class mobility' (2001: 150). Stills and Chowthis (2008), working with Filipino export processing zone workers in Taiwan, found that 91 per cent had college or university degrees. Moreover, Filipina women (and men) become increasingly exposed to universal Western models of parenting through migration, which reinforces prior local exposure to Western popular culture and its attendant normative representations of motherhood. Under such influences the feminisation of migration and the rise of 'left-behind children', roughly estimated around 9 million in 2004 (Parreñas, 2005a), become increasingly viewed as one of the hidden injuries of migration, prompting the establishment of charities and organisations dedicated to addressing this phenomenon.

ICTs and digital literacies in the Philippine context

If migration is one of the first attributes that academics associate with the Philippines, then mobile phone texting is perhaps the second, as from very early on the Philippines became known as the texting capital of the world, and it still has by far the highest rates of texting globally. The mobilisation of huge crowds in the protests of 2001 which culminated with the overthrow of President Estrada has been well documented by scholars (Castells *et al.*, 2006; Rafael, 2003; although see Pertierra *et al.*, 2002 for a more sceptical account) and has acquired paradigmatic status for what has been termed 'smartmobs' (Rheingold, 2003). Quite apart from the potential of texting for the coordination of political participation and protest movements, there is an additional, yet perhaps even more fundamental way in which texting has transformed Filipino everyday life. That is the way in which Filipino sociality, from friendship to flirting, is now very much conducted through texting, as Pertierra and his colleagues (2002) have demonstrated. The ubiquity of texting in Filipino social life and the ways in which this technology has been domesticated (Silverstone and Hirsch, 1992) point to the other way in which the Philippines can be understood as being at the vanguard of globalising trends.

In common with other developing countries, mobile phones dominate the Philippine media landscape while internet penetration rates remain low due to the scarcity of landlines.[3] Mobile internet represents an alternative, albeit an expensive one, for working or lower-middle-class families.[4] In 2006 when our research began there were almost 43 million mobile phone subscribers for a population of approximately 88.5 million (National Statistical Coordination Board, 2007: 1324), up from 15.3 million in 2002. This figure contrasts to only 7.2 million installed telephone landlines with 3.6 million subscribers in 2006 (National Statistical Coordination Board, 2007: 1322), more than half of which are located in the Capital region (ibid.: 1323). So for most Filipinos it is only the advent of mobile phone technologies that led to telephone availability.

The other conspicuous asymmetry is between the Philippines and the UK. For those without easy access to the internet, international calling from the Philippines is prohibitively expensive and therefore the opportunities to initiate communication with a significant other abroad are limited. Having said that, the cost of international calling has been significantly reduced from what it was in the 1970s when PLDT had the monopoly of landlines and it cost 250 PHP (£3.5) per minute to call the US. In 2008 a call to the US was 2.5 PHP (£0.035) per minute when using the pre-paid international card developed by Globe (the only one available at the time of fieldwork) although calls to other destinations are more expensive. For example, a call to the UK would be 40 PHP (£0.50) per minute. Still, such rates continue to be expensive relative to local salaries, which probably accounts for the asymmetry in inbound/outbound traffic at 7:1. However, representatives from both the major mobile phone companies suggested that a lowering of price might not shift the pattern of demand, which would remain greater for those who are abroad than for those left behind. According to mobile phone companies the average expenditure on international calls by OFW families is 300 PHP (approximately £4) per month, which is already very high for local standards.

Within the Philippines, the major discrepancy is between urban and rural areas, with metropolitan centres better connected in terms of landlines and fast internet connection. This combines with class, education and age parameters to determine the digital literacy of the Filipino population (see Livingstone, 2004 for a discussion of media literacy), confirming wider observations that class and socioeconomic status are digitally reproduced (see Hargittai, 2007 for findings pertaining to US college students). In our sample, almost all the Manila-based participants had broadband access to the internet, in stark contrast to our rural participants who very often relied on internet cafés in order to communicate with their relatives abroad. Access to the internet and a good connection can potentially correct the asymmetry of phone-based international communication, as the cost of webcam or chatting online is insignificant after the initial investment in hardware and the ISP subscription cost.[5] However, this in turn depends upon the mother also being connected, which in our sample was by no means always the case. Migrant workers' digital literacy also depends on education, class and crucially their type of employment (for similar observations see Merla and Baldassar, 2008). Domestic workers, for instance, who live-in with their employers are more constrained with internet-based communication, which usually takes place in an internet café or community centre. In addition some of our older informants struggle to adopt computer-based communication, even if they invest both in the computer and in classes, although we have encountered many participants who became media literate at the ages of 50 or 60.

The Filipino telecommunications landscape

As with many countries (e.g. compare Horst and Miller, 2006: chapter 2), Philippine telecommunications suffered for a considerable time from a monopoly control that led to unmet demand and poor coverage (see Ilano, 2005; Salazar, 2007). The Philippines was first connected by submarine cable in 1880 during Spanish control. The current monopoly derived from 1928 when four companies merged to form PLDT, first under US ownership and then from 1967 under local ownership. By 1990 there were only 1 million landlines – mainly in the metropolitan Manila region – for a population of 61 million. Prices set by commission guaranteed a

12 per cent rate of return. Not surprisingly PLDT was most vigorous in resisting attempts by the government to liberalise. The company was involved in various murky political interests, though to be fair even the World Bank at that time favoured monopoly control of telecoms. In 2005 PLDT still had 62 per cent of landlines, with low installation costs.

Liberalisation brought in several new players such as Bayantel and Digital, but these remained relatively small since very soon the only development of real importance was mobile communication. By 2003 there were already 20–25 million mobile phones and landlines were actually in decline. The company that most effectively broke the monopoly was Globe, which pioneered GSM digital backed by the Ayala family, one of the key oligarchical businesses of the Philippines. By 1999 Globe had overtaken Smart (first part-owned and then from 2000 fully owned by PLDT). But still in 2008 fixed-line teledensity remained at less than 5 per cent while mobile teledensity was 75 per cent and still growing.[6] The biggest revolution was in texting, which started as a free add-on to mobile phones but soon came to dominate voice calls, producing eight times the revenues of voice calls. From its inception the Philippines has had the world's highest number of users of texting, which by 2008 reached a staggering 1.39 billion texts a day (Reuters, 2008). By the end of 2008, Globe had 24.7 million mobile subscribers while Smart had 35.2 million. Although this is not entirely a duopoly, other players such as Sun Cellular are relatively small.

As in most developing countries (Castells *et al.*, 2006: chapter 8), the Philippine market is mostly pre-paid (some 95 per cent of the market) using low denominations ranging from 10 PHP (£0.14) to the very rare 500 PHP (£7.11). Unusually, credit (locally referred to as 'load') has an expiration date which means that a 30 PHP top-up card will expire three days after an account is actually topped up. This pressure to spend any credit before it expires is one factor that has led to the dominance of texting, such that within the Philippines we found that people were often quite startled by the use of voice calls for non-urgent purposes, and we quickly learnt that it was best to text people in advance that we were about to call them. Texting, which started off as a free service, remains very cheap at 1 PHP per SMS. Mobile phone companies have even developed products whereby SMS are sold in bulk thereby further reducing their price, as do recent products that allow subscribers to pay a flat rate for unlimited texting.

The OFW market[7]

The mobile phone companies were surprisingly late in appreciating the sheer scale and potential of the OFW market, creating targeted products since only about 2005. Today, however, the two major players Globe and Smart now place considerable emphasis on developing new products tailored to the needs of migrants and their families and are subsequently making inroads into this potentially lucrative market. Both companies now have dedicated departments for product development and marketing for overseas populations. Globe's marketing strategy for the OFW market included slogans such as: 'With Globe's Worldwide Services, the family will always be together.' (*Palagi buo ang pamilya.*) And: 'Christmas is more colourful and happier when the family is together.' Or: 'With Globe, you're always together.' Such slogans are echoed by one of their senior managers, who told us: 'we keep [the OFW families] together'.

However, 'this keeping of the migrant family together' emerged more from the way the companies have developed products to reflect the prior creative appropriation by migrants of already existing features within mobile phones. The most common way in which transnational families keep in touch is through texting via a roaming phone. This is effectively a SIM card registered with one of the Filipino networks, which can be used abroad to receive SMS messages. Although roaming voice calls are very expensive and perhaps only used in the first hours upon arrival in the UK (if at all), receiving SMS is free as sending an SMS to a roaming phone is priced at the local phone rate of one peso (£0.01). By contrast, sending an SMS to a UK number costs 20 PHP (£0.28). Not surprisingly, almost all Filipinos we met during our fieldwork have a roaming phone used for receiving texts, in addition to one (or sometimes two) UK numbers used for voice calls. Some companies in the Philippines now sell SIM cards pre-registered for roaming. Such phones merely require credit to be topped up once a month. Both Globe and Smart have dealers abroad (including the UK) who sell 'load', which can now also be bought online. 'Load' can also be passed on electronically (*pasa-load*) so that a child can ask his or her mother to send them credit for their phone to work (or vice versa – their mother can ask for her phone to be topped up by someone in the Philippines).

Apart from these widespread appropriations by transnational families, mobile phone companies are developing more sophisticated products such as a mini cell-site on board ships, introduced since 1999, which allows Filipino seafarers to use their roaming phones. Currently they are developing products to allow for the sending of remittances. For example, Globe have developed *G-cash* which enables the user to send money through the phone via SMS. Smart also had a similar product, *SMART padala*, but at the time of fieldwork it facilitated transactions only between Bahrain and the Philippines. Most remittances are still sent through specialist companies and banks.

During the time of our fieldwork, Globe had just launched the Tipid or IDD card for international calling (40 minutes to the US for 100 PHP, but only 12 minutes to the UK) in two versions: *sakto* which charges per second and is best suited for making several short calls, for example, to wish different family members Happy Christmas; and the regular one which the company calls *lambingan*, which means to 'show affection' by making longer calls.

Selling 'load' (especially as it can now be done electronically) has led to some entrepreneurial activity also among OFWs and their families. Smart in collaboration with the Development Bank of the Philippines started a franchising initiative targeted at OFWs, the idea being that they can set up their own business selling load, or a wireless internet café as a way of investing OFW remittances. This builds upon well-established observations about local entrepreneurial activity in selling 'load' (compare Horst and Miller, 2006: 118–120). This was the way some of our informants generated income to pay for their own communications. For instance, one of our participants sends at least 100 SMS daily to her husband's roaming phone in Saudi. She funds her prolific texting by selling 'load' to people in her *barangay* [neighbourhood].

Conclusion

This chapter has concentrated upon three aspects of the background to our study: the institutionalisation of migration, the diverse concepts and ideals of parenting and the provision and use of new communications especially mobile phones and texting. An essential point made throughout this volume regards the interconnectedness between these apparently very different contextual factors. The Philippines has garnered a reputation for being in the vanguard of globalising trends, both for the sheer scale and government support for migration and for quickly becoming the world's leading nation in the use of mobile phones and especially texting.

As shown in the last section there are clear links between the intensification of emigration and developments in the telecommunications industry, particularly evident in the domestication of mobile phones and the advent of devices such as the roaming phone. Migrant transnationalism, which affects almost every family in the Philippines, has had major consequences for the traditional ways of parenting and mothering in particular. The media are a key factor in spreading more universal models of appropriate mothering and new expectations for the way parenting should be expressed.

In this chapter we have concentrated on the structural and more impersonal factors of institutional and technical development. Even with respect to mothering, we have structured our discourse in terms of highly generalised models and the way these complement and contradict each other, something that is by no means unique to the Philippines. However, our actual engagement with these processes came through an ethnographically orientated research programme which was inevitably intimate and often poignant. To appreciate and understand any of the factors so far introduced we need also to convey their consequences at this more personal level and as narrated in the stories and experiences of our informants. For this reason the next chapter, which deals with the reasons migrants give for going abroad and sometimes for staying abroad, is derived from our more personal, ethnographic engagements. While many of these same themes, such as ideals of mothering and the problems of dealing with agencies and government bodies will reappear, we will come to see them more through the eyes of these individual migrants and the actual consequences they have had for their lives.

3

WHY THEY GO – AND WHY
THEY STAY

The reasons why women migrate and the reasons why they most often decide to prolong migration are crucial for understanding their relationship to their children, the nature of the communication between them and the role that media technologies play in these processes. This chapter examines these questions, drawing on the interviews and encounters with our participants in London and Cambridge. Although most of the interviews were with Filipina migrant workers who are also mothers, we also include material from our work with single women and some men (for more information on our sample, see Appendix). The intention is to complement the previous chapter which looked at the context of migration from the point of view of state policy and regulation by providing an ethnographic perspective on how migrants themselves understand their trajectories and decisions.

Academic theories of migration have often favoured economic or structural explanations and have often revolved around push/pull factors in order to explain migration flows. For example, neoclassical macro-economic theory, the oldest and very influential theory of international migration, focuses on the economic disparity between sending and receiving countries and the asymmetries in the demand and supply of labour. The microeconomic variant of neoclassical economics conceptualises migrants as rational agents who migrate in order to maximise their income (Borjas, 1989: 461). World systems theory, an equally influential paradigm, argues that migration is the result of global capitalism and the structural asymmetries created because of the industrialisation of the developed world at the expense of developing nations (see Massey et al., 1993). In Chapter 2 we demonstrated how migration is a clear economic policy of the Philippine state which actively sponsors and regulates migration. We also saw how the demand for health workers in the British NHS led to the intense recruitment of Filipino care workers during the early 2000s. Although we obviously acknowledge the structural political and economic reasons, here we argue that they cannot be the only explanations for international migration. Personal, family and social reasons emerge as hugely important. Our data suggest that the decision to migrate usually involves a combination of reasons and almost never simply a single motivation. Although economic motivations are central, they are certainly not the only ones and in some cases may be secondary. Several of the alternative factors are discussed below, for example, the importance of personal networks (Boyd, 1989), gender stratification and the wider gender inequalities including the physical violence that women experience (Parreñas, 2001: 78–79), the emergence of a 'culture of migration' (Massey et al., 1993: 452–453) and the 'cumulative causation approach' according to which 'migration causes more migration' (Massey et al., 1993: 461) as a combination of variables intersect and reinforce one another (Massey, 1990). Our evidence supports the arguments of these approaches and demonstrates that no single explanation can fully capture the multifaceted process of migration. However, what also emerges from our research is one comparatively neglected motivation for emigration, which is the desire for personal development and self-improvement, and this represents one of this chapter's contributions to the literature on migration. More generally, what we have found is that the experience of migration is far more contradictory and complex than allowed for by some of the top-down theories (see also Constable, 1999). This is partly a consequence of the discrepancy between the reasons for migration that are deemed socially and culturally acceptable and the often more personal, less readily acknowledged or openly articulated motivations which are evident in women's actual practices and decisions.

In addition, the socially acceptable economic motivations become less significant – while personal reasons become more salient – when explaining the decision to prolong migration, which is the focus of the second part of this chapter. As such, this chapter underlines the advantages of a more ethnographic approach that puts the migrants' own perspective as active, reflexive agents at the centre of the analysis and can provide a more nuanced picture of these contradictions.

Why they go

Trajectories

More than half of our participants came to London after stints in other destinations, usually in the Middle East or Hong Kong, but also Singapore or Taiwan. Several of our participants have migrated a number of times as return migrants before coming to London. Sometimes these migrations are seamless, in that one follows directly from the other; in other cases they are interrupted by a period back in the Philippines. Women may often migrate to the Middle East on a two-year contract, return to the Philippines, have children and then migrate again to the Middle East, and from there to London. London itself may be the final destination, or just a stepping stone for migrating to the US or Canada. The reasons for each migration often depend on the point of an individual's life cycle.

Marivic first migrated to Singapore when she was still single and in her early twenties, although even that had been preceded by an internal migration from Ilocos Sur, the region in the Northern Philippines where she was born, to Manila, where she worked in a clothes factory. At that time Marivic was having some trouble at home with her parents and 'wanted to get away from it', 'to clear her mind'. Although Marivic sent some remittances to her parents, she saved most of her income, as her parents were self-sufficient and as an only child she did not have any siblings to care for. Following her experience in Singapore, she briefly returned to her village in Ilocos Sur, but soon decided to leave again. This time she wanted 'the experience of a different country' so she chose Kuwait, which was soon followed by Hong Kong. While she was in Hong Kong, she met her husband – himself an OFW in Saudi – who courted her for five years by sending letters and audio recorded cassette tapes and with whom she fell in love. They eventually both returned to the Philippines and had two children. But when the children started school the couple realised that it was hard for them to make ends meet, so Marivic decided to leave once again for Hong Kong, this time to pay for her children's education and to buy some more land for the family. It was easier for her to get a job as a woman. In fact, most women of her age had left her village to work abroad. Her husband looks after the children and also works on their land. Marivic stayed in Hong Kong for five-and-a-half years until she came to the UK, following the relocation of her employers. When we met her she had been in London for four years and planned to bring over her children and husband.

Marivic's story illustrates the confluence of a number of motivations and how reasons evolve along with her life course. Her curiosity to experience a different country is a theme present in many of the life histories we collected. Also common were economic motivations such as the need to pay for children's education, and structural factors such as the demand for domestic workers which makes it easier for a woman to find work abroad. The fact that most women of Marivic's age have left the village to work in Hong Kong suggests a wider culture of migration which legitimates and normalises such decisions.

An important factor in this case was that Marivic had close family and a supporting husband to look after their children. Marivic's family was one of the very few in our sample where traditional gender roles were reversed and where the man became the 'househusband'. Marivic is from Ilocos Sur, in the Northern Philippines, close to the area where Pingol carried out an ethnography which uncovered exceptions to traditional concepts of masculinity to accommodate female migration (Pingol, 2001). Otherwise our evidence suggests that fathers are usually conspicuously absent from the upbringing of their children, a finding we share with Parreñas (2005a). Also unusual in Marivic's case was the absence of siblings as a factor in migration, a contrast with the next two life histories.

Edith was born in 1954 in the island of Samar. The eldest daughter of 11, she always had to look after her younger siblings, especially since her mother's death when her youngest sister was aged five. After graduating from college, she worked as a civil servant, but because of the low salary decided to migrate to Qatar where she worked as a nanny. She stayed there for four-and-a-half years, during which time she married an old friend during one of her return visits to the Philippines. After four years she 'got bored' and applied to go to Hong Kong on a new contract. All this time her husband remained at home and they only met every two years when she returned to renew her visa. Then in 1993 at the age of 39 she decided that she wanted to have a child and returned to the Philippines where she had a daughter. Edith left again for Hong Kong when her daughter was nine months old. At that time her daughter was taken care of by her husband and a *yaya* (a paid nanny) – who is also a distant relative of her husband. Edith continued to visit every two years, remaining with her daughter again for one month when Evelyn was almost three years old. Then when Evelyn was six, Edith decided to return because she wanted to tutor her, as she was starting school. But after six further years when Evelyn was 11, family hardship dictated that Edith, now aged 51, should go to Qatar, an 'easier' destination than Hong Kong where 'one spends too much money'. She had also applied to work as a teacher in the Philippines, but as she lacked the personal connections – 'a political backer' – she did not get the job. As Edith noted: 'But it's so painful to leave my daughter because she was 11 years old. It was so hard to explain to her that I had to go. I had no money to send her for school if I didn't go. I sent my daughter to a Montessori private school because I want a good education. It's so expensive.' From Qatar, Edith moved to the UK together with her employers. She describes coming to London as 'the greatest blessing' of her life. In Qatar she would earn US$200 a month, less than her weekly wage in London. While she may earn more, she also helps a wider range of relatives, paying her nephews' and nieces' school fees. She feels this requires her to stay in London at least until her daughter finishes college, which will be another seven years. She has no plans to bring her family over as she feels that it is best for her daughter to be in the Philippines: 'It's safer there.' Also her husband is happy with his life in Manila, where he owns a *sari-sari* store[1] and does not want to leave. He himself has migrated internally from their island to Manila, and only sees their daughter once or twice a year. This means that Evelyn at the age of 15 has been cared for by seven different people excluding her own parents. Even though Edith has spent most of her life abroad, she has not yet built a house or acquired other property as all her income has been channelled into her family's immediate needs.

Edith's life history illustrates the 'contradictory social mobility' in terms of her skills and education noted by others (Hochschild, 2000; Parreñas, 2001). Typical of other participants is that her decision to remain in the Philippines when her daughter reached school age was stymied by the impossibility of finding a job locally at the age of 51. Although these economic imperatives are highly significant, there are additional factors in Edith's sequential migrations and in particular for her continuing to stay abroad. For her, being in London is a 'blessing' and despite her daughter's wayward behaviour which she recognises is a cry for help, she does not intend to return. She feels fulfilled by her work abroad. To return to the Philippines would also mean that she would lose her empowered status as the relative who helps the family and thereby commands respect as well as her sense of personal development that comes with her English and computing classes. During our fieldwork Edith learnt to send emails and chat on Yahoo Messenger, and even though her daughter still has no access to the internet in the remote, rural area where they live, Edith is proud of her achievement and 'is now ready for when her daughter will be able to go online'. But we can already discern the tension between her sense of herself as a mother and increasingly as an independent woman.

Similarly, Elisa, a Cambridge-based nurse, first migrated to Saudi Arabia when she was still single. As *ate* (eldest daughter) she was expected to assist her mother with her siblings' education. She was proud to inform us that she had put her brother and sister through college. Eventually Elisa met her husband, also an OFW, in Riyadh where they had their first child. Elisa returned to the Philippines with her four-month-old son whom she left with her mother so that she could start a new contract. However, after her second child was born two years later she decided to return to the Philippines and become a full-time mother. This had been a difficult decision, since Elisa enjoyed her job and missed her independence. But when her husband had a stroke which left him incapacitated, their savings quickly dwindled and she decided to take up work again in a local Manila hospital. She soon realised that her nurse's salary was hardly enough to sustain the family's needs and particularly her children's school fees for one of the most prestigious Manila schools, so when she found out that the NHS was recruiting, Elisa decided to apply to come to England. She has been working as a nurse in Cambridge since 2001. Her eldest sons are university students in Manila (one studying nursing himself, as the 'passport for going abroad'), but her youngest is still at school and Elisa hopes that she can bring him over one day. Whilst in the UK, Elisa developed a rare health condition which requires a weekly treatment, otherwise expensive, but free on the NHS. Without staying in Cambridge, she would be unable to afford either her own, or her husband's medical bills. As her son in Manila acknowledged, his mother would be dead if she had not come to the UK.

Once again a plethora of reasons converge to explain Elisa's initial decision to migrate and her decision to stay abroad. Economic grounds combine with status and her aspirations for her siblings and her children. Any initial economic motivations are exacerbated by the absence of any public health system and insurance in the Philippines. Furthermore, although Elisa initially migrated to help her family, she also enjoys the independence and respect that she receives through her job. Each of these motivations, from the economic and structural through to the more personal, requires further elaboration, which is the substance of the next section.

Between need and aspiration: children's education and building the house

In a situation where labour migration is generally referred to as economic migration, it is those factors which dominate the established literature. But our evidence for the diversity of the OFW experience suggests that the precise nature of these economic needs varies widely. While some women migrate because they face crippling debts, or bills due to medical emergencies, for most of them the prime motivation is the improvement in the family's quality of life, which usually boils down to two things: paying for children's private education and building a better family home (Aguilar *et al.*, 2009: 100–160). Our informants rarely came from a situation of extreme poverty, reinforcing other's observations that those who migrate are those who already possess the necessary economic, cultural and social capital (see Portes and Rumbaut, 2006).

Nora had lived a comfortable life in the Philippines until her husband lost his job during the economic collapse of the Marcos years. Once their savings ran out, the family found themselves living in poverty, struggling even for basic essentials. They became dependent on relatives from the US who offered to take on the fees for her son's private education. Nora's husband tried to migrate to Saudi Arabia but was refused a work visa because of his poor health. So after insisting and almost begging her husband, Nora left for Riyadh to work as a nanny. After nine months in Saudi Arabia the family Nora worked for visited the UK and Nora decided to stay in London for good, where she has now retired.

For others, however, migration would be better described as aspirational. When Marcela, a nurse from Ilo Ilo, left for Ryadh to work as a nurse, her motivation was primarily to pay for her children's private education. Her remittances also helped to buy a house in Manila. After 11 years in Saudi Arabia, Marcela returned to the Philippines for about seven years. By that time her relationship with her first husband had collapsed and she had married Marvin, with whom she started up a business. However, the high expense of maintaining her various properties in the Philippines meant that she was open to the possibility of migrating again. In 2002, at the height of the NHS recruitment from the Philippines, she decided to apply for a nursing job in the UK. She described this as 'too good an opportunity' to miss. She passed the telephone interview and her papers were ready in three months: 'It was that easy.' When we met her, she already held British citizenship and her aim was to stay in England but visit the Philippines regularly.

Generally, although experiences vary, there are two main material goals that women seek to achieve by going abroad. The first is to pay for their children's education. There are expenses even if children go to a state school, but the vast majority of our participants send their children to private schools (often owned by the Church) which are very expensive relative to local salaries. The range of fees varies between 10,000 to 30,000 PHP (£142 to £426) for provincial private schools and 83,000 PHP (£1,180) a year for a highly esteemed school in Manila for grade 7. Given that a teacher's annual gross income is around 100,000 PHP (£1,422), it is obvious that private education is otherwise unaffordable. It is perhaps ironic that in order to achieve this, most of our participants were prepared to accept downwards social mobility (Parreñas, 2001), sometimes moving from college-educated professionals to becoming employed as domestic workers and nannies, to achieve higher salaries.

Children's education is viewed as a key parental responsibility. As Angelo, a male nurse from Cambridge, put it: 'In the Philippines it's our culture that education is the gift, the only diamond ring that our parents can give us. Nobody can take education from us, and if we have education then we can go anywhere.' State schools are regarded as having poor standards and private schooling is essential for good career prospects. Rodolfo, a male nurse from London, said that:

> People in the Philippines really care about the University you graduated from. Say, in the job ads they specifically ask for people coming from prestigious universities. That would be done on any Philippine magazine. Generally University of the Philippines is number one. Followed by Ateneo de Manila, and University of Saint Thomas.

The second main goal is building a house. Not everyone achieves this OFW dream even after many years of migration, as remittances often go to repaying the cost of migration and to relatives. More problematic is the abuse of remittances by families who syphon off money intended for house-building to other activities such as cock-fighting, drugs and mistresses. People rarely confessed to such events within their own family (though some did), but readily confirmed it for other families.

For those who manage to invest in property, these range from *nipa* (traditional bamboo) houses usually in the countryside, to large villas, or modern Manila condominiums. There is a vast industry devoted to selling the latter to OFWs, with a very evident presence in the main London barrio fiesta.[2] House-building may continue as a project even when an OFW has decided to settle abroad and managed to bring over their family. Aguilar observed such unoccupied mansions perched on the hills of Southern Luzon, where he argues they continue to symbolise the maintenance of ties of relatedness between overseas kin and the community left behind (Aguilar *et al.*, 2009: 157–160).

Such processes can exacerbate class differentiation both within the Philippines and abroad. Most nurses come from urban and predominantly middle-class[3] areas while domestics tend to come from rural and generally poorer areas. The higher salary of nurses may allow them to invest more in private education and property. The situation is more complex for domestic workers. Some of those who work in central London and live-in so that they have few expenses may achieve higher remittances than nurses. We gained access to several years' worth of remittance slips from Judy, a domestic who sent £48,117 between 2000 and 2005 in 165 remittances: an average of around £8,000 per annum (given there were some gaps in the receipts, this should be considered a minimum). Judy built three homes back in the Philippines for herself and her children. But others earn a good deal less. The explosion of nursing colleges in the Philippines (responding to the demand for care labour in countries such as the UK) is attracting students from lower-class backgrounds and quite remote areas (Amrith, 2010). An in-between category of care workers for the elderly and children, or nursing assistants, is also growing. Although on the one hand even low-paid domestics can now send back consumer goods previously the preserve of the middle class (Amrith, 2010), we also observed a sharp manifestation of class distinctions within the UK-based Filipino diaspora exemplified in the unwillingness of nurses to mix socially with domestic workers.

Remittances tend to be spread across the extended family following the pattern of bilateral kinship, which means that helping siblings and then nephews and nieces becomes a constant demand upon migrants. Ideally, the first to migrate is the *ate* though in practice it may simply be the first who manages to find work. There is an extensive literature on the degree to which Philippine migration should be regarded more as a family or an individual strategy (see DeJong *et al.*, 1983, 1986; Lauby and Stark, 1988). Tacoli (1996) finds examples of both among migrants in Rome while Rosario (2005) notes that even 'electronic marriages' can actually reflect a collective decision by the family for one woman to be married abroad in order to put the whole family through school, with the extended family taking her to the airport to send her away for marriage. Our data provide considerable evidence for individual motivations, but suggest these are often legitimated as obligations to one's family:

> *Elisa*: When I came to Saudi Arabia I had a dream. Because my father died when I was only twelve years old. So I said to my mother, you give me reason to study and she saved money for me to study. So in return I give her the best. We lived in the province. When I finished my study, I worked. As soon as I finished and graduated I had one advantage. That's why I let my brother and sister continue studying. Nobody stopped in our family. You still see the poverty there. So I said to my mother, don't worry. If I have experience I will go abroad. I will buy our own house and everything.

Although Nelia, a domestic worker in London, has never refused any of her six siblings the help that they need, she feels that there are often too many requests. Whenever she calls her mother, usually three times a week, 'my brother, he says he wants to talk to me. He says, "You know, your nephew wants to go to school, but he cannot go because we lack money to pay his school." Every time I call there's a problem.'

Clearly one cannot separate economic and social imperatives, since the primary demand for money derives from a problem of kinship recognised by Strathern (1996) that there is no point at which you can effectively 'cut' a network based on bilateral kinship. Cannell (1999: 54) suggests obligations to siblings are often seen as paramount, and we found considerable sensitivity when one relative seems to be recognised by a migrant more than another.

So although economic motivations, whether urgent or aspirational, are undoubtedly compelling, it would be misleading to assume that they are always fulfilled, or that they are rationally pursued. In fact, most women admitted that the cost of migration itself is very high and it takes years to break even. Several of our informants resorted to loans, sometimes under unfavourable conditions, took their valuables to pawnshops, and borrowed from other relatives, especially to pay the initial agency fees which can reach up to 280,000 PHP (almost £4,000).

When judged solely by economic criteria, migration can even be a gross miscalculation. Although Donna led quite a comfortable life with her husband, they found their needs increasing once their two children started school. The fact that the construction company where her husband was working was also hit by the global financial crisis added to their concerns. So when her sister-in-law, a nurse in England, suggested that Donna come to join her it sounded like an excellent idea. In 2008 this was only possible through a student visa scheme which requires a hefty agency and visa fee in addition to the travel and tuition costs. For Donna the total was over 300,000 PHP (£4,000). Even after her sister-in-law contributed half, the family had to borrow heavily to fund this. Donna's original visa application was unsuccessful, and during the appeal process she became unexpectedly pregnant. When the appeal was successful, she faced a dilemma between leaving her new baby or giving up on this 'investment'. Speaking to her sister-in-law, she sensed her disappointment and disapproval about not taking up this heavily subsidised opportunity. Donna had an *utang na loob* (a strong form of personal debt discussed in Chapter 6) to her sister-in-law and therefore felt obliged to take up her care worker's course in England, leaving behind her daughter of six weeks. What she had not realised was that as a student she could work for only up to 20 hours a week on the minimum wage. Since January 2010 the UK government further reduced that to 10 hours a week. Donna takes on any part-time cleaning or babysitting job she can find to supplement her income and estimates that it will take her at least two years to simply repay the debt her family accrued in order to pay the visa and agency fees. Until then she is unable to contribute to her family's financial situation. If, on the other hand, she returns home, she faces a crippling debt, impossible to pay off on Filipino salaries. In short, Donna is trapped.

Other structural factors: unemployment and the absence of a welfare state

The incentive to migrate comes not just from opportunities created abroad by the international demand for care work, but also the lack of opportunities for women in the Philippine labour market, such that the alternative to migration was often unemployment, especially for women over 40. Another factor already noted is the cost of medical care, either long-term or emergency. The Philippines lacks much by way of a state health care system while private health care is very expensive, and sometimes unobtainable. Parents may turn to remittances, as when Greta faced hospital bills after a new industrial site opened close to their family home in Pampanga and her children developed asthma and other complications which required expensive medication:

> And our children always get sick. It's very hard. My son is having allergies. He's having tonsillitis always. That's why it's very hard. We're always in the

> hospital, seeing the doctor, and it's very hard, even though my husband is working hard. [...] In the Philippines we're not covered. Only half of insurance SSS – Social Security System. They only pay half and it's once a year.
>
> *Greta, domestic worker and mother of three, London*

Similarly, Karen, a Cambridge nurse in her twenties, feels that she was able to save her father's life after he had a life-threatening motorcycle accident which left him paralysed:

> They had to open him twice. It left him paralysed. At least he is still alive. [...] The first hospital they took him to was a private one. This is the nearest hospital. They said to my Mum you have to decide whether you want us to operate or.... They didn't know whether he was going to live. [...] He was in hospital for nearly a month, ICU.

Without her wages in England, Karen could not have guaranteed the fees without which hospitals will not operate. For Irene, an aspiring artist in an *au pair* arrangement, a key motivation for migrating to London was finding treatment for her rare genetic disease. These issues of health reflect a more general sense of disappointment and disillusion with the Philippines itself as a failing state. As Donna put it: 'There is no order in the country.'

In addition, whatever the travails and forms of exploitation found abroad, care work itself is often regarded as being light compared to traditional work within the Philippines. Some of our participants have family working in farming and are unlikely to romanticise the backbreaking and dull routines of rice planting and harvesting. But improving education is creating expectations that the Philippines economy currently has little chance of fulfilling. As Aguilar (2002b: 444) puts it: 'in innumerable cases, the departure of workers for overseas employment is an indictment of a society that, while cultivating aspirations to modernity and life goals of higher status, has provided them with limited opportunities to fulfil the self'.

Relationship breakdown, domestic violence and gender inequalities

Relationship breakdown is a motivation for migration in which personal and structural reasons (relating to gender inequalities and the position of women in Philippine society) combine. Parreñas (2001) has described this as a 'hidden cause for migration' in the sense that it is hardly acknowledged in the theories of international migration. An exception is Aguilar (2002b) who suggested that around a quarter of the cases in his sample involved women who were at least partly trying to escape from problematic and unsuccessful marriages (Aguilar, 2002b: 429). A significant number of our participants attributed their migration to the unhappy or even abusive relationships they were in and the ensuing marriage breakdown. Judy and Janice both decided to leave when they could not take any more:

[I left to escape] from violence, yeah. And also to help my children. Because there's no future with him because there was one night when he came, he kicked my children, and I told him, 'If you are angry with me, just hit me, not our children. They are innocent.' It's good that my mother came because we are just in a separate house. My mother come because maybe I would have just blacked out already. I took a knife. . . . We struggled and were just fighting and it was good my mother came. [. . .] Because I really wanted to kill him, because when you're fed up already.

Judy, domestic worker and mother of four, London

Judy had wanted to leave her husband before their relationship had reached such levels of violence, but had encountered strong family opposition and pressure to stay with her husband. Her grandparents had told her: 'You stick with him because you're married already. If you want to separate with him, nobody will support you, what about your children?' The fact that divorce is still illegal in the Philippines[4] means that there were few options for women who want to leave their relationships. In Vicky's case, when her husband had a child with his lover, she was actually urged both by her in-laws and her own family to go abroad in order to avoid the stigma:

My marriage broke up. He was in uniform, you know, he was good look-ing, and women were after him. So he had another woman and that woman got pregnant, had a baby. We were fighting. And my father-in-law was very good, he took us to a big house for us to stay, and my father-in-law suggested . . . because they started recruiting for people to go to England then, so he suggested 'Why don't you go abroad, I will look after your children, I will finance everything you need.' And then I said 'This is a good idea, but then I will have difficulties being away from my children', so I got to my mum's house, and told them, and they said 'That is a good idea', because they wanted me to be happy and maybe to forget about . . .

Vicky, retired, mother of three, London

Vicky told us that the family lived relatively comfortably with her husband's salary as a policeman and her own as a teacher. She did not think that she would have left if it hadn't been for the collapse of her relationship, as she 'loved her children'. But it would have been impossible for her to sustain her children as a single mother and she would have had to depend on the generosity of her richer in-laws who either wanted her to tolerate her husband's antics or to go abroad. Even her own parents concurred with the decision to migrate: 'My mother said "You go abroad and try to make things [better] for you, perhaps you will be more happy there".'

Janice experienced both physical violence and humiliation by her husband's affairs. Although she admitted that 'life was very hard' for her family, she actually 'left because of my husband. My first reason is because of that.' Strikingly, all these women who reported relationship breakdown and abuse as reasons to go abroad had never wanted to get married to their husbands in the first place. They had felt that in varying degrees they had been forced into marriage, usually following a pregnancy. Janice was 18 years old and a civil engineering fresher at college when she met her husband. Getting pregnant meant not only that she had to marry a man she did not love, but also that she had to abandon her degree and experience denunciation from her own family. As the only one out of six siblings who managed to go to college, Janice always regretted that she never managed to study for more than one term. Her family were also upset at what they saw as her wasting the opportunity they had granted her. So when the relationship with her husband soured beyond repair and after a very violent episode in which 'they almost killed one another', she decided to leave him and their three children to go to Hong Kong. Such was her fear of her husband's reaction that she did not tell him or anyone else where she was and at first only sent letters to her children without disclosing her address. But when she sent some presents for her children through a friend her coordinates were revealed and she was persuaded to give her husband, who came to join her in Hong Kong, another chance.

One of the most severe consequences of the breakdown in a woman's marriage is the resulting financial burden – especially in cases when the husband has left to start a new family and abrogates sole responsibility to the mother to provide for their children. Usually this means that the mother has no choice but to go abroad. If the relationship breaks down during the mother's migration this may lead her to prolong her absence. For the children, this can effectively mean the loss of both parents, or alternatively, they find themselves pawns within a constant battle between estranged parents.

Our evidence so far supports Parreñas' arguments that escaping gender stratification is a hidden cause of migration (Parreñas, 2001: 79). As she puts it: 'In the Philippines, gender stratification spurs the migration of women in resistance to male abuse, the double day, labour market segmentation, and single motherhood' (Parreñas 2001: 79). But while Parreñas (2001: 79) argues that gender stratification is ultimately inescapable for migrant women, because they are largely employed in domestic and care work, and cannot effectively escape patriarchy (see also Pessar, 1999), our subject-centred approach has revealed that the issues are more complex as some of our participants experience migration as a form of empowerment and an opportunity for self-development.

Self-improvement, maternal ambivalence and social status

For women, the lack of prospects within the Philippines, especially following improved education, combined with traditional and conservative attitudes to gender relations explains the prospect of migration as self-improvement. Greta, for example, was a trained teacher who loved her job. After she married and had children she gave up her job and focused on raising her children because they could not afford a nanny on a teacher's salary:

And I was in the house, taking care of the children. [...] I missed my job. I was always upset. Always not in the mood. I was telling myself that my degree was wasted. My brother [in London] said I have a friend here looking for a job, a domestic helper, and he was a friend, a diplomat. He can easily get people from the Philippines.

Greta, domestic and mother of three, London

So when Greta's family ran into difficulties following her husband's redundancy and her son's health problems and concomitant medical bills, she 'found the courage' to follow her brother to London. Even though as a domestic she was doing precisely the same chores that she detested as a housewife, she did not feel that her degree was wasted, but rather felt appreciated and valued.

Similarly, Nelia worked in an administrative job until she met her husband. During her difficult pregnancy she had to resign from her job and stay at home and she subsequently never returned to work. Although she loved her son, she also missed her job and the independence that came with it. 'I was very bored at home', she told us. She was also growing increasingly frustrated with her husband, as he actively prevented her from going to a job interview by hiding the invitation letter. When she heard about the possibility of a direct hire nanny job in Taiwan, she took the decision to go and eventually convinced her husband to agree. Nelia stayed in Taiwan for just under a year and then followed her employers to London, where we met her working as a domestic. Even though she is overqualified for her job, she sees being in London as an opportunity not only to be autonomous but also to improve her skills by taking English and IT lessons.

Nina, who migrated when her daughter was 10 years old, referred to herself as getting 'itchy feet'. As a single mother, she combined a desire to earn more in order to help her daughter and elderly mother and a curiosity to see the world and satisfy her own ambitions. Like Greta and Edith, Nina was a fully qualified, experienced teacher who came to England to work as a domestic. She too saw this as an opportunity for self-improvement through taking up language and IT classes. She was particularly proud that during her 30 years in London she worked herself up the job ladder, finally working in an administrative post before retiring in mid-2000. Nina's example suggests that self development can also lead to economic gain which in turn further increases the status and independence that the migrant women come to value.

What Nelia, Greta and many other of our participants share is a tension between their roles as mothers and their identities as women. This provides a specifically Filipino version of the more general issue of maternal ambivalence discussed in Chapter 1 (Hays, 1997; Hollway and Featherstone, 1997; Miller, 1997; Parker, 2005), although locally this remains a sensitive topic. Maternal ambivalence takes on a far more explicit dimension in the context of migration when work, with its attendant respect and satisfaction, lies in England, while the children remain in the Philippines.

The issue of self-improvement for the individual is balanced by what may be much older issues of status for any given family within the community they come from. For example, Barbara who came to London in the 1970s as a domestic and now runs her own company, has helped not only her extended family but subsequently also many fellow villagers. She helped build an extension for the local school and church. She even had her old piano sent from London to her village church and regularly sends other household items for charity. Her house in London is full of plaques to commemorate her benefactions and she proudly displays these and talks about how highly regarded her family has become locally. Marcela, a London-based nurse and mother of three, who described her second migration to the UK as 'too good an opportunity to miss', was also proud of her role as a local benefactor.

Collective parenting

The other way in which these close kinship networks impact upon the decision to migrate is an expectation that children will be looked after by the wider family, in the absence of their mother. This is not inevitable, though there were cases of children cared for by *yayas*, exemplifying the model of transnational care chains (Hochschild, 2000). But many more of the children were cared for by their maternal, or less commonly, paternal grandparents or by aunts and uncles whom they had been close to from birth. In only two cases was the biological father the primary carer, confirming Parreñas' (2005a) conclusions about the unequal division of reproductive labour and our earlier observation that fathers were often already absent prior to the mothers' migration. The nature of the Filipino close-knit family and reciprocal obligations offered some reassurance to the mothers that their children would be well looked after (although as we shall see in Chapter 5 we encountered several cases of deceit and abuse). These expectations were already in place given the precedent of internal migration from rural to metropolitan areas, which as noted in Chapter 2 relates to significant class and regional differences. Emma, a trained caregiver, first migrated to Manila to work as a nanny and a domestic, leaving her children in a remote part of Negros with her mother. Even though she was in the same country as her children, she only saw them once a year, no more than some of our London participants who on average visited their left-behind families every 1.6 years, while the average period between first migration and first visit back home was 2.6 years.

Culture of migration

As the literature on migration suggests, the role of interpersonal networks underlies much of recent migration to industrial nations (Boyd, 1989; Portes, 1995). Tilly (1990: 84), in his overview of the history of migration to the US, has argued that it is actually networks which migrate: 'the effective units of migration were (and are) neither individuals nor households, but sets of people linked by acquaintance, kinship and work experience'. Having a relative abroad may not be the only reason to migrate, but it can certainly determine the choice of destination and also provide the catalyst for making the leap. All our informants without exception had at least one relative abroad, while many had several. This might be their parent(s), one or more of their siblings, or several of their uncles, aunts and cousins. Our participants often owed their education to the benefaction of these overseas relatives and were in turn now assisting their own nieces and nephews with their education. The precedent of migration set by networks of relatives – in this case the infinite networks of a bilateral kinship system – was almost universal, thus normalising the experience of going abroad. The presence of relatives abroad both facilitates migration and legitimates the decision to leave.

This can amount to a kind of 'culture of emigration' which is a pressure in its own right (Massey *et al.*, 1993: 452–453). Some of our participants like Marivic and Pillar told us that almost all their friends had migrated at the same time as they did, which reinforced their own decision. Several of our informants told us that the vast majority of their classmates (in many cases 80 to 90 per cent) were now abroad and this was particularly so amongst nurses, as nursing is seen as the 'passport out of the country' (Rodolfo, male nurse in London).

In this context we can understand why some participants told us that the whole process of migration was more of 'an accident' than 'an actual decision' (compare Búriková and Miller, 2010: 5–30). Although this applies more to childless women than to mothers, it reveals the extent to which migration is normalised and can 'just happen'. This was particularly the case in the mid-2000s when the NHS was recruiting systematically and opportunities for deployment were abundant, compared to the period of economic crisis that had developed by the time of our fieldwork:

> *Carmen*: Being here was an accident for me. The senior sister asked me to accompany her to this agency as she was applying for a job in London. Then when I got there they asked me what I did. I said I was a nurse – so they got me to fill out a form and then they interviewed me for the day. And then she said you passed – just bring in your resume. They told me – you have passed the exam, you have passed the interview. I didn't even apply! She said that she had an employer who was looking for someone with my line of specialisation. So then in two months I flew here.

Aguilar (2002b) sees a larger cosmological issue underlying this culture of migration, equating it with a rite of passage in which there is an increasing expectation that one should have tried to 'see the world' and that this leads to some kind of more or less profound transformation of the inner self (see also Búriková and Miller, 2010: 156–170). It is not just that going abroad gives them advantages in skills, knowledge and resources, but they see themselves as marked and in various ways enhanced.

This overall culture of migration concludes and encompasses the litany of more specific motivations we have now provided evidence for. What emerges is a complex and contradictory process whereby factors that have been traditionally recognised, such as economic (Massey *et al.*, 1993), family (DeJong *et al.*, 1983, 1986; Lauby and Stark, 1988) and social (Boyd, 1989; Portes, 1995; Tilly, 1990) motivations co-exist with other perhaps less recognised and less socially accepted reasons such as domestic violence and relationship breakdown, but also individual ambitions, or curiosity about life abroad, the desire for self-improvement and personal development. The balance between these shifts still further to the more personal issues when we turn from the decision to migrate to the decision to remain abroad.

Why they settle

Although most women leave the Philippines on the assumption that they will be abroad for only a fixed period of time, in reality migration lasts much longer (see Castles and Miller, 2009) and most, at least in our sample, look likely never to return. Amongst our participants the average period of separation was 15.65 years. The reasons why women choose to prolong migration and fail to return to the Philippines are as, if not more, important than their initial decision to migrate for understanding their relationships to their children and their communication with them. Constable (1999: 205) has been perhaps the most explicit about a fundamental ambivalence within migration that links the reasons for going in the first place to the reluctance to return: 'Even though most women stress their economic motivation for working in Hong Kong, that is but one of many complex reasons why they come, why they remain, and why they continue to return'. One issue Constable stresses is women's increasing identification with and interest in the place abroad where they may now have worked for many years. One of her informants felt empowered by the independence and freedom she negotiated for herself there. She described Hong Kong as a place where – despite the rules and regulation – she felt 'free' and where she could have much more 'fun and freedom' than in the Philippines, 'where she would have to learn to plant rice' (Constable, 1999: 216). In Hong Kong she had become 'her own boss' (ibid.: 214).

Of course, all this is matched by upward income mobility. As Szanton (1996: 186) notes, in the US median income for Filipinos is higher than native born Americans, which may be perhaps linked to the fact that they have the highest rate of naturalisation among all US immigrant groups (Szanton, 1996: 183), though this may be combined with the facilitation of continued close connections back home which leaves the boundaries of nationality quite blurred. Maas (2003), working in the Netherlands, has noted the importance of businesses set up by diaspora Filipinos. In our research entrepreneurial activity often involved links to the Philippines, such as setting up travel agencies or cargo forwarding companies specialising in *balikbayan boxes*, or real estate agencies specialising in the selling of condominium properties to the UK diaspora. Parreñas (2001) also notes factors that make Filipinos reluctant to return, which may include long-term pessimism about their economic prospects in the Philippines, for which there remains good evidence even at the time of writing.

This ambivalence about returning leads to various strategies to legitimate such decisions. Mozere (2005) notes that Filipinos in France are in many ways content with their life in Paris and the sending back of remittances partly justifies their desire to remain there. Faier (2007) notes that Filipinos in Japan tend to legitimate their role there by seeing Japanese men's attraction for them as confirming the Philippines as the most romantic place on earth and themselves as much warmer than Japanese people. She suggests that much of this is a means to defend their continuing presence there. Our own evidence substantiates many of these arguments but also adds others, especially with regard to more personal issues that speak to the wider context of maternal ambivalence which tends to be neglected in the literature.

Economic and other structural factors

There comes a point in the migration cycle when the initial most compelling reasons why women migrated have been dealt with. The house has been built, the children have been through college and the loans have been repaid. This is not the case, however, where remittances have been abused by relatives, sometimes including their own husbands who in some cases absconded with their money, leaving migrant women to start all over again. Deception was an issue for many of the women, who found that their good will and trust had been betrayed by relatives. Joan, for example, who was paying her niece's college fees was shocked when she found out that her niece's registration had lapsed for several terms despite the fact the Joan was continuing to remit money for that purpose. Anecdotal evidence suggests this is even more common than would appear from those instances of failure which our informants were prepared to divulge to us.

All migrants would expect to at least pay off the initial expenses incurred and to accumulate some further benefit. Beyond that, the concept of need is more relative, as the potential for material improvements are unlimited. There will always be possible home improvements, a new car or an additional plot of land. The ability to facilitate these will depend upon the circumstance of migration and its rewards. The UK is considered to be a good destination in that although it was expensive to get there, the relative strength of the pound[5] made it easier to make money and repay one's debts more quickly. Also the high degree of state regulation meant that minimum wages were relatively high and for legal migrants there was easier recourse to the enforcement of rights. Those within the state sector such as the health service were also relatively protected from discrimination. Our participants frequently described England as 'lovely' (Marivic), or 'a blessing' (Edith), especially compared to their stints in the Middle East where they would earn a fraction of what they could obtain in London and where they had also suffered from various employment constraints and sometimes even abuse. Of course, such observations should not deny the fact that for some, migration to England was often difficult and challenging. But most of our participants spoke positively about their experiences in the UK.

The other factor which we have already discussed in some detail is the way bilateral kinship systems promulgate endless requests from more extended family members and even fictive kin. This comes not as a demand specifically that they stay abroad, but is merely the incessant and insatiable requests for help. Indeed Tacoli (1996: 22–23) notes that parents strongly disapprove if a migrant daughter gets pregnant or marries, since that means less money for her siblings. Nelia helps more than a dozen relatives, apart from her husband and son. These are mainly her siblings and not a week goes by without a demand from one of her brothers. Although these are usually for small amounts, because there are so many requests they do have an impact on her outgoings. As we have already indicated, refusing such a demand is not an option, so Nelia obliges even though she feels burdened by the sheer volume of requests. This culminates in Nelia's visits to the Philippines when she is expected to have presents and money for the 12 relatives she normally supports and smaller gifts for at least another 20 people (which she often sends through a *balikbayan* box to coincide with her arrival). Taking into account the gifts for her own son and her husband as well as her airfare, her Christmas visit to the Philippines costs her more than £1,600, or over a month's salary. In our fieldwork we met Filipinas in their sixties who have worked on good salaries for decades but remain personally in debt as all their earnings been dispersed to relatives. However, we also meet some individuals who have long since reneged on such obligations and live a largely autonomous life in Cambridge or London.

Other parameters which promoted initial migration such as lack of employment, are in fact reinforced, given the further difficulties in finding employment for middle-aged or older women, especially if they have experienced downward social mobility giving up professional jobs for cleaning and care work. Similarly the health issues that may have been a factor even at the beginning become much more pertinent as our participants age, and the benefits of a free national health service seem irresistible.

Family breakdown is yet another factor which can grow rather than fade with migration. This follows from the evidence we have presented that migration is more likely to turn an abusive or unsatisfactory relationship into an actual separation. This can still create an atmosphere of shame and humiliation within the Philippine context. One year after Romalyn migrated, her husband absconded with another woman and never again made contact with her or with their children. Romalyn had to stay abroad to send money to support her whole family, as she was the sole provider. The absence of a husband back home also means that women's romantic interests shift more decisively to England, or anywhere in the world (we met several, especially younger, women who were looking for and often finding romantic relationships through social networking sites such as Friendster, or Yahoo chat rooms). Any actual relationship removes women still further from the prospect of a permanent return.

Finally, migrants realise from stories of those who have returned that this is not entirely straightforward either. Those who have not undertaken migration have many critical things to say about the arrogance and, as they might see it, inflated self-esteem of the returnees (Aguilar, 2002b: 432–433). In some ways both they and the returnees themselves may recognise the degree to which they have become increasingly alienated from their own land. The criticisms they had of the Philippine state may now become almost a hyper-discourse about its failings, which can be tiresome for others. For other migrants the experiences they had abroad and sometimes their failures to meet expectations at home lead to problematic issues of shame.

Personal development and identities: the ambivalence of transnational motherhood

All these are important reasons, but they can mask some still more profound underlying issues. Listening to women talk about their lives in England and their legitimations for remaining or returning makes clear the degree to which women, through the experience of migration, are likely to develop and change. As we have already seen, for many migration was the first time that they became recognised and valued in their families as the main breadwinners. The respect evident in the fact that women are now consulted in all family decisions provides a sense of empowerment, independence and autonomy that is very hard to give up. Listen to Nora, a retired domestic worker, now in her late sixties who refuses to return to the Philippines to stay with her now 32-year-old son: 'I do not want to be dominated. I don't want to be controlled by my sisters. They keep on controlling me anywhere I go.' Having been unable to build a house in the Philippines, she would have had to live with her son, which would have made her feel like a burden on him (a fear also shared by her son as he told us when we met him in Pampanga). After almost 25 years in London, Nora feels that it is easier for a woman to be in England than in the Philippines where 'you're being dominated by your husband, by your children'. Home is now in London where she has her own circle of friends from different parts of the world, but also from the Philippines whom she meets every Wednesday and Sunday where she works as a volunteer at a community centre. For Nelia, a domestic worker and mother of one, the autonomy and respect comes from having money, which is why people 'treat you well': 'Without money you are nothing in the Philippines, at least when I go back now I have money.'

Similarly, Vicky told us that she now finds that women are very constrained in the Philippines, 'especially if you are used to being on your own here': 'What would happen if I come home late? The teenagers, even now, they don't do that. They cannot do things by themselves. The woman cannot decide what to do, she calls her mum.' In fact, Vicky did attempt to return to the Philippines for good after six years in London, during which time she had been granted indefinite leave to remain in the UK. She had saved enough money to set up her own minibus business in the Philippines which, however, did not do well. After two years, Vicky decided to return to London. Rather poignantly, Vicky told us that although she had been very happy to be reunited with her three children, she also missed her life in London during that two-year period. She would often go to the *Ayala* shopping centre in the upscale Manila neighbourhood of Makati because it reminded her of London:

> Like, looking for big buildings, and the comfort, everything here, the water. . . . In Manila water is a big problem. Too many people there I must say. But I used to go to Ayala, to Makati . . . [. . .] Just to recall London, because it was a bit like London. [. . .] I missed London very much.

Through migration, women develop new identities centred upon their work and the respect and value they derive from that. They value their independence and autonomy and find it hard to give those up by returning to the Philippines and the near certainty of unemployment. This may be recognised within the Philippines itself. A recent highly successful film called *Caregiver* (2008) starring a very well known actress Sharon Cuneta tells the story of a migrant to London. While her children seem an important element at the start of the film, by the end the concerns have moved almost entirely to her relationships within London. As in our earlier discussion of the 'accentuated ambivalence of transnational motherhood', it is not that these migrant women are 'bad mothers' as some commentators have claimed (for a discussion see Parreñas, 2008: 22–39), but rather that they are experiencing the opposing pulls between work and motherhood which, because they are divided across different continents, are hard to reconcile. Work is (and can only be) abroad while the families remain in the Philippines. Beyond the issue of work, the sheer amount of time abroad may lead women to adopt different cultural norms and expectations. Tellingly, Judy, a mother of three and a migrant for over 20 years, finds it hard even to stay with her family in the house that she built in Laguna. Her children told us that in one of her recent visits she chose to stay in a hotel for part of her visit as it was quieter (something Judy herself did not disclose to us).

Related to this discussion is why these mothers cannot bring over their children to join them. In fact some do, and in our study five (out of our 53) participants had managed to bring their children over. But for most, such a reunification was not an option for a number of reasons. Many of our informants came to the UK after stints in the Middle East or other destinations where their temporary status prevented them from being joined by family members. Once they came to London their children were already adults, and therefore did not count as dependents who could legally obtain visas. So, for example, one mother managed to get a visa for the younger son but not for her elder daughter who had effectively parented her brother. For the son, coming to England to live with his mother for the first time marked a painful separation from the person who had been closest to him all his life. Apart from such legal and personal constraints, there are significant economic difficulties. For example, for live-in domestics the cost of renting their own property – an essential precondition of family accommodation – was prohibitive. Finally, we even have one example when a teenage daughter simply refused to

[margin annotation: ambivalence: simultaneous and contradictory attitudes + feelings towards an object, person, or action]

join her mother after the latter managed to obtain both the visa and the necessary capital. Although this is a rare case, it suggests that family reunification is difficult even when the legal or economic barriers are lifted.

When we asked our participants if coming to England was worth all the trouble and pain of separation, almost all (there were two exceptions[6]) unequivocally said yes. Sandra considers her decision 'right', 'happy and lucky'. Such a response does not contradict our argument about ambivalence. Despite her positive outlook towards London, Sandra often becomes emotional when she talks about her children and described herself as 'an incomplete mother'. She particularly felt this way when her children were still young and communication infrequent and expensive, at which point she felt the gap growing between them. Sandra had to bribe the *yaya* to send her truthful updates about her children's lives as she did not trust her husband's relatives. Sandra found she needed to assert her role as a mother to her own children:

> Because my daughter when I come back from Hong Kong says 'Go back to Hong Kong!' Just like that. I think she was 6. [...] Because I think they're trying to be far away from me because of the relatives of my ex. So I fight with them. I said 'I know you have money but you will never ever get my children.' And then my daughter don't want to come with me.... I could really feel that my daughter's feelings were getting far away from me. So what I did, I knew it was very naughty but I did show to my children my caesarean. I said 'Look, this place is where you come out of. I nearly died before. So there's no other mother.' And I always keep reminding [them].
>
> *Sandra, domestic and mother of two, London*

Conclusion

This example finally brings us to something that has remained in the background within this chapter precisely because it will come to dominate the rest of this book. Sandra's gesture symbolises her assertion of her maternal identity given the lack of other avenues to perform mothering on a daily basis. The above episode took place in 1992 when communication was mainly through letters and the occasional phone call, meaning that the opportunities for direct involvement in her children's lives were very limited. Contrast this to Sandra's experience today, when she justifies her infrequent visits by saying that she chats with her daughters on a daily basis using Yahoo Messenger, often including webcam. New media are playing an increasingly significant role in reconciling the marked ambivalence of migrant motherhood and in justifying decisions to prolong migration. As we shall demonstrate, new media transform the experience of long-distance mothering and ultimately migration.

So understanding why mothers decide to go abroad is crucial for understanding communication within the family context. Equally, if not more crucial, is to understand the reasons why they often choose to prolong their migration and

[margin handwritten note:] reconciling the marked ambivalence / justifying decisions to prolong migration.

settle abroad. We shall see how the media impacts upon this decision to remain abroad. Apart from the well documented motivations such as the need to build a house and pay for the children's private education (Aguilar *et al.*, 2009) and the more hidden motivations of migration such as domestic violence and gender inequalities (Parreñas, 2001), our chapter has highlighted the relatively neglected importance of personal development and self-improvement. Such personal reasons emerge as even more compelling when explaining the decisions to remain abroad. We have observed a discrepancy between what are the generally socially accept-able reasons for migration and these more covert, but equally powerful forces. Migration is a contradictory and complex process which does not always fall neatly into the explanations provided by more macro theories. These contradic-tions and paradoxes emerge in the personal accounts which dominate the evidence of this chapter in the form of the 'accentuated ambivalence' women experience in relation to their family lives and motherhood on the one hand and their work and the different experience of being a woman abroad, on the other (Madianou, 2012a). This ambivalence is at the heart of the relationship between mothers and children.

In the remainder of this book we will explore the way in which this ambiva-lence is often negotiated through the new communication technologies which the mothers see as allowing them to work abroad but also mother from a distance, a perspective not necessarily confirmed by their own children. But just as we require an understanding of the underlying forces that pertain to migration, so also we need to step back first and see something of the longer-term role of media in this experience. For which reason we begin our more specific consideration of the media with a chapter looking historically at the period of initial migration, espe-cially the mid-1970s to mid-1990s that were dominated by letters and cassettes. We will then look at the perspectives of the mothers and the children, integrating the issues discussed in this chapter with those raised by a more explicit consid-eration of the media.

4

LETTERS AND CASSETTES

Barbara, a 60-year-old entrepreneur living in London, remembers her first years in England in the early 1980s when she would take every opportunity to listen to the cassette tapes that her children sent her, even during her part-time cleaning jobs. She still remembers her excitement when she realised that the owners were still out as she turned the key to open the door of their apartment as that meant that she could listen to her tapes freely. Barbara suddenly looked forward to her two hours of cleaning: She closed the door, opened her bag and took out a brown envelope that had just arrived that morning. Inside was a tape, a red 90-minute SHARP. She recognised her daughter's handwriting which read: 'To Inay'. She rushed to the living room, turned on the stereo and put the tape in. The voice of her husband and her three daughters filled the room. She could hardly hold back the tears, and sat there listening to their news for a while. Lia had got top grades at school. Cory had bought a new pair of shoes with the money she had sent them last month. Anita needed some books for her tutorials. The land had been harvested and things had gone well but the roof was leaking and needed to be fixed soon. Elsie, their neighbour, was pregnant again, but her husband from Saudi had stopped sending money. Christy, her niece, was getting engaged to Nino. Relieved that there were no bad news and aware of the job waiting for her, Barbara went to the cleaning cupboard to get the dusters. She wiped the windows, dusted the surfaces and swept the floor, washed the dishes and ironed the clothes whilst listening to the recorded Sunday mass and sermon from her village church followed by her daughters singing songs after the Sunday lunch – they had made *lechon*, her favourite dish. When the tape was over, she hoovered the floor, put everything back in the cupboard, took her cassette out of the stereo put in back in its case and in her bag, locked the door and went down the stairs towards her basement studio where she would cook some rice and listen to her cassette once again.

By contrast, Marcelo, a 60-year-old man who had finally returned to Manila to live with his family, talks fondly about the letters he sent and received over 30 years of separation. Marcelo got married at 25 and within a few years his wife had given birth to their three children. But from the age of 26 he was mainly living away from the Philippines; first in Saudi Arabia and later in Angola, with contracts of up to two years at a time. He tells us how in the early days he would send a half-page letter about once a month and receive from his wife letters of three to four pages about once a week. Every few months he would send a cassette tape, but he preferred receiving letters 'because it is more personalized, and I mean, she can tell me the things I want to know, and I can, during my free time, I can read them all over again'. One has to imagine the circumstances. He would be putting up fences in the middle of the desert, miles from anywhere. There would be perhaps eight of them with their trucks, their food and their drink. His friends used to bring cassette players, but he felt the presence of a letter in his shirt pocket, near to his heart, was what sustained him. Alone, he could indulge in what he acknowledged to be his penchant for sentimentality, privately.

In a way it was ironic. It was only now at such a distance, alone, that thanks to these letters his relationship with his wife really developed properly. The problem had been that though he loved his wife he told us that: 'I'm not a good talker, actually. So when I'm with them, I do not talk much. But when we are far away, then I can write things I want to tell her.' It was precisely being away and communicating through letters that brought romance to their relationship. When in Saudi Arabia, he used to ask his fellow workers sometimes for help in getting the right words, the romantic words, he wanted to express himself. What he does not mention, but his wife in a separate interview told us, is that he sometimes wrote quite long letters especially when he had problems that he needed to share. When his contract took him to Angola, where sending and receiving letters was often an adventure in its own right, Marcelo continued to do so, entrusting letters to colleagues travelling back home, as sending letters would take months to arrive. Yet this is when communication was even more important, since life seemed so fragile surrounded by constant warfare. Could he even tell her about his Filipino comrade shot dead at a check point that he could just as easily have been passing through?

Having established this close relationship with his wife through letters, he was desperate to engage with his children through the same media. Even before they could write, his wife got them to make little drawings on scraps of paper to enclose with her letters. Later on cards became important, for Christmas or birthdays, and especially if he missed what everyone regards as the most important events of all, the school graduations. Today, his children and grandchildren, who in turn have migrated themselves, send him letters from the US even though they have access to every kind of new media from webcam to email. It is not that he specifically asked them to, but they seem to have sensed that for him only letters have that personal touch which he continues to value as the essence of a communication. The original letters were too precious to let go. He devised his own system, and would staple the letters to envelopes, punch holes and use fasteners and folders in order to store them all. He still has them. He showed some of them to his children when they were old enough, though now they just gather dust. There were some things no number of letters could properly convey. He still feels he missed out on the development of his children, when they first walked and talked. This is why in retirement he is so devoted to helping bring up his grandchildren. 'That's why with my first grandson, who is with us, I was the one taking care of him. To pay for the lost time. With my son. I missed time with my own son.'

He never developed the same kind of emotional attachment to cassettes. 'Well, the cassettes, first of all, you have to bring a player with you. You have to playback. As for me, sometimes I work kilometres away from our camp. So I don't have the means to bring along a player. Whereas with letters, I can just put it in my pocket. Then I can read it there, during lunch time.' But then cassettes had compensations, such as when his daughter sang him his favourite Frank Sinatra song. But he could not use cassettes to be romantic. When he tried to speak into the microphone, he would become tongue-tied, just as if they were actually together. Voice was just not his medium. Instead he would use cassettes more to give a sense of events and the landscape, retelling an incident in Jeddah or a visit to the sea, fishing, catching crabs. Also, his sense of sentiment was very private. He did not like to share this intimacy, unlike fellow workers who brought their cassette players with them into the desert where others in the group could overhear them.

As noted in the Introduction, this book brings together two themes: several chapters focus on migration itself and the relationships of mothers and children, while others then move towards a consideration of the media used in their communication, so that we can end with a theory of mediated relationships. This chapter is the first to focus more on the media themselves. While later in the volume we look at the complex situation of contemporary polymedia, it helps to clarify our approach by starting with the period of time prior to cheap phone calls and the internet. At that time communication was dominated by just two media, and we can start to see the interplay between the capabilities of those media and way they are utilised under the extreme conditions within which parent–child relationships had to be maintained. We will demonstrate that, even in this early communicative environment, we find the first evidence of polymedia, that is of media used as an integrated environment within which users exploit contrasts within media to manage their relationships. At the same time, because most of the examples come from our interviews about the past rather than the ethnographic present, this chapter also conveys the historical background to the present condition upon which the rest of this book is focused.

More than half of the parents we worked with in London (28 respondents) left the Philippines between 1973 and the mid-1990s. Most of those, as we saw in Chapter 3, first migrated to the Middle East and Hong Kong during the 1970s and 1980s. For many of these migrants the conditions of work and the overall experience of migration were significantly more constrained and difficult than today. For many, though not all, this period is remembered as being particularly stressful. Some participants reported quite appalling events and suffering. This was also the period when these migrants were most likely to have left behind very young children, often babies, and it was often difficult to secure visits home. Combined with the lack of media, this then is the most extreme exemplification of the issues of separation that this book tries to deal with, and is an essential background to understanding the rest of the content of this book.

There are no studies entirely parallel to this dependence upon letters and cassettes for these relationships. The study of epistolography has focused on the correspondence of famous authors such as Mary Wollstonecraft (Todd, 2003) or George Orwell (Orwell, 1968), though in recent years there has been a growing interest in the correspondence of ordinary people mainly from historical or literary studies (Barton and Hall, 2000; Basso, 1974; Danet, 1997; Decker, 1998; Earle, 1999; Jaffe, 1999). The classic sociological study on letter–writing in migration is by Thomas and Znaniecki (1996), who observed the formulaic nature of letters as manifestations of social obligations and solidarity among Polish family members who were separated because of work. With respect to audio cassettes, there is an excellent ethnography on the implications of almost all aspects of the materiality of the cassette for the circulation of music in Pakistan (Manuel, 1993; see also Abu-Lughod, 1989), but much less when it comes to a consideration of the cassette as a form of 'letter–writing' style of communication within migrant relationships (though see Richman, 2005).

As with letters and cassettes more generally, there has been little direct research on letters and cassettes amongst the Filipino diaspora, though Sampson notes with respect to Filipino men serving on ships:

> certainly they emphasized more openly their sense of loneliness and stressed the importance of receiving mail on board. They valued mail despite the fact that it could often take well over a month to get to them and as a result 'the news is already old'. It thus had significance beyond its contents representing perhaps a tangible connection with family and friends, or even the packaging and sending of love and affection (Sampson, 2003: 268).

In our research there is no such thing as a standard story. The two cases we have started this chapter with give a sense of our findings, but they are more contemporary and certainly do not fit every generalisation which we later explore; for example, other Filipinos commonly avoid talking openly about their problems. In turn, these differences between people derive from variation in their experiences of going abroad and prior to that different childhoods, resources and personalities leading to different needs and desires. The contrast between letters and cassettes will dominate our discussion. But we will also dwell on the contrast between the private and the public, which does much to explain why Barbara and Marcelo favour one medium over the other.

Letters: materiality and personality

Within our research the very nature and materiality of a letter is understood as both a capacity and a constraint in the crucial task of maintaining relationships. Typically a participant suggests:

> I think so 'cause when you're writing you get to think about what you're going to write. Like more time for you to compose what you're going to tell her.' Cause sometimes when you're on the phone, you forget a lot of things. So what happens is the things you forget to tell her, you write it. *Do you mean it's deeper or . . . ?* Yeah. It could be.

It is impossible to take such a discussion and separate its components as technical qualities and personal qualities. Price may also be integral to these issues: 'through letter you can express more. By phone . . . it's so expensive to talk and talk and talk.' Clearly once the costs of the phone decreased, its effective material quality changed and the same person may feel comfortable expressing themselves at greater length than through a letter.

The confluence of these qualities is often found in the way many women valued handwriting itself, which they believed added a personal touch to the communication. Katrina has always been a letter-writer and, rather unusually, still prefers to send letters, as she feels that handwriting is much more personal than typing an email. Irene also still sends postcards because it is more 'personal and unusual'. This way she can also offer her friends and family a glimpse of London. Edith, a 50-year-old domestic worker in London, would inspect letters to gauge her daughter's development through her handwriting, but also through her use of language and expressions. The letter was a crucial sign of educational attainment, where the move from cheap state education to more expensive private education for children is the most common priority in the use of remittances, a factor the children writing these letters are well aware of. Because communication through letters is not interactive, mothers scoured the letters they received for cues that would provide more information about their families. A question mark, a deleted word, or a little drawing could attract much attention and thought about what they might reveal about their writers.

Why should handwriting be seen as more personal than voice? Generally it seemed that because they are handwritten, letters require some thinking in advance in contrast to typing when one can erase any mistakes. A letter needs to be crafted and the effort put into that can be taken as proof of one's devotion and love. This sense that the letter is personal may also reflect a wider genre of traditional letter-writing that preceded its use in migration, which is the letter in courtship and the various forms of love letters, though our direct evidence for this is limited.

Even though Rodolfo (now in his thirties) came to London in 1999 to work as a nurse and was therefore past the letter-writing era, he nonetheless wrote one letter to his parents when he decided to 'come out'. He chose to write a letter, rather than an email or make a phone call, because he thought the letter would convey the seriousness of what he had to say. He also told us that:

> There's something about handwriting ... I'm obsessive and compulsive, and very neat in my handwriting, it's probably the exercise ... With internet you can erase any mistakes, but when you handwrite you have to think in advance about what you want to write. I wrote because I didn't want to hear any of those reactions people have at the phone ... With the letter I was safe. Actually my father wrote me back.

The materiality of letters is radically different from some of the new media forms which are inherently transient. A letter is a physical object, it takes a decision to part with it, to throw it away. That is why people find it hard to discard their letters even when they are unlikely to ever read them again as the memories they evoke are too painful. And that is why it can be upsetting when significant letters get lost. Apart from these emotional attachments to letters as symbols of significant relationships, there is another more instrumental reason why Filipinos and their families have kept their correspondence, which is that letters constitute legal evidence for the relationships and the separation experienced by transnational families. Such evidence is part of the routine screening procedure for granting visas to children who wish to join their parents abroad. The materiality of letters makes them perfect forms of evidence, although our participants also reported submitting print-outs of their emails and chats for such purposes. When Angela decided to apply to bring her two children over to the UK, they submitted a box full of letters as evidence of their relationship and length of separation.

The fact that they can be stored leads directly to another aspect of letter communication that our participants valued, which is that letters can be read again and again. In this sense, even if communication is not synchronous, it can be stretched in time. Many women told us that they would reread the letters and cards they received from their children and their other relatives almost every evening. For others, like Nina, a retired librarian who lives in London, rereading letters was painful after her daughter's death. However, she could not bear to destroy her letters so she decided to send them back to the Philippines where they are hidden away in a box 'for her own sanity'. Vicky also found rereading the letters uncomfortable as 'there is too much pain in those texts'. She kept only a few of them, but never felt like rereading them. In these cases the materiality of letters that remain become a way in which people may gradually come to terms with a loss such as a death. But they can also become a way to avoid acknowledging that loss. Andrea was one of those children whose mother ended up more or less abandoning her. Her correspondence was intermittent at best and later on more or less ended. But she too kept her letters in a box and read them again and again, and treasured a planner her mother had given her, using these as her way of trying to deal with the fact that no new letters came to replace the old.

Finally, another aspect valued by our participants was the capacity of letters to effectively convey information, especially detailed information and guidelines regarding financial and property matters. Edmundo, Barbara's husband, used to send her detailed accounts of what happened to all her remittances because 'she's working hard so she has the right to know what we do with her money'. Nina still writes letters to her niece who deals with her property in the Philippines as she thinks that it is easier and clearer to send instructions in a letter than it is in a telephone call.

Cassettes: emotion and presence

Apart from letters, the other medium that dominated family communication in the 1980s and early 1990s was audio cassette tapes. Unlike letters whose primary use is communication, we imagine that this was more a side effect of the cassettes' ready availability through their dominance at that time in music reproduction (and quite possibly other genres such as religion, as documented elsewhere by Manuel, 1993; Sreberny-Mohammadi and Mohammadi, 1994). These were recorded analogue tapes – either the regular sized, or micro ones – which were sent either through regular post, or carried by a fellow Filipino travelling back home. As it happens, they share a common materiality with letters, in contrast to much of the new media that has come to replace both. Cassette tapes could also be stored and listened to again and again, although it was usually the most recent one that would be played over and over until the new one would arrive. Barbara would carry the latest tape in her bag as she sometimes found opportunities to play it during her part-time cleaning jobs. Even though most tapes were now useless, as they were often broken or cut, they were rarely thrown out. Children sometimes discovered them hidden in the attic, or a cupboard and, if they were still functioning, they would listen to them, laughing at their young voices and naïve comments before storing them back into oblivion. But even hidden away in a shoebox together with a bunch of letters, they remain symbols of past relationships. Nico, now aged 36, remembered being told that when he was a baby he used to receive cassette tapes from his father singing and accompanying himself with guitar. He had rediscovered them a year ago and was listening to them with his mother, but the machine mangled the tape and he does not know how to get it repaired. This was quite distressing, since he was only two years old when his father died.

Tapes also have a perhaps stronger determining material structure than letters when it comes to their composition. If you have a C90 tape you more or less feel obligated to fill it with 90 minutes' worth of recording. It is harder to erase and rewrite and in other ways seems to impose itself as a format rather more than letters, which may be why it is often seen as the less personal of the two media.

As one person put it: 'It's very limited to time, and you had to consider both sides of the tape and what you think is worth telling. In a sense, you're trying to pick which story in your life you'd really rather share.' The very nature of a cassette may make it less suitable as a medium for instruction, since it is quite hard to mark a place that a person can come back to and be reminded of, while it is easy to scan a letter to find the place where a particular point is made. As we saw in the previous section, letters were (and for a few still are) the preferred medium for practical advice, detailed instruction and accounting of finances. In other words, letters have a large informational capacity. Furthermore, while a cassette depends upon a player to be heard, a letter requires no intermediating technology. As objects, cassettes are also a more homogenised form without the decorative elements that may adorn a letter.

What the machine-produced cassette tape lacked compared to the personal crafting of handwriting, it made up for in the significantly more emotional immediacy of voice and its stronger sense of a co-presence between sender and receiver. This emotional quality of the latter comes from the presence of voice. For a mother to listen to the voice of her child, especially if she had not heard their voice for months, or even years, is a very powerful thing. Barbara always cried at the beginning of each tape when she first heard the voices of her children. For Susan, who had been frustrated with the incompleteness of letter writing, cassette tapes were a breakthrough, as she could finally understand how her children were doing by listening to their voices. Tapes had a powerful effect on children too. When Sandra first migrated, her children were two and three years old. When she sent them a tape with her singing, her children – especially the eldest – got so upset on hearing their mother's voice that she never sent them another one. These qualities of voice as a form of communication make the cassette the clear precursor to telephone-based voice communication and later on, webcam calls.

Apart from the power of voice, cassette tapes were preferred because they allowed for a spontaneity that was not always possible in letter writing. If a letter needs to be crafted and thought-through, a tape can be recorded on the spur of the moment while the family is having a birthday celebration or dinner. In that sense, it can also be more naturalistic, offering a snippet of 'real life' from back home. Of course, we know from our interviews with the children that the recordings were sometimes staged, but even those were welcomed as opportunities through which the mothers could get a taste of family life. In the case of Barbara, recordings regularly included the Sunday mass and the sermons and she always looked forward to listening to those. On special occasions, like Christmas, the family would make a special effort by recording the whole Christmas service and then their dinner, which would take three tapes to fit in: 'Everything was there, the sadness, the happiness, everything.' When Barbara wanted to make a tape she would do it in one evening. She always chose the 90-minute format, finding 60 minutes too short. Barbara would recount what she did the whole week at work and what she cooked at home. She would give advice to her daughters about school and always end with a prayer. Other mothers would sing songs, or lullabies.

Tapes, unlike letters, could also include songs and even little documentaries on life back home. For six years Marivic received tapes and letters from her husband-to-be when he was courting her until they finally got together. He was best with cassettes and as he had a good voice, he would sing 'old English language songs' to her like 'My way'. Marivic fell in love with his voice. She found that her husband would express himself best on tapes and would even say things that he never told her face-to-face. As with letters, our participants found that their loved ones would often be more affectionate on tape than in face-to-face interaction. In this sense, the distance of mediation engenders proximity, a point to which we will return in the following chapters.

Cassette tapes could also work with the way children liked to present themselves to their parents. They could put on a little play that they had written, each taking on different roles, and record this as part of their tape. The tape became a mini-project in which they could get absorbed, and they were almost disappointed when it came to an end. They could also record things from the radio, and their favourite songs. Sometimes, because they could not think of anything in particular for this project, they would just leave the tape on. As a result, even their quarrels ended up appearing on the tape, which added a certain realism to the message. The other feature of cassettes is that they are performative, which children could use to convey what they saw as their personality or their contribution to family life. Antonio was one of those boys who saw himself as the funny one in the family, the joker. So he was the one who would make the cassettes, whose overall message was 'Mom, Pa, don't worry. We are so okay here.' This was where he could indulge his joke-telling. Nothing made him happier than when his Mom came back from abroad and told him 'You know what, when I was playing the tape, the group, my family was listening. Then they were crying out loud and laughing their arses off because of my famous line.' It was the same role he played when they were actually together; when the conversation was getting serious, he would lighten things up.

We do not want to exaggerate the contrast between cassettes and letters. Just as cassettes could convey personality, similarly letters could effectively convey emotion. We noted above how mothers might look for subtle clues in the handwriting of letters. They did not always need to. Edith will always remember the letter her daughter, Evelyn, sent her signing off, 'I hate you, your angry daughter.' 'It was so sad. It made me cry. Because she really expressed in the letter, very real feelings.' This example not only highlights the letter's capacity to effectively convey emotion; it also serves as a reminder of the limitations that some people saw in letter writing as a medium. Edith felt that she was not able to effectively respond to her daughter's raw emotions via the same medium.

Edith had received what amounted to an emotional letter bomb, but felt that the media available to her were inadequate to respond to her daughter's feelings. Since her daughter lived in a remote part of Samar island with no access to a landline, Edith could not call her directly. She could only call her husband who was based in Manila to ask him to explain to their daughter why she had to leave again. But even the husband had to wait until he visited their island and his visits were not much more frequent than Edith's. Although Edith replied to her daughter explaining her situation, writing the letter felt like a weak way to deal with her daughter's fiery emotional world. It was only when Edith returned to Samar for the Christmas break and took her daughter on a holiday that she felt – momentarily – that she was able to re-establish rapport with her. Evelyn's emotional outpouring in the letter and her mother's frustrated response revealed the biggest limitation to both letters and cassettes, which is the lack of interactive simultaneous communication. This brings us to the more general issue of temporality.

Temporality and performance

Depending on where in the Philippines the family was based, a letter would take between one to four weeks to arrive. Letters from the Philippines would take longer to arrive than when they had been sent from the UK. On average, most of our participants reported that they wrote and received one or two letters a month. They would reply to letters immediately on their receipt, as this was a way of keeping the communication as fresh as possible. The long time lag may have made it difficult to respond to emotions, but it also added an emotional intensity to the exchange because of the tremendous anticipation that accompanied waiting for the next letter or cassette. Even though almost two decades have passed since this period of intense letter writing, many of our participants recalled the anticipation and excitement of receiving a letter. Equally, the lack of letters was marked by anxiety about how their loved ones were. If Elisa had not received a letter for more than three weeks, she would go to the public booths in the hospital where she worked in Riyadh and queue to call so as to make sure her family was all right.

The children, especially the younger ones, had even more difficulty with the time lag than the parents. They simply did not experience life in terms of this *longue durée*. Mostly they would have no idea what they had been concerned with or thinking about in the letter or cassette they had sent months before, to which the letter they were now reading was trying to respond. They simply could not work with this kind of extended narrative or sustained emotional exchange that was in practice so intermittent. Their lives were punctuated by much more rapid emotional repertoires. So it is likely that at this early phase such communication was far more effective for parents than for children. The children might well write 'I love you' and 'take care', which may have been effective and meaningful to the parent who received this, but mostly such phrases were effectively taught to them as part of an etiquette of letter writing that felt to them more like a school lesson. Indeed so much of the parents' missives to them contained reminders and instructions to behave well and do well at school that their parents could become somewhat elided with schooling more generally. Children might find it easier to express emotions through voice and the parents recognised the greater authenticity of their children through the cassette: 'Because you can hear if there's something hidden. You can feel the voice, and the energy sometimes of the person.'

The formulaic nature of the exercise was one of the reasons Antonio did not actually like letter writing. But after a while he came to appreciate how important it was to his mother to receive this physical reminder of his concern, so he dutifully sent these on a regular basis. Many of the children recall letter writing in this spirit of a weekly chore imposed upon them by their carers, although as they grew up they might come more into sync with their parents' relationship to the medium. Indeed for an older child the lack of simultaneity in communication, which is normally a source of frustration for most of our participants, might actually be desired. This was the case for Roberto, who wanted to avoid confrontation through a telephone call, instant chat or even email. By the time his father wrote back to respond to Rodolfo's letter about 'coming out', time had lapsed and both of them had been able to dwell on the news. Rodolfo's sister had also spoken with her father, who turned out to be understanding and warm in his response. The fact that he too chose to respond by letter – something he had never done before – shows the importance he attributed to the matter. When his father died, Roberto desperately searched for that letter which he wanted to keep as a symbol of his father and their relationship, but was disappointed to realise that he had lost it.

There could also be a deeper relationship between the temporality of the communication and the ways children came to understand their new circumstances. Many children noted that their mothers almost hid from them the fact that they were leaving. They would try to protect the child from this traumatic revelation by making it seem more like a holiday they had gone for, or a temporary absence. But as a result, some children came to feel more alienated from the whole process, because there had never been a proper goodbye. The letters then became frustrating since they could not really understand what they represented within their relationship to their mothers or fathers. Did this show them how much their mother cared, or simply reveal to them that actually their mother was gone from their lives? They would place high hopes in any hints that their mother might return for some significant event such as a graduation. But if the parent failed to turn up, that completely destroyed the occasion from the point of view of the children.

An older child might have more of an understanding of what was happening and take on their new role with determination. This was particularly the case among older daughters (*ates*) who felt they were expected to substitute for their absent mothers in looking after young children, which in the Philippines is indeed a common expectation (Parreñas, 2005a, 2005b). While mothers generally recognised and trusted their daughters' help and responsibility, they often displayed a different behaviour to their sons, whom they sometimes continued to see as the young vulnerable child they had left behind. This was exacerbated by the long time lag of unreliable post, and left many of the young men just bewildered and at times frustrated. Like the mothers themselves, they might be desperate to hear and anxious when there was no news. But, for example, Ricardo recalls that when a letter finally arrived it related to old news and constant routine admonishments about getting on with school work that did not live up to the hoped-for sense of reconnection. This was perhaps a contributing factor which made him feel that there did not seem any point in putting deeper thoughts into his own response.

As result, many of the children might then concentrate more on just asking for money to buy things, or just asking their mother to send them this or that expensive foreign object – which in turn was hurtful to the absent parent. If their mothers recall their joy at the sight of a letter from their children, the children admitted to becoming far more excited by the site of a parcel or *balikbayan* box that suggested they were about to receive some new object. So although there is often a nostalgic and romantic portrayal of communication in this earlier period as though letters and cassettes were deeper and more substantial than the transient forms of communication that often replaced them, actually what is often revealed by these details is also their limitation and their failures to work as effective media in the maintenance of the relationship. What they also reveal is a marked asymmetry between the experience of the parent and the child: just because things managed to be emotional and personal for the one, did not mean they were for the other.

Public–private

The issue that emerges again and again in the children's memory of letter writing was a frustration with something that they understood at one level was supposed to represent their personal, or heartfelt relationship to their absent parent. The reality of letter writing was often that it was actually something determined by, supervised by, and often controlled by, the carer. The Philippines in any case is a more kin-orientated rather than individually orientated society (Jocano, 2001) (although, of course, as we saw in Chapter 3 there is evidence to suggest that this is gradually changing), and the letter was often regarded as a family construction rather than a personal one. A child might be expected to write just a small part of a longer family letter, or have their own note enclosed within the larger letter to save postage. As a result, anything they composed would be seen by others. Clearly the ability of letters to carry the emotional content discussed above depends also upon the context of their production. In many cases the letters that were received from absent parents would be read aloud to the family as a whole, before being distributed to each in turn to read to themselves. (Of course, letter reading as a public practice was also the norm in Western Europe until the early twentieth century; for a discussion see Earle, 1999.) In fact, the letter was often addressed to the family rather than the person. In that sense, anyone in the household could open a letter even if it was addressed to a different family member. Judy, originally from the province of Laguna who now works as a domestic in London, felt that letters may also involve a wider monitoring, as the whole neighbourhood 'will know that a letter was delivered at your address and neighbours will ask to find out what was in the letter'. This view may relate more specifically to Judy's marital breakdown and the way her estranged husband would show her letters to other family members, but we have strong evidence to suggest that notions of privacy of communication are very different in the Philippine household than they are in contemporary Britain.

This public nature of communication would tend to be ever truer of cassette tapes. Children often created these as a group in play rather than as a lone construction, and tapes received were generally listened to as a public performance. This issue of lack of privacy came up several times when a carer was found to have abused their trust, most often by siphoning off money that was supposed to go to the children. Because the media was public, the material it contained could be effectively censored in both directions, so that for years the parents were unaware of what was really going on at home, until a return visit, or because another relative, or in one case a priest, wrote to let them know the truth of their children's conditions.

Many of the children participants situated their letter writing and cassette production within the context of school, which dominated their lives during at this period. For them, making a cassette tape might be an exciting adventure more like the better kind of school project, or letter writing might seem a weekly chore most easily understood on a par with school homework. In more extreme cases the person they are communicating with became secondary to the task in hand. Especially when the children were young, these school-like tasks were easier to comprehend than an actual parent they were writing to, whose personhood had sometimes receded with distance and with time.

For parents too, these communications can fit into a number of relatively standard genres. There is the informational letter, or the formal letter exemplified in the 'accounting' style letters of Edmundo to his wife discussed earlier. Then there is the use of the media as narrative to retell an event or convey a story, such as a long account of something the children had done as told by a carer, or the kind of stories a person might tell when they came back from work in the evening. Much of the content, at least as written by children, is relatively formulaic, but fathers too often felt that they could express themselves only through ritualistic forms such as: 'You should take care of your health, do well in your studies, you have a very intense tuition fee, you should make the most out of everything. Usual father talk.'

The narratives suggest that a concern with more private and intimate issues tends to arise as the children become teenagers, at which point they may also be granted more privacy and individuality. They would wait around to be handed 'their' letter within the family communication. Letters may also be viewed as more private than telephone calls which, when they were dominated by landlines rather than mobile phones, were generally assumed to be family or communal events rather than individualised communications. So it was the letter that was often the medium for private gossip rather than the phone.

These concepts of public and private are rather more profound, however, than simply an interior personal world as against a social or impersonal world. They reflect the wider relations of power and discourse which control 'what can be said', which often derives from an interiorisation of a public discourse. Both private and public communication are infused with normative pressures on the appropriate forms of performative action and communication. An example of this, which was much discussed by our informants, relates to the issue of suffering. As migration develops, we see the emergence of a new public discourse that establishes the 'proper' narrative. This is a period which sees what Johnson (1998) calls a 'reformulation of tradition', as migrants objectify the Philippines itself in relation to their absence. Particularly influential is the rise of a narrative of suffering and the ideal of the self-sacrificial overseas worker. As Rafael (1997) and others have pointed out, the Philippines was unusual to the degree to which this attempt to construct an ideology as well as a practice of migration was heavily influenced by the state, although certainly not controlled by it. Instead we see various influences including public reaction to news about the treatment of Filipinos abroad as key factors.

When it comes to the material we collected, it seems that this wider public discourse has profound implications for the private communications within families. Often our participants noted that they were 'not supposed' to convey their problems or anxieties. Letters or cassettes were also understood as having a kind of functional role, and perhaps the most important function was to stop the person who received this communication from worrying. Therefore the communications should not include anything critical. This was noted by the three, now grown up, children of a domestic worker in London. As one put it: 'She said that she's glad that we were happy, that we'd never quarrel. Things like that. And how much she misses us'. So there might be jokes or banter, constant promising that one is studying hard and that everyone is completely well. Then there is the child who recalls that they would talk about their problems on tape, but always made sure that they did not cry. Which is why as soon as they had finished making the tape he would go to his room and cry and cry all the tears that he had bravely kept inside when in front of the microphone.

In contrast to the English notion of a 'stiff upper lip' with its connotation of individual dignity and privacy, not complaining is seen in the Philippines as part of a collective responsibility to not worry those who have gone abroad on the family's behalf. This echoes the public discourse that migrants are sacrificing themselves on one's behalf and that it is therefore a duty to pretend everything is OK. In this case a Filipino reticence to avoid public upset is linked to the typical 'myth' of migration found in many other contexts. In fact teenagers who often express themselves through opposition to the normative, might go to the opposite extreme of flaunting their unhappiness or sending provocative texts that they are drinking or unwell as a strategic subversion of this norm. This is evident in the film *Anak* discussed in the Introduction, but there are also examples within our own research such as Evelyn's negative outpouring in her 'I hate you' letter to her mother, as well as other cases complicated by impending marital breakdown. This may also reflect just how difficult things become when problematic issues do come out into the open, which in so many of our cases does eventually happen.

Conclusion

This chapter prefigures in microcosm many of the issues of this book. The discussion of letters and cassettes opens up a number of themes such as privacy, emotion and temporality, which we shall explore in relation to new media in Chapters 7 and 8. The perspectives of parents and children on the relationship itself are the subjects of Chapters 5 and 6. But what this chapter demonstrates, which will be taken up in our conclusion, is that ultimately these all come together as mediated relationships. At this historical stage media do not merely carry or convey content, but their nature and materiality profoundly mediates the relationships themselves. But as this book proceeds we shall see that this is only the start of our understanding of mediated relationships, which will need to go ultimately in quite other directions. This is because such mediation develops not in isolation, but within the dynamics of the migration process itself, and because we will also demonstrate how relation-ships mediate the media rather than just the other way around. These parents are being confronted by new ideologies and practices first in places such as the Middle East and then in the UK. New ideas about how mothers should act and the proper place of intimacy and emotion are opening up over these decades. The parents are becoming distant from their place of origin and the children are grow-ing from infants to teenagers and young adults.

Already, however, this chapter demonstrates the value of this particular case study. The deep suffering and anxiety created by these conditions of separation help explain the intense exploration of specific media such as letters and cassette tapes in order to eke out their potential and affordances in maintaining basic relationships. Letters, because they are handwritten, are seen as containing a trace of the letter-writer. The effort put into the act of physically writing them contributes to their recognition as 'crafting', especially if the letters are long and eloquent. Conversely, cassette tapes were often felt as powerful because of the emotional immediacy of the voice. While letters had a high informational capacity (for instance, allowing for detailed instructions to be laid out), cassette tapes could potentially introduce some realism into the long-distance communication and were therefore a preferred medium by mothers in terms of gauging their children's true feelings and state of being. The materiality of the media had implications for their temporality, meaning that communication was stretched over time, with mothers – and some-times children – reading and listening to the letters and the tapes over and over again. The fact that both letters and tapes were seen as carrying traces of their authors explains why they were never thrown away (for a similar argument relat-ing to photographs see Rose, 2004). But far from concluding that this letter- and cassette tape-mediated communication was satisfactory or successful (although there are individual positive stories), we have shown that both the letters' and tapes' key limitation, that is, their lack of interactivity and simultaneity, exacerbated inequalities and asymmetries already existing within the parent–child relationships. The time lag between sending and receiving these communications also partly explains how communication often ended up becoming a more formalised or ritual exchange that was as much an expression of cultural obligation as it was of personal feelings. These observations echo earlier findings about the standardised nature of migrant letters and their social function as confirmation of family solidarity and duty (Thomas and Znaniecki, 1996: 25).

All of this bears on the transformations of the relationships and dynamics in the ideologies of how such relationships are supposed to be. For example, we have noted the increasing openness in communication from the more formulaic compositions associated with childhood to becoming a teenager. During the same period the more infrequent earlier media which lent themselves to established genres of exchange give way to more directly interactive media which also provide more potential for confrontation and provocation. Later on we will explore these issues with respect to the still more complex situation of contemporary polymedia. The subsequent profusion of forms of media means that there can be still more specification as to which particular medium best serves which mode of performance and type of relationship, which was already evident in the ways in which our participants exploited the contrast between letters and cassettes whilst treating them as a communicative environment. This suggests that even in this period of old media we can identify early evidence of polymedia, that is media understood by users as an integrated environment. So to understand the contemporary iterations of long-distance relationships, we would argue it is helpful if we can bear in mind the clearer situation that developed during this earlier period, which was dominated by letter and cassettes.

5

THE MOTHERS' PERSPECTIVE

Every evening at about 10pm GMT when it is 6am in the Philippines, Donna, a care-home worker on a student visa in Cambridge, webcams her husband and two eldest sons, aged 12 and 10, while they are having breakfast and getting dressed for school. Early mornings used to be Donna's favourite time when she was back home. Now she will always make sure she is in front of her screen at that time in order to admire her sons in their school uniforms. This is the time when she asks about school and gives them advice on their homework. After a webcam session with her husband and sons, Donna webcams her mother who looks after her eight-month-old daughter. She asks her mother about how her daughter slept and what she will eat. She sings songs to her daughter and they often play peek-a-boo. Donna can stay up for hours chatting to her mother and playing with her daughter, but the thought of her early shift finally forces her to quit the call and go to bed. When she wakes up in the morning her first action is to read the texts that her sons have sent to her roaming phone. She made them promise before she left that they would text her at least once every day and she sends them extra money for this purpose. Donna almost always texts her second son to remind him to take his asthma medication. She will then call her husband and mother to ask about how their day has been. If they are at home she will webcam them briefly before going to work. And then she will briefly call again during her break at work just to say *Kumusta* (how are you) to her husband. All this intense communicative experience culminates in the weekends when she will webcam her mother and talk to all her relatives who gather there for the family meal. They often leave the camera on for hours, sometimes even for eight consecutive hours. Donna knows what her children have for dinner and what they do at school. She is heavily involved in the Facebook social networking game 'Café World' where she 'owns' her own café. Donna has made one of her sons her 'virtual employee' and they also interact daily through this online game.

Donna's intensive mothering extends to her attempts to monitor her sons' activities from a distance. She has both her sons' Facebook and email passwords and once a week she will check their accounts to monitor what they have been involved in. She justifies this as her way to check on them from a distance. To date nothing worrying has come up, but Donna regularly asks her husband and mother to make sure they keep an eye on the boys and ask their teachers about their performance.

If we compare Donna's experience to the situation described in the previous chapter, it becomes clear that new media have radically transformed communication for transnational families. Whereas Barbara, whom we met in Chapter 4, was able to send and receive 12 letters and cassette tapes in one year, Donna can send 12 SMS in one day, or spend eight hours on webcam. This chapter discusses the difference that digital media make for the performance of mothering at a distance. We argue that new communication technologies allow for the performance of 'intensive mothering' whereby mothers expend 'a tremendous amount of time, energy and money to raise their children' (Hays, 1997: x). The combination of internet- and mobile phone-based platforms have allowed for the experience of mothering to be 'more complete', as our participants have put it. However, to argue that mothering has become more complete is not to suggest that problems of separation are solved; on the contrary we will see that the constant communication afforded by new media often amplifies conflict by revealing problems. However, even in those instances mothers prefer to be aware of difficult issues, rather than not.

The performance of intensive mothering at a distance is hardly the whole story. New media are also having consequences for the way women reclaim and experience their maternal identities. After years of intermittent communication when mothers felt left out of their children's lives and described themselves as 'incomplete', women now feel able to reconstitute their identities and experience of motherhood. This is the theme that we explore in the second part of the chapter, when we also return to the notion of maternal ambivalence, which, as we saw in Chapter 3, is at the heart of the experience of migration. We will argue that new media allow women to negotiate the opposing pulls between work in the UK and family in the Philippines and thus negotiate the cultural contradictions of transnational motherhood. Interestingly, communication technologies do not just help in the negotiation of the resultant ambivalence, but also sustain it as mothers often refer to the media and the ability to mother from a distance when justifying decisions to remain abroad and thus separate from their children.

Intensive mothering at a distance

How 'intensive mothering' is performed depends on the age of the children. For those such as Donna with children at a preschool, or early school age, video-based platforms are particularly crucial for establishing the visual contact which matters for both sides. Mothers want to be able to witness their children's development, and they recognise that the children are more fully engaged during a webcam rather than a phone conversation. Mothers with infants are happy to simply look at the children and be reassured that they appear healthy and content. Parents with young children often ask for the webcam to be left on for hours so that they can get a sense of what is happening in the household. When children are so young, a good deal of the parenting consists of being in conversation with whoever cares for the children, offering advice and hearing reports on what the children have done. Some, like Donna, will also play games such as peek-a-boo and sing songs. Once the children are older, interaction through webcam can be more creative and we even heard of stories of mothers playing hide-and-seek with their children (with the help of an adult who moves the laptop around the house to actually find the children in their hiding places).

Once children start school, parenting becomes immediately focused on education. This is not surprising given that children's education is one of the two main reasons for migration and paying private school fees and tuition is one of the main areas to which remittances are channelled. In the past, mothers such as Edith chose to return to the Philippines when children started school in order to tutor their children. Edith knew that it would not have been possible to help her daughter Evelyn through letters, or voice recorded cassette tapes. But Greta, a trained school-teacher, finds that she can offer considerable help to her eldest children (aged 8 and 10) with their homework through Skype. For her younger one, however, she pays a tutor to come in some afternoons every week. So during weekends – or sometimes even early in the mornings London time when it is 4pm in the Philippines – Greta will dedicate some time to discuss her sons' homework on Skype. Donna prefers to give her advice on homework through instant messaging (IM) as she can type her answers to her sons' questions.

Looking after their children's diet is something that is a constant preoccupation regardless of the children's ages. It is often one of the first questions mothers will ask during a phone conversation, or even through text messaging, and it is not surprising that they always seem to know what their children have eaten each day. Sandra sent cookery books by Jamie Oliver and Nigella Lawson to her now 20-year-old daughter. Her children live in Baguio city, in the mountainous area of Northern Luzon, so they have access to plenty of green vegetables and ingredients that one can find in England. Sandra's daughter occasionally asks her mother for cooking tips on Yahoo Messenger and sometimes shows her on webcam the cakes she has made.

Perhaps because mothering is very much associated with feeding and nurturing, food and discussions about cooking remain important aspects of the transnational relationship. These are also relatively neutral topics and therefore constitute easy ways for bonding and developing small talk. This not something that mothers perform only through digital media. In fact, we have come across several examples of how mothers would mention food, or even occasionally recipes, in letters. Perhaps the most obvious and material way in which mothers have expressed this nurturing role at a distance is through the sending of *balikbayan* boxes – the tea-chest cargo boxes filled with goods which are sent periodically to the families back home. Barbara told us that she used to send all sorts of goods such as corned beef, spam, spaghetti, instant coffee, coffee-mate and nutella. When we first met Angela at her North London home, such a *balikbayan* box dominated the living room filled with clothes and food such as pasta, tins of biscuits and chocolates. Although Barbara said 'because when you try something here and you like it you want them to taste it too', looking at the lists of things included in these boxes it is obvious that most food items are also easily available in the Philippines, which suggests that the actual sending of food is an emotional and symbolic practice. Considering that the cost of living is higher in the UK and taking into account the additional cost of shipping, it becomes apparent that the sending of food cannot be explained economically as, in the end, a jar of instant coffee shipped from London will cost more than if bought from a Manila supermarket.[1] This is particularly exemplified in the example of the mother who filled her *balikbayan* box with rice among other things. Sending rice from London to one of most intensive rice-producing countries in the world can only be explained as an act of nurturing and symbolic 'cooking' for one's children. One can also see this practice as a form of controlling how the money is spent – if the women would send remittances instead, these could be spent on all sorts of things which they might not approve.

Although it is obvious that this type of nurturing from a distance is not something introduced by new technologies, what has changed with new media is the intimate knowledge of how such gifts are actually received and more generally what the left-behind children are actually eating. The arrival and opening of a *balikbayan* box is now incomplete without a parallel phone call, a sequence of text messages or, even better, webcam with Yahoo Messenger or Skype where mothers can actually witness the happiness of their children when they open the gifts that they selected for them. Cheap communication, whether through internet- or mobile phone-based platforms, also enables the frequency of contact which allows mothers to call several times a day to ask trivial questions, or to remind their children about important matters such as to take their medication as we saw in Donna's example earlier. Even if such communications are absent, it is again through some new media platform that the mother will seek attention, assurance and thankfulness. Such is the case of Donna, who recently complained through her Facebook status update that her relatives did not even thank her for the box she had sent, prompting an outpouring of messages on her 'wall' from all the embarrassed family members.

The other aspect of mothering is that of discipline and control which, as in offline parenting, can often require negotiation and be resisted (see also Chapter 6). Nelia calls her nine-year-old son to check whether he's playing computer games. They have a rule that computer games are allowed only on Friday evenings or in the weekends, so she calls her sister-in-law who looks after Marco to check on her son. Angela has an agreement with her sister to send her an SMS once her daughter is home from a night out. If Florencia is late, the aunt texts Angela, who will then call her daughter on her mobile to ask where she is. Social networking sites present a new opportunity for finding out more about the children's everyday lives by looking at their pictures and also reading the messages their friends leave on their walls. For mothers this is invaluable information about what the lives of their children are really like, although that is not uncontested, as we will see in the following chapter. Popular in that regard has been the social networking site Multiply, which is very much geared towards the sharing of pictures.[2] But social networking sites also serve a monitoring purpose as mothers check their children's profiles and wall messages for any worrying signs of trouble.

As children grow older, much of the communication begins to revolve around money and practical issues and it is often the eldest daughters who are expected to look after the mother's remittances (a finding also highlighted by Parreñas, 2005b). In general, mothers attempt to micromanage their households at a distance and expect their daughters to be their assistants in this process. Angela sends all her money to her daughter Florencia, who then reports with details on bank accounts and the building of the extension of the family house. Needless to say, such responsibilities are not always welcome, or uncontested by the children, and such matters can often give rise to conflicts.

But mothering is not only about control or monitoring. Once children become teenagers or when they go to university, mothers attempt to bond with them – particularly their daughters – in different ways. For example, discussing clothes, or even trying on clothes during a webcam session in order to get expert advice. In some cases, it is now the mother actually seeking advice from the daughter and not the other way around. A number of mothers told us that they became closer to their teenage or young adult children after they migrated. At one level they interpret this as 'not being taken for granted any longer' and being appreciated for being the main household breadwinners. But it is also possible that the distance of migration and the mediating process of communication give teenagers the ideal combination of autonomy (since the mothers are not physically present and perhaps not as oppressive) as well as emotional support (provided through new media).

Structural factors

'Intensive mothering' takes time, effort and money, all scarce resources for the migrant mothers. It also requires a considerable amount of skill in the form of digital literacy. These resources are not distributed equally amongst our participants and such asymmetries have consequences for the type of parenting mothers can perform. For example, domestic workers often do not have access to a laptop or internet connection in their own rooms. This might change with the prevalence of wireless routers in the homes of the families that they work for, but at the time of our research most domestic workers would mainly go online either in internet cafés or at the Centre for Filipinos in London, a key site in our fieldwork. This means that any synchronous internet-based communication (such as IM or Skype) with their children has to be planned in advance, which was not always convenient. Most nurses and care-workers, on the other hand, had their own laptops and internet connection at home – although, of course, there were exceptions. But nurses too, due to their demanding schedules and the fact that they often work overtime, may also find it hard to schedule communication in advance and prefer the mobility of the phone. Quite apart from access issues, is the question of digital literacy. Although more than half of our participants were, or became during the course of our fieldwork, digitally literate, several were not confident enough to use new media for communicating with their families.

The other asymmetry concerns the media available to the families back home. Those whose families in the Philippines do not have landlines, which usually also means no internet access at home, have to resort to mobile phone communication at a much higher cost. Nelia will call several times a day, as will Judy, and both reported significant budget issues, having spent at times up to £400 per month on phone bills and telephone cards (even the more typical bill of £150–£200 is still high relative to their salaries). However, the recent emergence of UK networks dedicated to international calls at competitive rates has made a difference. For example, one such network offers calls to the Philippines for 10 pence a minute. It is perhaps not surprising that one participant said: 'God Bless Lebara!' (the network in question). If we compare this to the early days of telephone in the 1980s or 1990s when most women had to queue to use the public phones in the hospital compounds in Riyadh, or the telephone boxes in London 'which were so expensive [. . .] they [ate] your money up' (Nora), then it becomes apparent how developments in mobile communications and the advent of competition in the mobile phone industry driving prices downwards represents a significant improvement. Women also tend to have multiple mobile phone contracts so as to take advantage of different plans and tariffs.

For families in the Philippines where calling by phone is prohibitively expensive and who cannot afford internet access at home, the only way children can initiate communication with their mothers is by sending an SMS on their roaming phones at the price of a local text. It is not surprising that historically it was the children of OFWs who first got mobile phones, invariably as gifts from their mothers who saw the phone as an opportunity to reach their children, but also providing their children with the possibility to contact their mothers. As noted in Chapter 2, the ratio of inbound/outbound calling between the Philippines and the UK is 7:1 and this communicative asymmetry was at times a source of frustration for some of the left-behind families. Internet access, once established, corrects this asymmetry significantly. Even though the cost of an internet connection is higher in the Philippines than in the UK, once obtained, families can reach their relatives abroad with the same ease that their relatives can reach them.

Not having access to the internet also makes a qualitative difference to the type of parenting the mothers can perform. For example, those who regularly use Skype and IM find that they often offer help with their children's homework. Such is the case of Greta who, as we saw earlier in the chapter, often takes the opportunity to tutor her children when they need some extra help. Elisa on the other hand, who only has access to the phone to communicate with her three sons, feels it is hard – and expensive – to help her youngest one, whose grades have plummeted since she left home, with homework over the phone. Although she is proud of the academic achievements of her two eldest sons, she feels deeply concerned about the performance of her youngest, especially as he is 'the brightest of them all'. Recall that paying for the children's education is one of the two key economic motivations for Filipina migrants as we discussed in Chapter 3, which explains the weight that mothers place on their children's school performance and their desire to monitor it. Mothers spoke with incredible pride about their children's academic achievements, which also legitimate their absence abroad. Conversely, any drop in grades is often experienced in an almost devastating fashion given the almost ontological significance attached to children's education.

'A more complete experience of mothering'

Overall, being able to see their children makes mothers feel more confident. Sandra is always concerned with how well her children are eating, and being able to see them reassures her that they are doing well. This relates to Sandra's past experience when communication was infrequent and mediated via her in-laws. During that period she found out that her children were being mistreated and even actively turned against her. Sandra has very much valued the ability to communicate directly and frequently with her children as, being unable to travel home frequently because of her irregular status, she has been able to develop a relationship with them within that mediated context. As Sandra put it referring to Skype: 'I feel confident now. I feel the trust because I can see them. This is a very big difference.'

For mothers, having access to numerous technologies and platforms makes mothering, in the words of Donna, 'more complete' as each technology is used for different purposes (see Chapters 7 and 8). For example, mothers use webcam for specific practices, such as helping with homework and generally for generating 'a feeling of co-presence', especially when they leave the camera on for hours. Webcam is particularly popular and successful with the parenting of younger children, as the visual aspect better meets both children's and mothers' needs. Conversely, mothers prefer phone calls when they wish to have more private discussions regarding family problems, or money. In general, even for mothers who are regular internet users, the telephone remains the preferred medium when it comes to understanding how their children really are and for conveying depth of feeling. Texting is a facility that often has a phatic function, an emotional reminder of the distant significant other, while social networking sites, such as Facebook or Friendster, provide context and an opportunity to share children's social life (although that is not uncontested). The combination of the different technologies and their functions contributes to the performance and intensity of mothering. Of course, 'intensive mothering' can also be performed by mothers who have access only to the telephone. But the combination of different new media, each attending to different senses and structuring communication in different ways, can provide women with increased communicative options to feel able to perform mothering in ways that suit them.

Conflict and the burden of communication

Although generally welcomed by mothers, the proliferation of new communication technologies does not simply solve the problems of separation: on the contrary, it may allow for the emergence of problems, or often amplify conflicts. In the past, because communication was infrequent and asynchronous, it was easy to conceal problems, whereas now, because of the constant and interactive nature of communication, not just with one's children, but also with a number of relatives or even neighbours who are willing to volunteer information, such concealment is more difficult. As we saw in the previous chapter, the main purpose of letter writing in past decades was to reassure the family that 'all is well'. Mothers did not want to divulge the difficulties of life abroad so as not to burden their families, whilst children recall being told by relatives to focus only on the good news so as not to sadden their mothers abroad who are working so hard. As a consequence, the whole 'genre' of letter writing was aimed at suppressing problems. Although not wanting to burden the family is still valued today, it is more difficult to hide problems. Of course, this does not mean that family members no longer keep secrets from one another, as Baldassar (2007) has also observed. In fact, as we shall see in later chapters, each individual appropriates the various media at their disposal and takes advantage of their different qualities in order to control their end of the relationship. But even when the children will not openly talk about problems, technologies themselves may offer cues which may alert mothers that something is wrong. When Mimi's son, Raul, dropped out of high school it was impossible for his mother not to find out, as she chats with her children on Yahoo Messenger everyday where she immediately noticed that her son was at home online when he was supposed to be at school. For Mimi this was particularly poignant, as paying for her son's education was the reason she migrated in the first place and his dropping out challenged the validity of the whole project of migration. Despite her devastation, Mimi preferred to know, rather than be oblivious to the problem and thus unable to do anything about it.

Mothers often recognise that conflict is an inevitable aspect of parenting, and that new communication technologies allow for a more 'realistic' experience of mothering. The main instances when the communicative opportunities afforded by new media are experienced as a burden are when the requests for help from other family members proliferate, something which can become a source of stress for some women. For example, Nelia, who as we saw in Chapter 3 helps at least a dozen relatives, sometimes finds the constant flow of requests upsetting. Every time she calls her mother, her brother will come to the phone and ask for some help: 'You know the children cannot go to school, we are struggling.' Of course, most women, especially those with younger children, agree that the most difficult aspect of new media in the context of separation is the realisation that they cannot actually hug, kiss or smell their children. Although one can simulate a situation of co-presence through having a meal in front of a webcam, the experience falls short of being physically present and this realisation is often painful for mothers, who often cry after a webcam session.

Donna had been hoping her first visit back home would be for her daughter's first birthday. However, the fact that she was still paying for the enormous debts (approximating £3,000) she accrued in order to come to the UK on a student visa meant that she could not afford the airfare and the cost for the trip. So she settled for a long webcam session which would allow her to witness her daughter's party. At 9am GMT on a warm midsummer Sunday Donna webcammed her mother's house where her extended family and friends had gathered. The living room was covered in balloons and pink decorations. Her daughter looked pretty in her white and pink dress, which Donna had sent from England. Relatives and neighbours had arrived for an evening of celebrations and ample food. Donna had also paid for an entertainer for the children. When her daughter was about to blow out the candles on the pink Barbie cake Donna was overcome by emotion. Perhaps because she had been desperate to be with her daughter on her first birthday and did not make it in the end, perhaps because she realised that already 11 months had passed since she left her children and it would take a lot longer to pay off the debts, Donna could not hold back the tears and abruptly hung up the call. She later told her mother and brother that the connection was too bad and the call was dropped. Later when her sister uploaded more than 300 pictures of the birthday party on Facebook, Donna spent hours perusing them, looking at all the details: the photographs of the cooked dishes, the decorations, the clown's performance, her daughter's smile and the endless pictures of the presents.

Such poignant moments reveal the limitations of digital media in overcoming the spatial and temporal constraints of long-distance relationships. Despite these, however, what also emerges quite clearly from the previous discussion is that developments in new communication technologies have changed the way that women can mother at a distance. Mothering can now be practised intensely with women doing most of the caregiving and emotional work, which is associated with traditional gender roles in the Philippines. At one level this finding is in agreement with Parreñas' (2005a) observations about how mobile phones tie women to gender hierarchies and perpetuate gender inequality despite the fact that through migration they are also the primary household breadwinners. Yet women themselves say that they find this ability to micromanage their households and control their children's upbringing empowering. They feel they now have a better idea of where their remittances are spent. While we have endless examples of how women in the past returned to the Philippines only to find their children wearing the same old clothes despite their mothers' hard toil and remittances, such examples of deception and abuse do not seem to be as common today when women can ask their children directly how much money they received and even see them online.

Maternal identities and ambivalence

Apart from being empowered through being 'in control' and being able to perform mothering in a more 'complete' way than in the past, mothers take pleasure from seeing their children and from being recognised as the ones who care and provide. In other words, what webcam allows them not only to see, but to be seen, which is linked to women's identities as mothers. One of the most poignant moments in several interviews with mothers who had first migrated before the new communications explosion was when they described their first visit back home, usually two years after leaving their children, and their deep sadness when their then young children no longer recognised them. When Vicky returned to the Philippines for the first time after six years her children called her 'auntie' while they called their grandmother '*inay*' (mother). Likewise, Elisa who had left when her son was less than a year old, returned when he was almost three to find that he no longer recognised her. She was devastated that he cried whenever he was left alone with her. Although Vicky, Elisa and the other mothers often managed to reestablish a rapport with their children, they described their experience of 'mothering' as incomplete. Sandra, whose six-year-old daughter ordered her to return to Hong Kong during one of her visits, said 'I gave to them whatever I wanted, but my presence. I didn't feel [like] a complete mother.' Mothers, especially those with younger children, experienced disappointment and a sense of failure in their role as mothers, which was encapsulated in this rejection.

Contrast this with the situation today when Donna proudly announces that her eight-month-old daughter, whom she left when she was six weeks old and whom she sees daily through webcam, points to the PC screen when her *lola* (grandmother) asks 'Where is your *ma*?' Donna told us that her daughter is aware that her *ma* is not in the room (so she does not confuse her mother with other female relatives) and always smiles when she sees Donna's wedding photo in her *lola's* sitting room. For Donna, apart from her own desire to witness and admire her baby daughter growing up during this period of rapid transformation, the fact that her daughter recognises her as her mother through webcam is also a confirmation of Donna's own identity as a mother. Being able to 'feel like mothers', or reclaim their identity as mothers, is something which matters a lot to the women we worked with and something which extends beyond the performance of dedicated mothering.

For mothers who had migrated before the recent explosion of communicative opportunities, new media represent a chance to feel like mothers again. In this context it is not surprising that once they access these technologies they often go on what we can call a 'communicative binge', frequently texting, calling or webcamming their loved ones. Whether this is welcomed by their children is a different matter, which we explore in the following chapter, but the gap opened up during the period when communication was expensive and infrequent often proves hard to fill. For those who left after the mobile phone boom, keeping in touch has always been taken for granted and it is perhaps not surprising that in this case women explicitly refer to new media and the ability to remain in constant communication with their children as one factor justifying the decision to migrate. Some mothers reported that since migrating they have become 'even closer' to their families. Being away makes them feel more appreciated and less taken for granted. That they are also the main breadwinners has added to their recognition and appreciation. However, it is conceivable that it is also the consequence of the media which allow the bridging of the distance and it is precisely in that space that words such as 'I love you' or 'my baby' are first uttered. Sandra and Elisa both mentioned that both they and their young adult children will consciously make an effort to find the time to talk to either via webcam (in Sandra's case) or the telephone (in the case of Elisa). Before migrating neither Sandra nor Elisa could easily find that extra time to communicate with their children, given that they both worked very long hours. Hence, almost paradoxically, migration and the affordances of mediated communication have in some cases brought mothers and children closer together.

As noted in Chapter 3, more traditional models of mothering, especially from areas further north of Manila, may have eschewed overt declarations of love and emotion (McKay, 2007), but when mothers go abroad they are more exposed to what are becoming more universalised expectations derived from schools of psychology which teach that the direct expression of love and emotion are essential to proper mothering. More intensive media communication allows them to adopt these new ideals of how to be a mother just at the time when they may feel increasing pressure to perform motherhood in this fashion.

Yet for all those stories of empowerment and success, there are some cases when the possibilities for cheaper communication have not been able to fill the gap of separation. This is usually the case for mothers who migrated when their children were still young, or who left at a time when communication was still infrequent and expensive. Such is the example of Edith, who has found it hard to develop rapport with her daughter even though she calls her frequently and sends her packs with her favourite celebrity magazines such as *Hello* and *OK!*. In Chapter 4, we saw how the daughter used to sign off her letters to Edith as 'your angry daughter'. Her mother is still concerned that the daughter is behaving awkwardly towards her and sometimes even towards others, although we should mention that hers was a unique case in our sample. Edith's daughter lives in a remote part of the island of Samar with no internet connection at home. Yet, even under these circumstances, Edith has embraced the idea that adopting new media is part of her duty as a mother. Edith takes IT classes at the 'Centre for Filipinos' in London, where we spent many Sunday mornings meeting and catching up with our participants. She hopes that one day her daughter will be able to access the internet and therefore, she, as a mother, ought to be ready for that. For Edith, digital literacy, apart from being a useful skill, becomes a practice through which she can improve herself as a person and as a mother. Even though she may not be able to use these platforms to communicate with her daughter, at least not until Evelyn gets online (and even then the outcome will be uncertain), for the time being, practising how to use these technologies becomes a way of articulating her identity as a mother. In this sense, it is even possible to think of new media as more than just technologies for relationships. In the absence of the child as immediate object they become the form through which, at least some of our participants, construct and articulate their identities as mothers. These practices that produce subjectivity (in this case motherhood) can be understood as technologies of the self (Foucault, 1988).

Most participants viewed communication with their children as a natural part of the duty that accrues to them as a result of separation, and as being just as important as sending remittances. When we asked Nelia, whose story we discussed earlier, whether migration had been the right decision given that she missed her family so much, she said:

> Yeah, for me it's the right decision because if I was still there I might have lots of children, but my life might involve just staying at home and not having time for myself. I've [achieved] more here. As long as I support them. I give them what they need, and I keep calling them.
>
> *Nelia, London-based domestic worker, mother of one*

Nelia's comment sums up the ambivalence at the centre of several women's experiences. On the one hand she feels valued and respected for her work in London, not just by her employers, but also by her family in the Philippines. This respect and fulfilment coupled with her family's continued economic need make her think that her return to the Philippines is unlikely. Like Edith earlier, Nelia describes coming to London as 'a blessing'. At the same time, Nelia loves and misses her nine-year-old son, often crying when talking about him. Nelia is torn in two. Her identity as a breadwinner and independent worker is at odds with her identity as a caring, loving mother. What makes this conflict particularly salient is that the two identities are spread geographically across two continents. Work is (and, as we saw in Chapter 3, can only be) abroad, while her child is in the Philippines. As a live-in domestic she cannot afford to bring her son over, unless she finds a regular job paid well enough to allow her to support her family in London. Under such conditions of separation Nelia cannot negotiate her sense of maternal ambivalence in a situation of co-presence. Thus new communication technologies do not just allow for the performance of intensive mothering at a distance; they are also the main vehicles for the negotiation of this accentuated ambivalence (see also Madianou, 2012a). If women return to the Philippines they will be with their children but they will lose the economic capital and autonomy that comes through work; staying abroad, but in constant communication, is one way of reconciling both, given that they can at least mother at a distance. It is not surprising that women increasingly refer to these new communicative opportunities when they justify their decisions to prolong migration. This role of digital media in legitimating such decisions points to an important, yet so far unacknowledged, consequence.

The difference new media make is evident not only in mothering at a distance but also in grandparenting. Nora is in her sixties and has been abroad for more than two decades. As is typical with many of our informants, she first migrated to Riyadh as a domestic and after one year she moved to London. Although the primary reasons why she left were financial (her husband had been made redundant and they were facing huge debts and poverty), she described her married life in the Philippines before her migration as comfortable but also boring, as she missed the time when she was in paid employment. Nora left one son who was 13 at the time of her migration. She did not return to the Philippines for 13 years – when her son was 26 and married with children. Most of the communication during that long period of absence was through letters and subsequently phone calls. Although Nora never lost touch with her son, she was not involved in the day-to-day business of his upbringing. Later on she missed his wedding and the birth of his two daughters. During our fieldwork Nora started using webcam with Yahoo Messenger and now schedules frequent sessions with her son and grand-children. They have even had a meal together as a family, toasting their glasses in front of the computer screen (though given the respective time zones these are different meals). The webcam has allowed Nora to see her granddaughters as they develop and the visual aspect, compared to the disembodied voice over the telephone, helps them relate to her. Nora has become very fond of her granddaughters and often talks about the presents she wants to send them. She also plans to increase the frequency of her visits to the Philippines. However, she does not want to return to the Philippines for good even though she is now retired, as she does not want to lose her independence and autonomy – especially as she would have to live with her son as even after all these years of hard work in the UK she has not been able to build her own house. Likewise, the prospect of her returning to the Philippines is not attractive to her son and his family (whom we also met in Laguna), as they see it as a potential burden at a time when they are overcommitted financially. So, in a way, we can begin to think that webcam and IM can offer this transnational family an 'ideal distant presence' which can ensure the viability of their relationships. The webcam allows Nora to be a grandmother and yet maintain her autonomy and independence, while it offers the granddaughters the opportunity to connect with their grandmother and develop a meaningful relationship with her.

Emotionality and mothers' own needs

Although this chapter has focused on the ways that new communication technologies have transformed women's ability to mother from a distance and their identities as mothers, it would be an omission not to refer to the ways in which new media may meet their own emotional needs. This has to be seen in the context of women migrating to a foreign place and often feeling lonely or bewildered by the experience. Women often recall their arrival to England with poignancy. Those women who arrived in the winter months were shocked by the cold weather and lack of light. Those who came from Manila to work as nurses in hospitals in and around Cambridge were shocked by the quietness of the countryside. And all invariably were shocked with the lack of rice 'three times a day', which for a

Filipino is basic to their sense of welfare. We have stories of women not being picked up at the airport, of luggage getting lost and of a general feeling of disorientation. In those early days the mobile phone – initially through the roaming SIM and soon after a UK number – and the ability to call back home was their life-saver. There are many stories of phone bills taking up a high percentage of their income in those early days. The women still say that they call more frequently when they are more lonely and budgeting issues remain important, as it is easy for bills to get out of control. However, this has become less of a problem with the advent of some technological developments, such as webcam and Skype (including the PC-to-mobile phone option) and other internet-based platforms. For example, when Donna's husband senses that she is sad, he is willing to stay up all night on Yahoo Messenger to comfort her, which he could never do if he was calling on his mobile phone. The importance that our participants placed on their mediated relationships is also evident from the several stories of women who leave their laptops on throughout the night and may even wake up if they hear sounds indicating that their loved ones have come online on skype or Yahoo Messenger.

What women also do in times of loneliness and homesickness is to read their text messages again and again, the same way they read letters as we saw in Chapter 4. The portability of the mobile phone means that they can read their texts pretty much everywhere and take solace that their loved ones are thinking about them. Very often the women's roaming phones are full of religious messages that are popular to forward even within the Philippines. Rather than seeing such messages as impersonal, women report that they see them as signs of love and indicate that their relatives are thinking of them. In that sense SMS, even the most impersonal ones, have a phatic function. Donna, who does not share this view and avoids such forwarded messages, sees her daily texts from her husband and sons as a key motivation and source of strength: 'I feel happy when I wake up in the morning and there is a message from them. It keeps me going.'

It is not just when they are sad or lonely that women may turn to communication media. Flirting and romantic relationships are a crucial motivation for single women. Most of the single women we met were actively seeking to meet fellow Filipinos through online platforms. Very popular were the chat rooms dedicated to Filipino OFWs on Yahoo Messenger through which several of our participants met partners or potential partners. Boredom is another factor. Janice, whose employers are in Hong Kong for half of the year, which means that she mainly house-sits when they are away, is beginning to spend more time on social networking sites such as Friendster and Facebook. She looks at the pictures of her children, of course, but she also looks up old friends and sends them messages. Vicky, who is now retired, told us how excited she became when she found out about what the internet can do. She has become very close to a group of Filipino nuns who provided great – virtual – support when her second husband died. They still send her an email every day, which she always looks forward to reading. Vicky is also close to her former priest, who has now moved to Africa and with whom she also communicates via email. Given that her family is dispersed across four continents, she regularly sends emails (usually with photographs as attachments) and SMS to her sisters in New York, Australia and her brother back in the Philippines. Vicky had already organised a reunion of college friends back home – all via emails – and was planning a follow-up event at the time we met her. All these activities kept her busy everyday. Such observations confirm earlier findings about the internet revitalising diasporic connections (Miller and Slater, 2000), but also suggest that women use new media in ways that fulfil their own personal needs and extend beyond their roles as mothers.

Conclusion

The explosion of opportunities for cheap and synchronous communication through digital media and platforms has allowed for 'a more complete' practicing of intensive mothering at a distance. Different technologies and platforms fulfil different aspects of mothering, allowing women to be in control of their households and children's upbringing. The digital divide both nationally and transnationally has implications for the type and cost of 'distant care', affording more opportunities to those with access to internet-based platforms. However, intensive mothering is also performed though mobile phones, which are widely available and represent a significant improvement over the past situation when communication was asynchronous and prohibitively expensive. Even though the frequency of communication through new media can often involve conflict and disappointment, for mothers it represents a more 'real' experience of mothering and an opportunity to 'feel like mothers' again. In this sense, communication technologies have implications not only for practices of mothering, but also for maternal identities. Even though there is evidence for the persistence of traditional gender roles, transnational communication cannot simply be understood as confirmation of asymmetrical gender relationships (Parreñas, 2005b). We have argued that new media have become pivotal in the negotiation of the accentuated ambivalence of migrant mothers by allowing them to maintain and negotiate a plurality of roles and identities across distances. In that sense, new media can also be seen as solutions (albeit painful) to the cultural contradictions of migration and motherhood. In fact, our evidence suggests that communication technologies feature increasingly in women's justifications for both the initial decision to migrate and the subsequent decision to remain abroad, exemplifying the manner in which transnational communication has become an inextricable factor within migration.

6

THE CHILDREN'S PERSPECTIVE

Cecilia, aged 23, was born in Manila. Her parents raised pigs, but the business folded and her mother felt she had to leave to pay their debts, going to the US as a caregiver, although entirely without training for this job. As was typical in our fieldwork, underlying the mother's decision to leave was an estrangement between wife and husband. Cecilia's father was already seeing other women and taking drugs. After ten years in the US, Cecilia's mother returned only once to the Philippines, the year before we met Cecilia. Cecilia felt that this period of absence between the ages of 14 to 22, was pretty much exactly that period of adolescence during which she expected, following what has become a common trope in discussions of modern parenting, that her own parents would evolve from being more hierarchical figures of discipline and boundedness to becoming more engaged in equal friend-like relationships. In her case Cecilia felt that she had grown much closer to her mother after she left, and that their separation, combined with frequent communication, had provided just the right degree of autonomy to facilitate such a transformation in their relationship. In fact, Cecilia told us that she and her two siblings hardly saw their mother prior to her emigration. As their mother worked in a different town, she had to leave the family home before Cecilia and her brothers were awake and would often return at night when they were already asleep. Ironically, only after her mother left for California, did she consciously make the time to communicate with her daughter, first through a satellite phone and, once the family got internet access, through webcam. This equalising process was greatly facilitated by the fact that Cecilia was dealing with her parents' separation. In Miller's recent fieldwork in South London (Miller, 2008a), children often refer to this event as forcing them into the position of having to 'parent their parents' because divorce often brings out the most immature aspects of both parents' behaviour. If her parents' divorce had not been enough to contend with, Cecilia had then taken on the task of rallying her other relatives in the US to support her mother when she became stricken with cancer and had to undergo chemotherapy. She is also consulting with both of her parents on how to support her younger sibling, who has had a much more negative reaction to their parents' departure. Finally, and most recently, she finds herself talking to her father's new partner in California about their recently born baby, and having to overcome the initial awkwardness of that relationship in order to empathise both with this young mother and her father's devotion to his new infant.

Under all these circumstances it is not surprising to report that Cecilia's use of internet communication is intense. She and her parents may be online through webcam when eating meals, comparing the food they are eating (though different meals in different time zones). Her brother plays guitar to serenade his mother, and on another occasion she places the microphone next to his head just so that she can complain to her mother about his snoring. Cecilia and her mother frequently go shopping together, based on simultaneously visiting websites, after which her mother pays for a garment and has it delivered to her daughter. Both her mother and her father are on social networking sites such as Facebook and Multiply. And her parents have a habit of viewing pretty much everything she posts. Not only that, but also going further and viewing the postings of her friends, which as her friends point out, seems to them a little weird. 'My friends would say, "Hey your mom viewed me." I would say "Ooh sorry!" My mom is a cyber freak.' Cecilia does, however, use privacy controls to prevent her parents seeing the kind of party pictures almost any daughter would not want her mother to view, for example, evidence that she went to see a boyfriend that her mother particularly disapproves of. This problem is compounded by her habitual use of a Multiply account as a kind of visual diary, within which she includes photographs of more or less everything she does.

Cecilia acknowledges the importance of social network sites in facilitating this desirable shift in her relationship to her mother. A traditional parent–daughter relationship would sit awkwardly on Facebook, while the rather loose category of 'friend' that pertains within Facebook may have helped with this shift towards kinship taking on the idiom of friendship. It will also be no surprise that we found this 23-year-old to be a remarkably composed and mature individual whom we could only describe as rather awe-inspiring. Cecilia's case goes beyond the argument that intensive media use can resolve issues of separation. It also implies a new modern form of parenting in which autonomy itself is regarded as critical to the maturing of such relationships. This model of mother as 'new best friend' derives mainly from the Western popular culture of magazines and television shows throughout the world and marks a departure from traditional Filipino norms.

At the other end of the spectrum of children's experiences we find the story of Ricardo, a 28-year-old professional born into a middle-class family of health workers. Ricardo's parents met as OFWs in Saudi Arabia where they married. When Ricardo, an only child, was born in 1980 his parents briefly returned to the Philippines, but left again for Saudi Arabia when he was three months old, leaving him with his 60-year-old grandmother who brought him up. Ricardo's parents recently migrated to the US, effectively making the family separation a permanent one. During most of his childhood, Ricardo would visit his parents for the entire duration of the summer holidays when schools were closed, and his parents would visit him twice a year. So until Ricardo was 15, when he decided he would rather spend his summers having fun with his friends, he would, on average, live for three months a year with his parents in Riyadh, and nine months apart. Yet despite these periods together, Ricardo mostly felt distant from his parents. Partly, Ricardo thought this was because they were 'disciplinarian', 'very strict' and as a consequence he always felt 'overpowered' by them. This was reflected in their communications, whether in the form of letters in the early years to emails and mobile phone calls more recently. Ricardo described his letters as attempts to 'show off' and 'impress his parents' with his achievements and school grades. To achieve this:

> If I remember correctly, there was like a template to my letters. Like the first part was, 'Hi. How are you? How are things in Saudi Arabia? Blah blah blah . . .' Then the next part was I give them updates, like in academics, then in general, in my life. It was never that personal. [. . .] Now that I'm reflecting about it, I really think it was a lot about impressing them. Because even though I had this thing for independence and all that, I still think that, at the very bottom, I still want to make them proud of me.

Although Ricardo craved his parents' approval and appreciation, he never felt entirely accepted. That is why when his grades 'started failing in fifth grade [. . .] I couldn't tell them about it and I felt really bad. And I didn't want them to know about the grades, and I couldn't tell them that I was having a hard time.' Conveying 'bad news' to one's parents seems to go against one of the norms of what constitutes proper behaviour towards one's parents. We have already discussed in Chapter 4 how such views shaped letter-based communication as a genre that suppressed family problems. For Ricardo, the asymmetrical power relationship with his parents reflected in his communication by letter became even more accentuated with the arrival of phone calls. In fact, Ricardo told us that he 'dreaded' his parents' calls as they would be opportunities for them to 'grill' him on a number of counts:

> My parents' letters, they weren't personal as well. They were more like commands; like things you should do, things you shouldn't do. I always felt the letters were like a disruption, like there's a new set of edicts. (laughs) Even when we transitioned into phone calls, I always dreaded their phone calls because that would mean they would ask me to do something for them or they ask me to give them updates about school and then they would tell me, 'You should do this. You should do that.'

Ricardo's parents would call once a week for around an hour or so and these weekly calls were experienced as a form of monitoring. 'At least, that was how I felt, that I was being watched all the time.' The transition to the mobile phone exacerbated this sense of surveillance as his parents could call any time without warning, something which Ricardo found very stressful. We will discuss later how Ricardo handled this feeling of oppression by switching to different media (Chapters 7 and 8). But what emerges from his discussion is a more traditional model of parenting, noted in many of the other participants' descriptions where the parents remain distant and authoritarian and where, in contrast to the case of Cecilia, media, both old and new, cannot help overcome the problems of separation.

These two case studies represent the extremes of success and failure of parenting by media from the perspective of the child. The contrast between them helps explain why, when we turn to the children's perspective in general, we should not anticipate any simple or homogeneous finding. Nevertheless we are responsible for coming to some kind of conclusion with regard to one of the main questions that motivated this research, and which was central to the previous chapter. What is the impact of new communication technologies on the very possibility of parenting? One of the key issues in the literature on Filipino migration has been simply to assess the impact upon left-behind children (e.g. Edillon, 2008; Parreñas, 2005b; Reyes, 2008). What the last chapter revealed was that usually mothers welcomed the massive increase in potential communication as it allowed them reconstitute their role as parents and alleviated some of their anxiety about the consequence of separation. So we shall start this chapter by showing how, for many, but by no means all of the children, this is entirely untrue.

When it does not work

In contrast to the accounts of the mothers, who seem mainly unequivocal about the benefits of improved communication, we found that approximately half of the children were either ambivalent or negative about the consequences of new media. For these children, not only had new media failed to reconstitute their mothers as actual mothers, but the belief by their mother that, thanks to these improvements, she could reassert her role as a mother, was itself seen as more negative than positive. By the time we interviewed them, they were no longer children, but themselves young adults, which could imply that they were better able to reflect upon these past experiences. Grace, a woman in her mid-twenties, in reflecting upon the improvements in communication noted:

> You'd think that we'd have a better relationship or that she'd be more present in my life, but it wasn't really the case. I think it just makes it more convenient. I use 'convenient' because it's for practical concerns, like 'Are the bills getting paid' or 'Are you still in school' or 'What are you doing now?' or 'Are you sick or well', but then for the depth and quality of relationship you want, it's not dependent on those things.

In such cases the clearest evidence for this failure comes during their mother's return visits. Several children suggested that their mother tries to demonstrate her own parental role by challenging norms that they have established with their carer:

> My grandmother wasn't that strict about these things. And then she comes and says 'I confiscate your phones, you can't use them over dinner.' And it's like, 'Whatever, mom, you're not even here.' And then she'd get all our phones and say 'You can't read at the table.' And we'd had this life for the longest time. Suffice it to say that it wasn't easy. We all couldn't wait for her to . . . we were kind of torn because we were all waiting for her to go back, so we could get on with our lives, but then there was also a side that just missed her so much and she wasn't there for the longest time so we just want to spend time with her.

An even more extreme case is with Bea, now 22 years old, who clearly felt that the improvement in communication is more there to satisfy the mother that she is now a parent again than having any actual benefit to the child. When asked how often her mother phoned she said: 'Once every two weeks. Or every time she feels bored there. . . . I thought it was a lot because sometimes, especially if you're not together, you don't really have anything in common anymore. . . . She talks to us for about an hour and then we'll get really irritated by then. And then we'll just find someone to pass the phone to.' In fact in this case having failed to elicit the children's engagement, the mother most commonly would end up having very extensive conversations with the *yaya* who was employed to look after the children.

Of critical importance here is phatic communication, a topic with which anthropologists have been engaged since the time of Malinowski (1923), who used the term 'phatic communion' to refer to the important social function of seemingly trivial small talk. 'Phatic' could be translated as communication about nothing much at all. What matters is not the content of communication, which might be about the weather, or an event, which neither side is much interested in, but the sheer awareness that there is communication. Phatic communication may play a vital role simply because at least both sides feel they are still communicating. It can represent a bedrock to relationships where there is a mutual desire to express this underlying bonding, but we found it can also expose the discrepancy between what a relationship is supposed to be and what it actually is. On the positive side are many examples of children who feel that just texting, or sending a message on IM, achieves precisely this aim. It reveals to their parents that they are thinking about them, and reassures them that they remain present to their parents. But other children note failures in phatic communication. Instead there are only stilted and forced exchanges about what has been on television, what one ate for dinner and other excruciatingly boring discussions, because really the children are just desperate for this embarrassing and awkward conversation to end so they can go back to playing with friends. Paolo saw it as something of a service to the family that he was good at as he liked to chat and could more or less use up his mother's phone card single-handedly by talking endlessly about what he was doing, his problems with their father, and other matters. His brother would just mumble the answers to a few questions and rapidly hand the phone back, while Paolo would gossip so much that it spared the rest of the family from an ordeal they had come to dread.

Mothers in the past would often have a particular time of the week when they would phone, but so far from this being seen as a reassuring ritual, the children could find this irritating, complaining that they are left hanging around during a weekend for a phone call when they had better, more interesting, things to do. In some cases we found that the mother and child were not aware of the discrepancy between their respective experiences of new communication. Because of constraints in their circumstances, Andrea's communication with her mother had become reduced to a 10-minute call once a month. Her mother continued to work for the money that would allow Andrea to join her, at which point normal parenting would, presumably, be resumed. So it came as a complete shock that when finally the mother had the resources to bring her daughter to Britain, Andrea refused. As Andrea put it: 'First of all, I'm not close to them. I don't know how they think. Sometimes I don't even know if they really love me. So I decided not to go. I don't want to be far away from my relatives here, especially from my grandparents because they really took care of me'. After all, from the daughter's point of view this is a mother she only remembers meeting once, for a couple of weeks, during a return visit when she was 14. So although her sister is also living with her mother, she feels she would be joining strangers and leaving her actual family, those she is close to and who have looked after her. Given that 'going abroad' is the most common ambition amongst Filipinos, the fact that a young woman turned down her mothers' invitation to join her in the UK is very poignant and revealing of the daughter's emotional state.

One of the most common ways in which this failure of parenting is expressed by the child is for them to tell stories about the degree to which, although the parent was trying to be present, they were clearly quite unaware as to the actual age of their children. The children resented the parent's apparent inability to acknowledge that they were growing up. For example, Ricardo states: 'Even when I was working already, for the first two years of my work, I was a High School teacher, and they still treated me as if I were a student, because they don't see the changes that happened here. They still think that I'm a young child.' This was often made painfully evident through the presents parents chose to send them, which were clearly suited to children some years younger than they actually were at the time. Bea thought her mother 'got stuck in time' and lost track of how her children were growing up when she sent baby shampoo for her teenage brother. Such examples demonstrate that even though the parents had increased contact with their children, this did not necessarily mean they had a better understanding of whom their children had become.

For teenagers this took on a somewhat different complexion. They were subject to representations in films and other popular culture, where mothers might typically have been portrayed as important for discussing intensely intimate and emotional problems, such as the first boyfriend or girlfriend. But trying to do this without an established background of sustained and successful phatic connection mostly failed, and was sometimes disastrous. Instead of an empathy with her daughter's anxieties, a transnational mother was portrayed as reduced to a shrill 'Don't have sex' which made the daughter simply angry and above all embarrassed. These were sometimes the worst conversations that children ever had with their mothers. Given the nature of our fieldwork and that it was often easier to broach this sensitive topic of parental absence by talking first in general terms, we would often have some discussion about the film *Anak*, which almost all the children in their twenties had seen. It was during these teenager years that participants could identify with the bitterness and resentment over prolonged absence that is central to the film's narrative.

In essence, several of these children are stating something they regard as quite evident, and which is also articulated in the film *Anak*. For them the mere presence of frequent communication does not of itself bring one's mother back home. On the contrary, what it achieves is quite the opposite. It makes for a daily reminder that one's mother is absent. The fundamental point is that with only occasional communication, a child can become reconciled to a stable alternative set of relationships, with the absent parents occupying a sometimes idealised but distant position. But with new communications this stability is disrupted and an actual parent deviates from this projected image, sometimes leaving the children confused and conflicted.

While even such extreme cases of absence could lead to reconciliation, it does not detract from the larger conclusion of this section. For many children, in fact about half of those in our sample, the impact of new, cheaper and improved communication came to be seen as negative rather than positive in its consequences. This is not simply for the aforementioned reason that it comes as a more constant reminder of the mother's absence, and the way they disrupt a projected ideal that had come to fill that absence. It is also what they see as their mother's belief that they could return to a parental role, turns instead into a clumsy attempt to micromanage and even monitor their lives. The intensification of media contact merely demonstrates the continued distance that exists between children and their mothers, and exacerbates the problems of separation. As such, this evidence would seem to contradict the mother's perspective. But before concluding, we have to acknowledge that such views apply to only around half the children we worked with. Cecilia, with whose story we began this chapter, was by no means the only example where children, as well as mothers, saw new media communications as a positive boon.

When it does work

In the case of Cecilia it was not just that improved communication helped to sustain a relationship, but the distance created by her mother's absence allowed for a positive transformation and maturing of their relationship, which might otherwise have been difficult. Zoilo also clearly feels that his mother's absence allowed him to come closer to her:

> I became more likely to talk to her about those things. I think it was a feeling of longing. I think that's a manifestation of me missing her, but she's not around, so I tend to share more about myself to her. So we became more close, actually. During the early stages, actually, not much – but around late high school, when I actually had my first girlfriend. I would tell my mom about my girlfriend then. And when she would call, she would ask about her. So I'm happy to share about, telling my mom about my girlfriend – what she does, what we're doing, we're going out – something like that. So those kinds of personal things were, like, were brought up. Whereas normally if she were here, I wouldn't normally talk to her about it upfront.

One aspect of this more positive side of parenting by media is the way in which, in at least two cases, it was not assumed that the absent parent was a more distant or less involved parent. In both these cases the father who remained present was seen as introverted and relatively uncommunicative or uninvolved in the minutiae of family life, which confirms findings by Parreñas (2005a). In contrast, the absent mother was now sufficiently involved, thanks to new media, to be the mainstay of family organisation, whether through her practical role in obtaining and dispersing money or the gossip that united the family networks.

There were also several cases where relationships that were tense and oppositional during the teenage years, softened and improved in the post-teenage years. The evidence suggests that new communication frequency is most positive when it dovetails with the frequency and content that might anyway have been expected of that relationship at that time. As children become older and leave home, they would expect to interact less frequently but for longer, more intense communication when they do meet. At this point such less frequent interaction no longer implies lack of care or affection. As one put it:

> When we get the chance, we would talk, like, for two hours. We would talk longer, but it was more infrequent. I would still tell her about the things going on in my life. *But how close do you feel you are now?* Closer than before. Yes, I think. Because probably the reason I think that we can survive not talking more frequent than before, my mom and I feel like our relationship is stable. I think I'm confident that she would understand me. I think she can get what I'm trying to say. So there's a certain, I think, trust already between me and her.

These occasional long chats are probably just about the same kind of communication they might have had even if both were present in the Philippines, but living apart.

One of the other points made by Cecilia, as also several other participants, was that mediated communication has the potential to reduce the embarrassment in expressing intimacy. She noted that it is easier 'to say things on the phone than to talk to [my mother] in person'. Zoilo, too, would be more affectionate on the phone, while others such as Florencia and Lisa preferred text-based media, such as letters or email to express feelings. Even Bea, who as we saw earlier had an ambivalent relationship with her mother, mentioned that 'I would make it a point to say "I love you" to her, or "Goodnight" whenever we talked with her on the phone. But we really didn't usually do that while she was here because it was embarrassing, and we didn't see the need to.' Such cases tend to follow the model of contemporary popular culture in which expression of intimacy and emotion is regarded as essential in positive parent–child relationships.

Many of those who felt that they really came to appreciate their mothers only after they migrated, were those who were old enough to understand the reasons behind this migration. Even Bea, despite her ambivalence towards her mother, recognised that migration had been an empowering and transformative experience during which her mother metamorphosed from someone without voice in the domestic context to an equal partner who supported the whole family through her remittances. Bea's account of her mother's metamorphosis oscillated between some admiration for her mother's empowered status (reflected even in the way she started dressing in stilettos and expensive clothes) and disappointment when the mother retreated to her traditional more submissive role on her return.

This understanding sometimes arose when the children themselves became parents. Such is the case of Domingo, who has developed a close bond with his mother after the birth of his two daughters. Nora had left Domingo when he was 13 years old. Partly because of her irregular status, Nora did not visit for 13 years, a period when communication was infrequent and expensive. As a consequence Domingo became distant from his mother. It was only after he himself became a father that he sought her advice. It was fortunate that this happened at a time when new media were becoming more readily available. For Domingo the break-through happened through webcam, which has also made a difference to the relationships between his mother and his daughters: 'Although she is far away from us, my feelings for her [do]n't change. I still need her as my mother. I still need her guidance [...] I usually get her advice from my mum through webcam.'

As we saw in Chapter 5, Nora similarly feels that webcam has allowed her to rediscover her son. Their newfound bond was consolidated during Domingo's recent trip to the UK, when together with Nora they travelled across the UK and Ireland.

Other participants also developed a closeness to their mothers once they became old enough to relate to them as mature adults. Paolo, for example, after years of mediating between his parents' conflicts, finally started talking to his mother about her new relationship. During one of her visits, he even accompanied his mother when she decided to have a tattoo on her fiftieth birthday – an event which he photographed and blogged about. Even Lisa, who for years felt resentful towards her mother for abandoning her, described how she understood her mother's position only when her father's new girlfriend moved into the family home. It was only then that it occurred to her that her mother may have experienced this humiliation long ago, prior to her migration. Her emails have become more affectionate now in an effort to show some solidarity with her mother.

The most extreme case of separation and eventual reconciliation through new media is the story of Grace, who had been effectively abandoned by her estranged father since she was a young child. In Grace's case, the social networking site Friendster opened the road for some kind of reconciliation with her father. When Grace started using Friendster she thought of typing in her father's and half-brother's names to see 'what comes up':

> And there's a profile under that name, and I click on it and it looks exactly like my dad. So this is my [half] brother. I messaged him, then 'I am his daughter. I don't know if you know me. I'm not looking for anything, I just want to know how he is.' He answers, and then he goes, 'Fuck you, my dad doesn't have other kids.' So this guy, who's 27 years old, doesn't know that I exist. He didn't know! So I say, 'Hey, it's not my fault that he's my dad. I'm not looking for anything.' Although I knew that my eldest half-brother knew that my dad had other kids. He's met us, so he knows. But this brother says, 'How can you talk shit about my dad, blah blah blah.' And then I said 'I can prove to you that I'm not looking for anything, that I'm actually his daughter. If you don't want don't tell me where he is.' So I forgot about that. But then two months later I receive an email from my half-brother, the eldest brother, who knows about us: 'I'm sorry, my brother doesn't know about you guys, blah blah. I have a kid and I'm married now.' And I say, 'Okay, that's fine. How are you?' Just a polite exchange. And then a month after my dad emails me. 'My son gave me your email. How are you guys?'

Grace's encounter with her estranged father ended quite well – at least given the circumstances – with the father agreeing to start contributing towards the children's education, a gesture which has become almost the bedrock of Filipino remittance-based relationships.

Amongst these more ambivalent and fluctuating relationships we also encountered Carlito and Ofelia, both of whom had a profound connection to their mothers, before and during their migration. Carlito may speak to his mother for only 20 minutes each week, but that has not diminished how close he feels to her. His mother's visits (usually once every two years) are like month-long celebrations: the family have meals together and go for outings to the mall and the bay. By contrast, Ofelia feels that her constant communication with her mother through the new media environment which we term polymedia simply allows her to maintain and continue to develop what was always a strong bond. Similarly to Cecilia, her mother is her 'best friend' to whom she will confide everything. Tellingly, it is not just Ofelia that turns to her mother for advice, but even her own boyfriend.

Age, media and the pre-existing relationship as factors

It appears that many of the participants who reacted negatively to improvements in communication were those whose mothers migrated when they were still under 10 years old. This was also a time when transnational communication was still expensive and infrequent. Some of these became close again when they became adults despite years of emotional distance, but often these relationships remain unresolved by new communications. Conversely, most of those who report positively on the impact of new media on parenting relationships were older when their mothers left, which was also when with mobile phones were not such an extreme scarcity in communication. Moreover, because of the expectation of frequent communication, these families seemed to be prepared to face the higher costs of telephone bills.

As the children become adults, they may also become more empathetic towards their parents' situation and their needs, including loneliness, boredom and the stress of their work. Eventually they may come to see this communication more in terms of their ability to help their parent live through their difficult circumstances. A key factor may be when the children start their own families, since even where an absent parent could not reestablish their role as parent, there may be a more natural transition to becoming an effective and affectionate grandparent. When it is a son who is left behind, who never develops a strong affinity with the phone and with long chats, it may then be the daughter-in-law who takes up the reins and engages in long conversations with her mother-in-law abroad, conveying all the news and dealing with practicalities with far more patience and good grace than the son. This reflects Parreñas' (2005a) point about women in the Philippines being expected to be more responsible for the maintenance of relationships generally.

Another obvious factor in explaining differences in these long-term relationships after migration is simply the state of those relationships prior to migration. For example, when they still lived together, Ofelia and her mother had a very strong relationship. When her mother went abroad to work, Ofelia felt able to use communication technologies to sustain and develop their relationship. Ofelia and her mother are one of the pairs who had good access to a range of communicative options (broadband internet apart from mobile phones) and were both equally conversant in using these technologies. In this case mother and daughter used the range of media at their disposal to suit the different aspects of their relationship in a way that echoes the concept of media multiplexity (Haythornthwaite, 2005) whereby the closer the relationship, the more complex the media that are used to support it. But ultimately, although media availability matters, the quality of the relationship is an influential predictor of the type of mediated interaction. Carlito has remained very close to his mother Eliza, even though most communication is telephone-based.

Our conclusion that the younger the child left behind, the worse the prospect for their future relationship, at first seems almost diametrically opposed to some recent arguments of Aguilar *et al.* (2009: 224–251), that Filipinos believe it is more important to have their parents around them once they reach the age of moral discretion (*bait*) around 12 years, such that parents may even return at that stage. This in turn is diametrically opposed to popular psychology influenced by figures such as Bowlby (2005) and Winnicott (1971), which implied that the key to subsequent parental relationships lies in the initial bonding with the infant. These writings have filtered down to become the assumptions of popular magazines and global popular culture (Riley, 1983; Rutter, 1981; Smart and Neale, 1999). It is possible that our material differs from Aguilar *et al.* (2009) being mainly situated in the Manila region and therefore closer to these more cosmopolitan influences which are further heightened by our participants' experience of migrant trans-nationalism. We have also noted the impact of the media themselves in the sense that the older children experienced much more continuity thanks to the improvements in phone and other communication that had developed by the time their parents migrated.

The wider family relationships

So far our focus has been on the simple dyadic relationship between absent mother and left-behind child. Most anthropological work in the Philippines would instead emphasise the wider role of kinship and extended family. Several authors (Aguilar *et al.*, 2009: 114–128; Cannell, 1999: chapter 2) place the primary emphasis on sibling relationships as the core to all kinship relationships. Our evidence suggests the importance of a variety of wider relationships, especially the *lola* (grandmother), and not just the relationship between siblings.

The importance of sibling relationships is partly the differentiation within that category, where the eldest female sibling (*ate*) often has a prominent role in taking responsibility for left-behind children. Even when it is the *lola* who is officially designated as caregiver, we have several cases of older siblings who in effect become responsible and concerned for the problematic behaviour of younger sisters and brothers in the absence of their mother. This was particularly true where the older sibling is a daughter, in which case she effectively becomes the parent of the rest of the family (for similar arguments see Parreñas, 2005a). In some instances, such as that of Cecilia, even quite a young eldest sibling may become the principle carer. In such cases much of the communication is often about effective co-parenting, where the older sibling has to translate the desires and demands of the absent parent with respect to their younger siblings. It sometimes seemed that the older sibling used this role to express their resentment of their own lack of parenting. Lisa sees herself as showering love and attention on her younger brothers and sisters and thereby being an exemplary 'parent' partly as someone who is overwhelmed with bitterness and anger at being abandoned, as she saw it, by her own mother.

Not every older sibling felt comfortable with this role. In one case an older sibling felt a failure since he reckoned, if anything, he could not but set a bad example in his own behaviour. This substitute parenting may also put the older sibling in an invidious position with respect to their responsibility for financial issues. How remittances and gifts are distributed is an obvious cause of sibling rivalry. In one case a mother became convinced that under the influence of his wife the elder sibling was siphoning off money intended for the younger siblings, and cut off her relationship with him and his wife, passing on responsibility to the next sibling, at which point suspicions started to mount against him in turn. Financial responsibility may also mean being expected to follow the parents in migration to help earn money for younger sibling's education. So just as eldest siblings are initially committed to being present, they may also see themselves as subsequently committed to being absent.

A variation on this theme came with Amelita, who already had children of her own to look after when her mother went abroad to work. Her mother left with extreme reluctance but saw no other way to pay for the medical expenses for Amelita's brother who had a severe illness. Sadly soon after the mother left, their father, who had not been separated from her in 27 years, became depressed to the extent of having to be hospitalised. So Amelita is now responsible for her own children aged seven and five, a brother with increasing disabilities and a hospitalised father. On top of this she had her unfair share of other problems having to deal with a younger brother who drank heavily. She was forced to have long telephone calls that consisted of her absent mother expressing her anger at this brother. After a while she moved their conversations entirely to emails so no one else could overhear this anger.

Expectations of siblings may be sequential, as when the eldest leaves for college or employment and the next eldest takes on the pseudo-parental role, sometimes leading also to serial migration. Other than the eldest, it is common also to see the youngest sibling as a special category. Jezza felt that being in that situation she tended to be spoilt and treated more leniently than her other siblings even when her parents left to work abroad.

Apart from sibling relationships, the other crucial nexus of family relationships consists of that between the two parents. As noted in Chapter 3, the deterioration of this relationship may be one of the causes for migration and equally one of the consequences. Given that divorce is still a very rare occurrence in the Philippines, often the relationship is effectively dead as both spouses have alternative partners. In such a context, Bea became rather more concerned with the relationship between her parents that with either's relationship to her. In particular she becomes almost obsessed with what she sees as the inequalities and basic unfairness in the treatment of her mother by her father. Her own role becomes central when she is the one who comes to spy on her father's infidelities and report on these to her absent mother. She fervently hopes that the experience of migration will make her mother more assertive, and is disappointed when on her return to the Philippines her mother reverts to her more traditional and subordinate position in the relationship, although through this process daughter and mother end up having a closer relationship. A similar situation is experienced by Ricardo, who effectively mediates between his parents when his mother discloses that his father not only had an affair but also another child with another woman.

When the parents break up, the child is often faced with the difficult decision as to whose side to be on. There are no longer parents, only two disputatious individuals. Most commonly the identification is with the mother because, more than we had anticipated, the father came over in our fieldwork as frequently a strict disciplinarian and in most cases (although there were a few exceptions) not closely involved with the children. Many of our participants recalled corporal punishment, often being hit with a belt. As Paolo noted, this was often for quite small misdemeanours when he was young, such as not going to sleep in the afternoon when he was told to. In one case there was even a fear of being beaten up. In Paolo's case there was an informal agreement that each parent paid a certain percentage to the children's upkeep. But because his parents remained in acrimonious conflict this resulted in him trying to allocate 60 per cent of their textbook cost to one parent and 40 per cent to the other and both parents disputing their responsibilities largely because it is a way they can get at each other. Paolo, whose mother was in Saudi Arabia, would be holding the phone while his parents engaged in vicious arguments about money through him, neither wishing to speak directly to the other. Eventually he felt the only solution was for him to leave home.

There are, of course, exceptions, where the absent father is able to use new communications in a conciliatory way. For example, Gregorio recalls that he would have the usual little flare-ups and quarrels with his mother in his teenage years, over issues such as having to do housecleaning or mowing the lawn. But in his case it was the father who took on the neutralising role, asking him 'to understand your mum'. With improved communications it was possible for such triangulation to operate even though all three parties are living in different parts of the world.

Access and cost

Several factors discussed in earlier chapters, such as the asymmetrical structure of transnational communication at a 7:1 ratio of inbound/outbound calls, and the urban/rural and class divides in internet access, impact upon the child–parent relationship. Our participants confirmed their infrequency in calling abroad, an act which usually signified an emergency, such as the time when Lisa's brother became ill with dengue fever and she had to call her mother for help. Children mainly text a roaming phone, or make a missed call to initiate communication. Although mothers would almost always respond, this asymmetry often caused some resentment. Also frustrating was the reliance upon the calling card by most mothers. Some, like Lisa, found these calls too short, especially as her mother would call her on her mobile which is more costly. Lisa felt irritated that her mother would have to hang up after only 10 minutes, when she was just getting into the conversation. Conversely, Paolo sometimes felt his mother's desire to use up the whole card was burdensome, especially if he was busy with his own work.

The other significant asymmetry was in internet access, with many of the left-behind families having only dial-up connections, inadequate for webcam-based communication. Zoilo, an avid user of webcam, found this especially difficult since he knew the positive effect visual communication could have on his migrant mother. Those in rural areas were usually dependent upon internet cafés, such as the family of Arnel who have to go to a nearby town in order to webcam their father in Dubai. Apart from the lack of infrastructure, several, such as Glenda from semi-rural Laguna, lacked the basic digital literacy and were therefore entirely dependent on mobile phones. Carlito is fully equipped at home; it is his mother's reluctance to get a laptop that prevents him from using internet-based platforms to communicate with her. He told us how much he would love to be able to see his mother's face, whom he has not seen for two years. 'That's a long time', he added.

Would co-presence be different?

The question posed at the start of this book was whether a situation of cheap polymedia would resolve the problems of long-distance parenting for migrants. By this point it is clear there will be no simple answer. This chapter has revealed both marked discrepancies in the accounts of different children and also between those of the children and their own parents. To some degree we have been able to point to factors which help explain these differences, such as the age of the children when the parent first migrated, the quality of the pre-existing relationship, the range of media available, and wider contextual factors involving the extended family.

One of the problems in interpreting this evidence is that often the children are talking negatively about a situation that developed during their early or later teenage years. It is entirely possible therefore that what we are documenting has less to do with failures of communication and more to do with the kinds of tensions that in any case arise between a teenager and their parents. It may, for example, be a problem that a parent uses new communication to increase the intensity of their relationship at the very time when the teenage child is looking for greater autonomy. Our material may be compared to Wolf's (1997) research with Filipino diasporic families based in California. She starts by noting that although in many ways Filipinos are considered model migrants, nearly half of the female students she worked with reported that they had contemplated suicide within the previous year. The problem in her study is clearly not one of separation from parents since the families live together. Rather she argues that the parents retain a Filipino model of parenting which is incompatible with the much more liberal expectations in California, so that the daughters are torn between the expectations they derive from their peers and the lack of freedom or autonomy together with huge pressures on academic achievement from their parents. It is the presence of the parents, not their absence, that exacerbates differences in cultural expectations, which in turn manifest powerful generational differences. This suggests that factors such as age, media, separation and culture are not simply causative of each other, but co-present. To properly interpret our material we need to look more deeply at what is involved in these relationships, and appreciate the sheer emotional charge, but also the layers of intimacy and abstraction they involve.

Relationships as mediation

The concept of mediated relationships was introduced at the beginning of this book and will be expanded considerably in the concluding chapter. But at this point we have completed two chapters that focus on relationships, and before turning to the consideration of new media, we may begin our theorisation of relationships. The content of these last two chapters have brought starkly into focus the questions: what is a mother and what is a child? One problem is that we do not know what a 'traditional' Filipino mother would have been several generations ago and we probably now never will know since there are no records analogous to the nuanced situations of the ethnographic present. But we can make some suppositions.

The first is that it is very unlikely that there was ever any one clear normative model, given the diversity within the Philippines (see Chapter 2, also Cannell, 1999; Johnson, 1997; McKay, 2007; Rosaldo, 1980). The importance of this is evident in the recent work of Aguilar *et al.* (2009). He argues that for the rural *barangay* in the Southern Luzon province of Batangas where he and his colleagues worked there was a clear distinction between a young child who lacks moral discretion (*bait*) and an older teenage child (*talubata*). In strong contrast to Western psychological models, it is felt that separation from a child without *bait* was not problematic, as explicit emotional bonding with an infant is not integral to parenting. It was separation during the later stages from a *talubata* that could cause long-term problems (Aguilar *et al.*, 2009: 224–293).

Our participants' discourses, perhaps because of their exposure to Western models of parenting through their experience of migration, did not seem to correspond to this regional model. Instead their views seemed closer to the more international models presumed in studies such as Parreñas' (2001, 2005b). But our informants were also often well versed in alternative *Tagalog* terminologies and expectations that pertain to the regions around Manila. These formed the basis for a debate in the 1950s (e.g. Lynch and Guzman, 1974) and were reprised in an influential historical study by Rafael (1993). The two key terms are *walang hiya* and *utang na loob. Walang hiya* translates roughly as to be 'without shame' and is pretty much the worst possible thing a Filipino should be seen as exhibiting. *Utang na loob* by contrast is generally regarded as a positive trait, and refers to a particular kind of debt (*utang*) that is felt to be deep and interiorised. It may be the debt that it is incurred when someone goes well beyond the norms of kinship or friendship in the help they have given you. We have noted the case of Donna who migrated in order to fulfil her *utang* to her in-laws (Chapter 3). It also corresponds to a debt that all children owe to their parents for the gift of their birth. *Utang na loob* is a debt that can therefore never be fully repaid.

While we discussed these concepts with several participants, their implications were best observed in one of the most extreme cases we encountered, that of Andres. In this case Andres' mother had done just about every wrong thing that a mother could. She had more or less abandoned her children; she had only intermittently kept in touch and only occasionally sent any kind of financial support. She only once ever returned to see them, for a month, with hardly any notice that she was returning. After the shock of this sudden encounter, she then went back to a state of near-disappearance, within which communication and remittances returned to being intermittent and unpredictable. Her son knew, for example, that at one point she received quite a large legacy that could have gone to her children, but she insisted that the entire sum went to her abroad and nothing to them.

Since she had left when he was an infant, her son's sole face-to-face experience with his mother was this single month's return visit. He was well aware that there were mitigating circumstances, in that his mother had originally suffered considerable abuse, which precipitated her initial departure. Nevertheless none of these things seem to have marked her son as much as his subsequent encounter through Friendster. Several years after effectively losing contact, he received out of the blue a *friends* invitation request to his Friendster account from his mother. It is hard to convey the way he then spoke about what followed. Starved of knowledge about his mother, he immediately went to look at the pictures of her and her *friend's* on her account. While scenes of drinking and partying are the norms of social networking sites, he stated – and he could hardly bring himself to utter these words – that they were 'like ... prostitutes'. Within a month he had closed down his Friendster account. No other point in our fieldwork so clearly demonstrated the sense of a woman who was revealed to be *walang hiya*, without shame. And of all the people who really should not be *walang hiya*, the very worst would be one's own mother.

But against *walang hiya* stands *utang na loob* – the debt due to one's mother simply by virtue of her giving birth to you. At the time we encountered him, the son was again in communication with his mother. The circumstances were that his mother had maxed out her credit cards and was begging her children for money to help pay off her debts and avoid being thrown into prison. Despite everything that had happened, the son had absolutely no doubt that his priority in life at this moment was to save his mother from going to jail by somehow earning that money and sending it to her. He would leave college and get a job in order to achieve this. Why would he do such a thing? In her behaviour this mother had pretty much repudiated the role of mother as a given category. But the son still desperately felt the need for a mother. So he employed an aspect of debt we have come to appreciate from the writings of Mauss (1954), but rarely encountered with this degree of nakedness, free of encumbering factors. Here debt, in and of itself, has the power to reconstitute his mother as a mother. Despite *walang hiya*, neither she nor her son can escape from the fate imposed by *utang na loob*.

While undoubtedly an extreme case, this example demonstrates both the continued presence of different and competing models of motherhood and childhood, and also the need to think more deeply about the fundamental nature of relationships. In contemporary anthropology the dominant approach to kinship today has been highly influenced by the work of Carsten (1997, 2000), also on Malay populations, though in her case, within Malaysia. Her approach is central to Aguilar *et al.* (2009) analysis of migration and its consequences. The emphasis in this approach is on kinship as a highly fluid and flexible process, in which the actual behaviour and experience of people relative to each other comes to constitute the sense we have of them as kin. We may come to see the person who acts as father, eventually as being our father. Such writing has swung the pendulum from traditional anthropological studies of kinship as formal modelling of categories within structures and systems.

More recently Miller (2007) has argued that neither these earlier formal studies, nor the more recent processual studies exemplified by Carsten, are sufficient in themselves. Rather, most relationships contain a dialectical tension between these two extremes. Miller argues that what we call a relationship has three fundamental components: Firstly, the idealised model of that kin category, i.e. what mothers and children are respectively supposed to be like. Secondly, there is the actual person who inhabits the category of mother or child, and finally there is the discrepancy that inevitably exists between these two. The evidence from our research strongly supports such a theory.

In a situation of constant co-presence it is easy to assume that a relationship is almost entirely composed of the experience and knowledge that each person has of the other. But every time we discuss either local or global ideologies of mothering or childhood, we recognise that we are also paying attention to normative conceptions of the role itself. How should a mother, or a child, in general, behave? In a situation of extreme separation where there is limited experience of the actual person, that person is largely a projection of these expectations and norms. A child one left as a new-born baby is in essence a projection of an aspiration to become a good mother to a child who should secure top school grades. Such ideals can form without knowledge or experience of the child.

While this is particularly clear in a situation of transnational separation, Miller (2007) argues it is the case generally. For example, even in the UK studies of inheritance show that British people tend to divide their main assets equally, that is according to the fact that all offspring are equally one's child, and only to divide sentimental objects unequally according to their experience of the actual individual that occupies that role. Similarly we have seen that older siblings in the Philippines are almost invariably seen as a different kind of person than youngest siblings. But when a person fails to behave as an eldest sibling, then the response to them changes accordingly, while the next sibling may be given that role and status. Even in such a successful and sensitive maturing of relationships as represented by Cecilia, we have analysed the case as a movement between two idealised models of what a mother is supposed to be: from a figure of discipline to a sort of best friend.

Conclusion

So before we turn to the role of media as a form of mediation, we need to be clear about the conclusions from these last two chapters as to the nature of these relationships. Most of the specific content of these last two chapters can best be understood as a constant dialectic between models of kin categories, *the mother* and *the child*, on the one hand, and on the other the diverse individuals we have tried to bring to life through examples of what they said or did. These are the actual individuals who occupy these given kinship categories. At the heart of this chapter is a constant dilemma of how to reconcile actual people to the projected ideal that these same people simultaneously represent. Such ambivalence was echoed in the experience of several of our participants and is expressed here by Ricardo:

> Although the weird thing was, when they would come home, there was this long period where I have to readjust myself to their presence. So that although I wanted parents, it was like a vague idea of wanting parents. But when they were here, it was really hard for me as well because I'm used to being alone and not having parents give rules and stuff like that.

So notwithstanding the multifaceted nature of these relationships and the complexity created by factors such as generational difference, cultural diversity and the media themselves, it is possible to theorise the underlying core to our enquiry – that is the relationship. If we can understand this dialectic in the nature of the relationship itself, we are much more likely to also understand the role of media and mediation within the relationship. The task of the final chapter will be to bring these two together.

7
THE TECHNOLOGY OF RELATIONSHIPS

The emphasis in the last two chapters has been on the nature of the relationships, while this and the following chapters will concentrate more on the media used within them. The task of the final theoretical chapter will be to find the right balance between these two different dimensions of our study. In Chapter 4 we examined letters and cassettes from the perspective of their propensities as technologies and then considered some of the issues they bring out such as temporality, materiality and privacy as precursors of new media. In so doing we recognise that a historical perspective can shed light on current uses of digital media, as suggested by recent writings on remediation (Bolter and Grusin, 2000; see also Marvin, 1988). In this chapter we will look at each of the new media that our participants use. While here we will focus on each particular new medium and its associated affordances (Hutchby, 2001), we recognise that in practice our participants, as well as others in long-distance relationships, do not rely on just one medium, but use a range of different media in parallel with one another. Analytically, it is still important to identify the particular functionalities and affordances (Hutchby, 2001) of each discrete medium. This is because users exploit these functionalities and affordances when navigating the communication environment which we term polymedia. In this sense this chapter is a precursor for Chapter 8 where the focus is on polymedia as an integrated communicative environment within which each particular medium is defined relationally to the other media. As we have already noted, although the seeds of polymedia can be found even in the early days of letters and cassettes, the proliferation of communicative opportunities made possible through new media developments have only existed to any great extent for the last two years for populations such as Filipino transnational families. Most people are still in a transition to polymedia, but given that we are never likely to retreat back into a simpler state, we need to confront its consequences now.

A single chapter cannot represent a comprehensive treatment of all that media could be, or are used for. Inevitably, we will emphasise those usages that emerge as salient within this study. Media in this chapter emerge as those which our participants construct from various technologies, and not necessarily what we would have anticipated as somehow the natural propensities of those media. In fact it is not simply what people make of any one given medium that is important, but how they exploit what they find to be significant differences and possibilities among a plurality of media. This was already evident in Chapter 4, where even though we were only dealing with two media, letters and cassettes (apart from occasional expensive phone calls), the response was to exploit the key distinctions between those media, such that the strengths of one could complement the other. Although we will continue to focus on the experience of both the migrant mothers and those left behind that has informed the book so far, we will also begin to move beyond the specificity of the particular ethnography as we attempt to develop some more general arguments about the different media and their affordances which result from the intersection of personal, social, cultural, economic and technological influences. The ethnography thereby becomes a foundation for discussions of much wider relevance.

In moving our discussion forward we will need to leave behind some of the conventional distinctions between technology, medium, platform and application. For example, in the past the mobile phone or the personal computer have been regarded as technologies, while email, IM and SNS are viewed as web platforms or applications that operate within a particular medium, that is the internet. However, some platforms, such as email, can be accessed through two different technologies, as when, for example, one checks one's emails through a mobile phone. In the case of VOIP calls made through software such as Skype, the internet functions like a phone sharing more similarities with other voice-based platforms such as landline voice calls, than other text-based internet platforms. Convergence makes it difficult to retain categorical distinctions such as those between technologies, media and platforms given that all these continue to hybridise and overlap.

Our ethnography suggests that, perhaps not surprisingly given the potential confusion and conflation, our informants prefer to use the term 'media' to refer to all the above. We will follow their example in that almost all of this chapter is organised by a sequential focus on what the participants would have generally regarded as specific media. We do, however, retain one distinction that seems to us to retain some analytic clarity, that between voice-based and text-based communication. In the case of letters and cassettes, the contrast between text and voice was crucial in framing usage. Some of the functionalities associated with literacy and orality (see also Ong, 1982; Goody, 1968) continue within the new media environment as a form of re-mediation (Bolter and Grusin, 2000). The chapter will therefore be organised in three large sections: voice-based communication, text-based communication and multimedia communication.

The other concept that informs this chapter is that of affordances (Hutchby, 2001) which was developed as part of a conciliatory effort between the opposing poles of technological determinism, whereby technology is seen as an external force shaping society (see Carr, 2010; McLuhan, 2001) rather than as something which is itself socially shaped (see Williams, 1984), and social constructivism, according to which technologies do not have any inherent qualities apart from the ways in which their users decide to use them. For Grint and Woolgar (1997), for example, technologies are understood as open texts 'written' and 'read' by their producers and their readers respectively. By contrast, Hutchby (2001: 444) drawing from the psychology of perception and the work of Gibson (1979), sees technologies neither in terms of their users' interpretation, nor their essential technical properties, but in terms of the possibilities that they offer for action, which he terms affordances. In practice, the term now has a much wider reach that largely implies what it is that people find easier to do thanks to this technology. It can retain this third-way position as long as we understand this only as a propensity not as a determinant of what people actually do with any technology. This may be equally a product of the wider economic structures, idioms of practice, or media ideologies (Gershon, 2010), but also the actual relationships in question.

In our analysis we will examine each discrete medium and identify the affordances that emerge as significant from our participants' experiences. For example, we will focus on the interactivity of each medium and its temporality, as well as its replicability, storage capacity, persistence of content, searchability, mobility, reach, social cues, private/public nature and informational capacity. All these have implications for the blurring of public and private boundaries. But first, we need to start with an acknowledgment that the materiality of these technologies is also something that retains a presence and influence, which can easily become taken for granted and thereby missed, so it is worth starting by making these consequences explicit.

The phone and computer as objects and technologies

Even retaining a distinction based on the idea of communication based on voice as against text would in practice be cross-cut by the materiality of technologies such as the phone and the computer. For example the phone, its size, ringtones, brands and capacities is itself a significant object of material culture. So we need to briefly digress with a reflection on the presence of these technologies as objects.

The mobile phone's potentially fetishistic quality, where an object comes to stand for a person, is evident in a well known advertising campaign by the Filipino mobile telecom company SMART, which featured an OFW father returning from working abroad. When he arrives back home his young son fails to recognise him and hides behind his mother. So the father calls the son on his mobile. His son is then able to visually connect the voice, with which he is very familiar, to the person in front of him using that phone, who had become unfamiliar, and following that recognition runs to greet the father. The phone's presence can become a material signifier of absence, as when Marites, whose husband works abroad, notes:

I would say that [before he left] I would survive without a cellphone. For a 24 hour period. Let's say I lost it, or it whatever, it's okay. I have a [landline], if anyone needs to reach me, they can call me. . . . But after he left, I sleep with my phone next to my ear on the chance that . . . I might get information. When he's here, I can actually . . . leave the phone downstairs, and sleep upstairs. And just check it the following morning. But when he's not here, I always have that feeling that if something happens, that if there's something he needs to know, or if he wants to get in touch with me, then I need to have my phone. The cell phone is, more than anything else, my link to him.

Previously we looked back to the historical conditions where communication was dominated by letters and cassettes. The phone came in gradually. For the mothers, initially phones were the public phones in Saudi Arabia or the streets of London which were prohibitively expensive. Elisa and Joan remember queuing for hours patiently until a phone became available in the reception area of the hospital where she worked in Riyadh to hear her children's voice for only a couple of minutes. For those working as domestics it was their employers' family telephone which they might occasionally access. The arrival of the mobile phone was a breakthrough for women, such as live-in domestic workers who because of their employment and living arrangements were not in a position to own a landline, or for nurses who may have had landlines in their apartments, but worked long hours and may not have had ready access. It is not surprising then that so many of our participants described the phone as their 'life-saver'. In addition, almost all our UK participants had a roaming phone so that their families in the Philippines could contact them. Some had a third UK number on a different contract so that they could take advantage of different packages. Mobile phones were treasured possessions and could account for a considerable proportion of their income.

For most of our Philippine participants, especially those outside Metropolitan Manila, their relationship to telephones started with the public phone of a village, usually located in the PLDT office or even a *sari sari* store. In some cases the nearest phone would be in a neighbouring town, which meant receiving a phone call would represent an outing. Mark remembers how the family would be picked up by a tricycle at an agreed time to take them to the nearby town which was one hour's drive away. Others recall being summoned to return home for a scheduled call or a call with advance warning. At that time a phone call could mark a special occasion, something one would do for Christmas or to compensate for the parent being away for a graduation ceremony. Later on people obtained landlines in their own homes. Then the phone call becomes a different kind of ceremony, a collective gathering of the household, with the call moving sequentially from one member to another, and all conversations having a public airing. Almost invariably, such calls were very short as all involved were aware of the high cost. Later still, most of these children obtained mobile phones. Because they were usually purchased by the absent parent, many of them obtained such phones around the ages of 12 to 15, often earlier than their peers, partly because it was their mothers' desire to be able to get hold of their children, and partly because the children themselves were asking for such phones as gifts from their mothers. It is usually OFW children who are known to have the most fashionable phones. Mobile phones changed the situation radically since having one meant they now could engage in private communication, and after a while texting became an additional potential channel of communication. However, it is worth noting that several of our participants, especially those in rural or semi-rural areas, still do not have access to landlines so for them mobile phones are the only telephones that they have ever had access to.

There are additional material forms that complement the phone itself. For example, a crucial object in our research was actually the humble international phone card. Participants constantly reported structuring their communication around the card, although for those who use new media systematically this is becoming less relevant. Technically this is not a determinant. It is not that hard to leave a card unfinished, or to start another one (although that can be expensive). But some participants allowed the card to assert an apparent materiality because it gave structure and discipline to conversations which otherwise might have been still more fraught and ambiguous. At least people knew when things would end and what was expected of them. A person did not have the burden of showing how much they cared for the other person being measured by how long they were prepared to speak to them.

Turning to the personal computers and their materiality, we observed three main constraints in using computer-based media: the cost of hardware and the high cost of internet connection for those in the Philippines, the availability (or not) of internet in certain locations,[1] and the lack of media literacy by some of our older parents within the UK. For all these reasons, personal computers have nothing like the ubiquitous presence of the mobile phone, though desktops, and increasingly laptops, would be markedly more present with families who have overseas relatives than otherwise, both because they are often paid for out of remittances and because of the importance both sides attach to communication itself. In many households that we visited, desktops were often like landlines, single machines in public places shared by the family. The desktop computer has much more potential than the mobile phone for shared online use although the situation is changing, especially among the middle-class urban young professionals and students. The difference in our participants' media literacy (Livingstone, 2004) can itself greatly impact upon a relationship. For example, Zoilo might prefer to communicate more with his mother, but finds that it is his father who dominates because his mother has been unable to learn to use a computer. So his father reads out emails to his mother.

Voice-based communication

In discussing voice-based communication, we cover a period when the technologies themselves keep changing. We have already seen the constraints posed by the scarcity of landlines, both for the mothers (who as domestics got their own private number only with the arrival of mobile phones) and the children (due to the scarcity of landlines in the Philippines). Another constraining factor, of course, was the previously high cost of international calls. So voice-based communication has been subject to constant change, from scarce landlines to abundant mobiles, from extremely expensive to quite affordable.

As phones replace letters, the issue of time difference comes to the fore. The difference between the Philippines and the UK is eight hours, which necessitates some planning and coordination. Most families seem to have developed a pattern for calling. Many mothers, especially those with younger children like Donna and Greta, would know exactly what time it was in the Philippines and would, whenever possible, organise their schedules to call when their families would be at home. We also have examples of partners staying up late to comfort each other although there are also examples of people getting the time wrong, especially if they are communicating with relatives in America or Australia.

Currently, voice calls are made mainly via the following platforms: mobile to mobile phone; international card to mobile phone; international card to landline; VOIP PC to PC (free service after hardware and connection costs are met); VOIP PC to mobile phone. Although international cards are ubiquitous in London as in other global cities (Vertovec, 2004), they remain expensive within the Philippines and only one of our Manila participants had purchased one, and even they had not yet used it once, reflecting the imbalance between our UK and Philippine-based participants *vis-à-vis* phone communication. Our focus will be on the particular characteristics of the main genres of calling, followed by what these have in common in terms of the qualities of voice, and finally the richness in social cues that they afford, which results in a high degree of emotional salience.

Direct international calling via mobile phones is expensive and is used mainly in emergencies or for very short calls, so almost invariably women use international calling cards via their UK mobile phones. Such cards make calls far more affordable, though of fixed duration. Most recently, international cards have been replaced by mobile phone networks that now offer comparable rates of around £0.10 per minute for a call to the Philippines, which circumvents the issued noted earlier regarding the materiality of the card. A new free application for voice communication is facilitated by VOIP such as Skype through the computer. Greta, a London-based domestic, used Skype to call her sons' mobile phones, which incurs a cost, but a considerably smaller one compared to what she would have paid using an international card. Crucially, she did not do this to save money, but rather to speak to her sons for longer periods without increasing the expenditure from her monthly budget. For Greta, using the free Skype service is not an option as her family live in an area without internet connection, or landlines.

Voice-based communication is by far the Filipina mothers' preferred mode of communicating with their children. The synchronicity and interactive nature of the call gives them an immense sense of satisfaction that they can get the answers they want when they want them. The dialogical nature of voice communication removes ambiguities (and some of the potential for misunderstandings and conflict) as the participants can ask for clarifications if something is not understood. Although there are no visual cues in voice communication, participants report that the aural cues are accentuated. This is related to the quality of voice and the way that it can convey emotion.[2] Recall the powerful ways in which mothers experienced listening to the recorded voices of their young children on audio tapes (Chapter 4). It is indicative that mothers invariably told us that it was only through a phone call that they could really tell how their children are doing. 'I can hear it in their voice', or 'I can feel them through their voice', are typical quotes. These same cues as to what the other side is really feeling, or thinking can at times give rise to negative emotional situations, although as we saw in Chapter 5, mothers at times welcomed this as an opportunity to perform more realistic mothering. Voice calls through mobile phones are more private, which is also at times welcomed by some participants. Mobile communication also has the benefit of spontaneity and 'reachability', although that can also be potentially intrusive, especially from the children's point of view. Generally, phone calls 'on the move' are short and the environmental distractions often detract from the attention that emotional engagement requires.

Perhaps the single most unattractive feature of voice call is its steep cost. However, such expenses can also be interpreted as a sign of one's love and devotion. So the high cost of calls is just part of one's duty as a mother and ultimately part of one's identity as a mother. Conspicuously spending on phone calls can be a means of showing how much one cares for someone (Miller, 2006).

Text-based communication

Texting

The Philippines is unique in its specific relationship to texting. Within a relatively short time it become something of a cliché to note that the Philippines was 'the texting capital of the world'. One particular story about Filipino texting that became internationally prevalent was their initial claim that texting had been central to the overthrow of a government, though more recent literature has suggested this was exaggerated (Castells *et al.*, 2006; Pertierra *et al.*, 2002; Rafael, 2003). Pertierra and his colleagues in a detailed monograph (2002, see also Pertierra, 2006, 2010) have also documented the significance of texting for Filipino socialities. Our evidence entirely confirmed the central role of texting in Filipino everyday social life. Participants in our study routinely sent 100 texts a day, especially if texting was involved in their work. In a developing relationship they might send 20, 30 or 40 texts a day to their new partner, as well as additional texts to other friends and relatives. This is not just an expression of their affection, but also it is a way they integrate each other in the minutiae of their lives. That texting is cheap (one peso per text or even less if purchased through a bundle), together with the fact that 'load' expires quickly after it is bought, may further explain the spectacular popularity of this mode of communication in the Philippines (see Chapter 2 for a detailed explanation of the pre-paid system).

Despite its extraordinary popularity, texting does not have the prominence within this study that previous writings might have led us to expect. As we will show, although it has certain roles in transnational communication, these are far less prominent than those observed for relationships within the Philippines. The key usage of texting transnationally was as a signal to parents that a conversation was desired. Almost all parents in London or Cambridge had Filipino roaming phones precisely so their children could text, at the local rate of one peso, to let the parents know they wanted to speak to them, which helped to balance the power asymmetry represented by the parents' control over costly international voice calling. Texting can also be used as phatic communication simply to remind the other that they are in one's thoughts. Texts could serve pragmatically to announce that a remittance had been received or a *balikbayan* box had been sent. Texting was also used to coordinate other forms of communication, as when Nora texts her son to ask him to get ready for a webcam call. It has also become a cheaper alternative for children to sending a Christmas card or birthday card, although parents are not always happy with this substitution.

A possible class distinction in the use of texting arises from the circulation of joke texts and religious homilies. These are important genres in lower-income families within the Philippines and are the text usage which most commonly migrates to transnational usage. For example, Glenda selects from the religious texts that circulate amongst her friends particularly 'beautiful' examples to forward to Judy, her mother-in-law in London, with whom she has become close. For the older women working in London this was often a great comfort. Many would store such texts on the phone, or even write down the best examples in a note-book, as did Vicky. They saw these as valuable resources they could turn to at times of loneliness or when feeling oppressed. The replicability and storage capacity of the phone and its mobility (the fact that women could access and retrieve these messages on the go, or during their break from work when they had no access to a computer) underpinned this emotional or phatic function of texting.

Texting could also become a medium of parenting, including instructing the caregiver as well as the child. An example first reported by Angela was subsequently confirmed by her daughter Florencia in the Philippines, who said 'because whenever I go out late at night, mom would tell me to text the person at home, like my auntie for example, regarding what time I'll be going home. And my aunt would be the one to text mom. And when I don't text my aunt, that's when mom would text me and remind me to tell my aunt what time I'll be home.' Parents might also use texting to remind their children to take their medication, check on their homework, or send them religious texts as exhortations.

These would be the typical uses of texting associated with some of its affordances such as mobility, low cost, replicability, storage, as well as informational capacity, albeit limited. But the lack of social cues made texting an undesirable medium for regular communication. As always, there were some exceptions to this pattern. This was the case of Juanita, in a semi-rural area north of Manila, who had demonstrated an entrepreneurial spirit in order to fund her insatiable appetite for texting, including to her OFW husband in Saudi. Juanita sent about 100 texts a day only to her husband, 10 of which concerned their young daughter, the remaining being local gossip or just banter. So as to afford such extravagance, Juanita had set up a small business where she sold 'load' to people in her *barangay*. Effectively, she bought the electronic 'load' herself and sold it, 'passing it on' – what she gained was the bonus texts that the company offered her for being such a heavy user. So, effectively, the 100 texts were 'free' in the sense that she did not have to pay for them.[3] But Juanita, who found texting an entirely satisfactory mode of communication (she always knew what her husband had for lunch and dinner and what he was up to every hour of the day), was the exception, as we did not otherwise come across such extensive use of texting for transnational communication.

Email

Email, rather better than the phone-based texting, seemed to bring out the key distinctions between voice-based and text-based communication. Letters are the precursor to email. Like letters, email was seen to have a large informational capacity, allowing for detailed instructions regarding money, property and legal matters. This capability was enhanced by the ability to attach textual or visual documents, such as certificates, contracts and copies of scanned bills. These may be vital for negotiating practical steps such as house buying, or investments. As Ricardo notes:

> And so, I started emailing my parents that it was going to cost around 300k pesos, which is big here. And then my dad replied, 'Why is the amount so huge? Why are you spending so much? Maybe you're inflating the sum and you're taking some of the money.' And I was like, 'I have all the receipts with me. And why would I do that?' So, what I did was I scanned all the receipts and emailed it to them. I told them, 'These are the receipts. I'm not cheating, you can count it down to the last centavo. I accounted for all of it.'

This recalls the use of letters as evidence and as detailed instruction. Another parallel to letters is the capacity for storage. Emails can be retrieved, re-read and even printed out when required as material evidence, for example for consular authorities considering applications by the children to join their mothers abroad.

Less formal than letters, email along with instant messaging, may encourage the development of a hybrid literacy which incorporates something of the more informal inflection of orality (Ong, 1982). Given the massive use of texting, email may also be used to extend that genre. Zoilo would use texting for what he regards as inconsequential random matters. 'But for important matters – like if we're going to pay taxes or register something – I would email it instead to my dad because I can compose it, think about it, the details. I'm not really time-pressured versus phone calls or webcam or chatting.' For all the above reasons, mothers preferred email for communicating practical information and for giving accurate instructions. But as we observed earlier in this chapter they would not choose email when they wanted to find out about how their children were doing. This suggests that the preference for voice-based communication which we observed earlier in this chapter is not just a product of mothers' digital literacy. Migrant women were keen to acquire IT skills by attending Sunday classes at the Centre for Filipinos and ended up using these facilities quite regularly and effectively, although there were some exceptions. That they do not prefer email for personal communication with their children relates more to what they see as the medium's affordances, as well as their views as to what the medium is appropriate for, what Gershon (2010) terms 'media ideologies'.

What is striking is that the children sometimes prefer to use email for exactly the same reasons that their mothers prefer not to. For example, in the previous chapter we saw that Ricardo found his parents' calls disruptive and intrusive, especially when they would call on his mobile phone. He much preferred emails as they allowed him to reply at a time of his own choosing, composing his reply in advance. So for Ricardo, email's low interactivity and lack of synchronicity were its attractive features, at least for communicating with his parents. Lisa found email gave her the space to develop her ideas and express her feelings, as compared to her mother's voice-calling cards which only lasted 10 minutes. While her mother preferred to call, Lisa would rather write when it came to deeper issues. Both Ricardo and Lisa turned to email in order to assume control of communication, showing that their own media ideologies clash with those of their parents.

Perhaps what everyone would agree on is email's lack of social cues compared to other platforms such as voice, webcam or social networking sites. The relative lack of cues can make communication ambiguous, which can often cause misunderstandings. Unlike the 'crafting' of letters, the informality of emails and the rapidity with which they are typed can exacerbate ambiguities and thus potential conflict. This was somewhat corrected with the use of emoticons – the standard way of introducing emotional cues in text-based types of communication (see Baym, 2010: 60–62), which were popular also in the case of instant messaging discussed below.

Instant messaging (IM)

Chat or instant messaging (IM) is a form of real-time text-based communication based on shared computer software packages. Philippine usage is dominated by Yahoo Messenger (YM) and this is what it is usually called. In transnational communication YM seems to have achieved greater prominence than either email or texting, especially following its combination with webcam (see below). The key affordances of IM are interactivity and simultaneity, the downside of which is that unlike email this requires real time co-presence at the users' respective computers.

So YM may be complemented by leaving messages to be picked up later. Both are possible within social networking sites which have their own IM facility. Time-zone differences present particular problems for such synchronicity. In the UK this represents an eight-hour difference, often exacerbated by conditions of employment, such as night shift for nurses. For Marites, whose husband also had very prescribed and long hours of work, or for Vilma and her mother, YM became limited to scheduled conversations at agreed intervals such as fortnightly or three monthly. It is usually those abroad who try to accommodate their children's or relatives' schedules. Some women, mainly nurses in Cambridge who had their laptops in their bedrooms, would leave YM or Skype on throughout the night and some reported even getting up if they heard sounds indicating that their children were online.

Being a text-based medium, IM shares some features with both email and texting. Like texting it is often used for phatic communication, essentially as an affirmation of a relationship. Like email it can also work well for conveying information and practical instructions. Because it combines the information capacity of email with enhanced interactivity and synchronicity, some mothers (and their children) found IM useful for helping with homework.

The 'status' facility of YM (as well as other IM software, including Skype and Facebook) allows users to see which of their friends or relatives are online. Even in the absence of direct communication this provides an important emotional bond as a kind of minimal unit of social contact. In Chapter 5, we saw that this was how YM revealed to Mimi that her son had dropped out of school – his online status demonstrated that he was always at home. Unsurprisingly, some children choose to make themselves 'invisible' precisely to avoid pressure to communicate with their mothers.

Multimedia communication

Social networking sites (SNS)

During our fieldwork, social networking was far more readily associated with the children than parents, and the dominant platform was Friendster (for a discussion see Pertierra, 2010). Since then we have seen a migration to Facebook in line with global trends (compare Miller, 2011). During our fieldwork in Manila and the surrounding provinces in 2008/9 use of Facebook implied class, or at least educational capital (Bourdieu, 1984). While Facebook had become common mainly amongst graduates in Manila, Friendster was almost universally used and all our participants had an account. Class could also be connoted by whether people communicated in English, Taglish[4] or Tagalog. Filipinos have a clear correlation between status and the quality of English used.[5]

There are some grounds for seeing Friendster as initially more commensurate with Filipino predispositions, including its greater emphasis upon friends in common and reciprocal testimonials that come from Friendster's origins as a dating site (boyd and Ellison, 2007). These seem closer to Filipino ideals of social relationships based on debt and reciprocity. In many respects usage in the Philippines seems common to that of other countries at that time, with a strong youth orientation, and a tendency to see friends quantitatively as well as qualitatively, so the children talked of filling up their initial quota of 500 or 1000 friends, and then adding a second account for further friends. More typically Gladys has 380 friends, many of whom are ex-college and school. About 30 per cent of all her friends on the site are from her local island. Out of these she has her three best friends, who have access to her private photo albums. She has been using Friendster since 2004 on a daily basis, but on her day off work she would be on the site for two or three hours. She has posted testimonials for 24 friends. A point made several times was that, within the Philippines, requests to be a friend are essentially unrefusable.[6]

At the time of our fieldwork the dominant usage was within the Philippines, catching up on peers from school and college, but SNS were also used to keep in touch with relatives abroad. This is the main way Florencia keeps in touch with her brother, who has recently come to the UK to be reunited with their mother.[7] Florencia always notes when he has added photos or changed his account in any way. SNS are heavily used for posting photographs that keep one in touch with diaspora family, through mutual awareness of activities such as holidays and family gatherings and meals.[8]

However, SNS usage is intensified when it comes to transnational parent–child relationships because those mothers who were users found Friendster, Multiply and Facebook invaluable for learning about the context of their children's lives. Since they could not pick them up from school or take them to parties, they would search for cues on their children's profiles. Such is the case of Donna, who takes this a step further by obtaining her sons' passwords and checking their accounts periodically to see if there are any worrying signs. Donna is adamant that she would not be doing this if she was still in the Philippines with her family. But she felt compelled by the distance to try to keep an eye on her 10- and 12-year-old boys in any way that she can. Parents would scour photographs, including their children's friends, to get as many visual cues as possible about what their lives are like. For mothers, SNS were mainly about looking at pictures – and sometimes commenting on them.

When we started our fieldwork it was rare for parents to have SNS accounts, but this changed dramatically during our research. For example, Edith at the age of 55 is starting to use Friendster regularly, has 100 friends, and even if she still does not have confidence in uploading she can at least frequently look at the photos and updates of her friends and sisters (unusually her daughter does not have a Friendster account). Already one of her godsons in the Philippines found her and started communicating with her. Olivia at nearly 60 is using it to communicate, but only with her children. In fact, several of our participants in London told us that they started using SNS after they were invited by their, usually adult, children.

The children's perspective is, as can be expected, more ambivalent. All the extended case studies discussed in the last chapter are largely dependent upon SNS. Recall how Cecilia uses it as the medium to transform her mother into her sort-of-best-friend while Andres is traumatised by his friending of his mother and the revelations that brings. There were, of course, plenty of less dramatic instances of SNS communication. Vicente puts up pictures of his children so his mother can see them, and his mother uploads photos of her holidays in turn. Estrella persuaded her mother to use Friendster for much the same reason. This proved important when the daughter of her brother-in-law died two days after giving birth. 'I put all the pictures on the Friendster so that Mama can view what happened to the child.' These benign and straightforward uses, though, are matched by much more problematic instances of contact through Friendster. In particular, SNS can bring out the issues of how far the parent recognises the maturity of their children, and equally how far the child feels comfortable with their mother being exposed to what might be considered evidence of their immaturity. The question of how to respond to a mother's friend request has become something of an international cliché in terms of the juxtaposition it creates of friendship and kinship, although here, as elsewhere, it is now becoming quite normal to accept this overlap. One important factor is the age of the children, with older, adult children inviting their parents onto SNS so that they can enhance their connection, including with the grandchildren if there are any. The other factor, as always, is the pre-existing relationship. It seems that when problems arise, it is usually as a consequence of the above factors but also, crucially, the way that Facebook blurs the public and private boundaries (see boyd, 2010).

Four affordances of SNS are crucial here: the increased social cues made possible by the combination of image and text; the persistence of content (as online interactions are recorded); their searchability; and, finally, their reach and visibility, reach implying less control over who comes to see content which may enter a more public domain (see also boyd, 2010).[9] Mothers become part of this 'invisible audience' (boyd, 2010: 48) when they inadvertently see the profiles of their children's friends. These affordances blur the boundaries between the private and public and create new fields of monitoring and surveillance, and thereby potential conflict. A tension at the heart of SNS communication in the context of transnational parenting is the way it can never be entirely dyadic. This may often be desirable when it offers the opportunity for a network of kinship to materialise through mutual testimonials (in the case of Friendster) or messages on someone's wall (in the case of Facebook), but it can also be felt as intrusive when one simply wishes to have a private conversation.

An alternative strategy to deal with the blurring of boundaries is to differentiate groups through multiple social network sites. Ricardo has made his Multiply (the second most popular SNS in the Philippines after Friendster during our period of fieldwork) site known to his parents and posts there 'parent-safe' photographs, but he would be devastated if his parents came across the Friendster or Facebook accounts which he sees as quite inappropriate. He also uses Facebook for non-Filipino friends while Friendster remains dominated by Filipino friends. Others target specific social networking sites, such as gay dating sites, kept separate from other networks.

Blogging

Most blogging in the Philippines is synonymous with SNS, since blogging is done almost invariably within facilities provided by the SNS sites. For example, Multiply is the software that most of our participants would use for blogging and for uploading their photographs. None of our informants used Twitter at the time of fieldwork,[10] although several referred to the status updates facility of Facebook as a kind of microblogging. A critical distinction between blogging and other media is that blogging is almost exclusively the preserve of the children and not their mothers. But it is important here because of the role it plays in the way children deal with parental absence. For some of our middle-class, college-educated informants blogging was almost ubiquitous (nearly a quarter of Pertierra's [2010: 221] respondents in the town of Buenavista have a blog). Irene saw her initial blog as relatively constrained in readership when she first blogged, using her local island language, but then following wider interest she decided to open it up and now blogs in Tagalog. Francisco maintains multiple blogs, some more public using Multiply and another on Wordpress that almost no one knows he possesses.

Although superficially like a diary, a blog is public and viewed as an effective way to inform a large number of people about one's feelings and activities without having to tell each separately. Although some use it mainly to share information about events or other publicly available information, others seem to see it as cathartic and exploit it to write about what previously might have been assumed to be highly private or intimate matters. In practice, blogs circulate mainly in the same groups as offline friendships and people expect their friends to respond and comment on postings. This makes it mainly a semi-public conversation between friends. But as their parents become more technically savvy, the possibility arises that these discourses will be seen by them.

To take two contrasting examples, Ricardo has been blogging for two years now, posting around once a week. In his case he feels confident enough that his parents are not internet savvy enough to find the blog. 'There are a lot of explicit personal references to my parents, so I'd be dead if they actually saw that.' Blogging allows him to write about his intimate problems, as in the traditional diary. He has huge resentments about the way his father treats his mother and her failure to stand up to him, but also a general feeling that his parents only gave birth to him as a vicarious expression of their own status. Yet he also wants their respect and affection. Being able to express his ambivalence in text is cathartic in itself and sharing this with his friends brings them closer together.

More problematic is Paolo, who takes this a stage further in that his blog is actually directed at his parents and family and becomes the public domain, where he too feels he can express things better in text than in conversation:

> Like when my dad hit my brother real hard, and I wanted to do something about it, I think this was within this year or last year. He was a teenager, and he failed to go home on time. Yeah, he went out with his friends. And

then, my dad hit my brother and I wanted to stop him. It was pretty much a lot. And then I blogged about it. It was a pretty emotional blog. And then, when my mom and my relatives from abroad read it, they were actually crying. I wasn't exaggerating. And they called me. My aunt from New York, and my dad's brother would say, 'You know, just understand your dad. He was from an abusive . . .'.

Paolo has thereby used his blog for washing the family's dirty linen in public. More typically, young adults with similar experiences share with their friends a common sense of anger with their immediate family. He notes that often when someone posts something this personal, others will respond immediately, ' "Oh, I can relate!" And you can actually post a similar blog, it happens all the time. And, you get to know and talk about it in real life.' He used to have a diary and then a personal website prior to blogs. Blogs are commonly used for peers to talk about the teachers they hate or other classmates.

Ricardo continually shifts between posting hate blogs about his father and blogs that talk about how he accepts his family and how important it is that they are there to support him. But while such ambivalence could be resolved within the privacy of the diary, a blog is far more revealing, and by blurring the boundaries between public and private, also potentially more destructive.

Of course not all blogs are so intimate and profound. Mostly they are simply diaries of the mundane and they tend to increasingly include photographic diaries as well as text. Multiply is designed to facilitate photo-based diaries, as in the case of Gladys, who mainly blogged and posted pictures during a very difficult and stressful stint in Taiwan, when she needed to remain engaged and feel connected with home. As with most blogging, the pictures came from her camera phone, and are intended for contemporary circulation rather than for embedding memory, although, as is the case with SNS, such content persists. Others use blogs entirely for political postings or jokes, but avoid anything personal. Even these can have unintended consequences, as for Joel, where unusually it was his mother who blogged. He became resentful seeing how often she posted during a period when she rarely seemed to have time to contact her son. Blogs share a number of affordances similar to SNS: persistence of content, reach and visibility, search-ability, replicability and high levels of visual cues (in cases of photographic blogs). It was less common to protect the privacy of one's blog (compared to controlling privacy settings on Facebook, for instance). Even in the case of anonymous, or 'hidden' blogs there is always the potential that they can be discovered by people other than the intended readers.

Webcam

The period of our fieldwork was, as we anticipated, quite revolutionary in terms of the changes in transnational communication taking place before our eyes. Perhaps the most dramatic example was not the spread of SNS and blogs, but the rapid adoption of webcam combined with various forms of VOIP, most commonly YM but increasingly also Skype. A few regarded this as inconsequential or declined to use it, such as Francisco: 'Just only once. We're not really fans of webcam technology. It's good that you see the face of the person there. But really you just see the face.' But for many more 'just seeing a face' revolutionised their sense of being in touch, creating some key relationships such as between grandparents and small children, that prior to webcam simply could not exist. We saw in Chapter 5 how webcam in particular made an enormous difference to a mother with an infant left behind. The webcam was the only medium through which Donna felt able to communicate and to be a mother to her year-old baby. The visual cues meant that her baby girl recognised Donna despite her absence and this recognition made all the difference to how Donna herself felt as a mother. Communication via webcam facilitated several other practices, such as helping with homework and cooking, which we analysed as part of the performance of 'intensive mothering at a distance.'

Many users of webcam had at least one story of how they took their laptop with webcam to view either an event or a scene, for example taking it outside to show what snow looks like. The most poignant example was Jezza, who heard that her father had died in the Philippines. She would certainly have gone back for the funeral but for the fact that she was pregnant and unable to fly. So a relative took a laptop computer with integral camera to give her a sense of participation in the mortuary rituals and ceremonies that she otherwise would have missed.

The increased visual cues are of the essence here. People often noted whether their correspondent was getting big or losing weight, a shorthand for whether they were looking after themselves. A woman would show concern as to whether a husband or a child was eating properly. In one case there was tremendous concern over an older man working abroad who was clearly looking gaunt, and one could almost feel the frustration that it was impossible to immediately send him a proper home-cooked meal. A Filipina mother in London, where the discourse on healthy eating is far more prevalent, has quite changed her views on the eating habits of her children. So she now complains 'Oh, you're getting bigger! Lessen all your food! Lessen eating fats, avoid eating fats, avoid eating too much carbohydrates.'

At first a webcam session may be taken as a rather formal appearance. Grandparents left looking after children may want to show how well they are coping and caring for their little charges. As a result, they will carefully dress and comb and spruce up the children in readiness, as though for a photo shoot. But the children promptly spoilt the effect as soon as they came online by failing to show any interest in their parents and within seconds turning the conversation to their demands for a new video game or playstation. We also encountered instances of the formal introduction of a girlfriend or boyfriend to parents through the webcam. For example, Zoilo thought about this for quite some time and finally found the opportunity at a Christmas party with his girlfriend's family, who had a webcam. First he broached the subject with her: 'She did feel awkward and she felt more conscious about, actually, of my dad. She was, like, refusing "No, no." "It's okay.

You can do this." So she didn't really do much about fixing herself up, but she did feel a little awkward about it.' The event itself was therefore somewhat awkward, but Zoilo still felt better once it was done, in that at least when he talks to his girlfriend about his parents, which he often does, he feels she has more sense of who he is talking about and the nature of their relationship.

The webcam also enters into parent–child relationships as a form of evidence, or even surveillance. It is linked to sending gifts and *balikbayan* boxes, as the sender can ask to see the gifted clothes on the recipient. Vicente noted that they also showed the chocolates they received, and had the children play with the toys they were sent. Perhaps less commonly than might have been expected, people working in more affluent countries use the webcam to show the goods they now have access to. There was an ironic comment upon this when a relative in the Philippines declared on webcam ' "Oh, we're drinking Bailey's here! We're also drinking red wine here!" She also brought up grapes! I also brought up grapes. "We have grapes also (in the Philippines)!" '

A topic avoided when talking of one's own circumstances, but often referred to when discussing migration generally, was a more serious use of surveillance, when recipients failed to use remittances for the purposes intended by the sender. Much of the money sent for house building and similar purposes was said to have been siphoned off for other more hedonistic or selfish uses. We also know of webcam surveillance with respect to accusations of infidelity within couples, including a story of a husband working in the Middle East where the wife demands that their webcam is on 24/7. Of course, she does not know what he gets up to in other people's rooms, but her intention is to monitor what time he gets home, and whether or not he got home alone.

The most sustained and radical transformation associated with webcam is communication between very young children and their parents, or their grandparents. Those who feel disconnected when limited to voice-only communication utter squeals of delight and recognition when encountering their grandparents through the webcam. Grandparents who dislike the technological demands of new media can be equally positive about simply having to appear in front of the camera and see their grandchildren without any technical know-how. Generally, we observed that the attraction of webcam was a prime motivation amongst older Filipinos for developing some elementary digital literacy (compared to all the media discussed here, Skype or YM with webcam require the least technological expertise). Toddlers clearly relate to the computer as a kind of extra-special toy and on both sides they may play with it, pressing lips to the screen, making silly faces, singing bits of songs, playing games – and also challenging the limits of the technology, as when a little girl asks her relative to throw her some snow through the computer screen. The result can be both a sustained basis for grandparenting, and the potential for hours of transnational babysitting, allowing the parents themselves time to undertake other tasks.

By the same token, webcam as well as phones can be accused of giving only an illusion of co-presence, and being an even more poignant reminder of separation.

People often reported crying after a webcam encounter. It may particularly upset young children who become confused after such a session and want to know why mummy is not actually there. But mothers routinely cry as well, as was evident in Donna's experiences recounted in Chapter 5. It also can come to be seen as a mechanism that disrupts the ability of a child to be reconciled to separation and loss, with negative consequences, although this seems to improve with age. At the most extreme were cases of people who simply could not bear to use the webcam at all. For example, the father who became clinically depressed when his wife went abroad to work and who refused all attempts to get him to develop a communicative relationship through the webcam. He will agree when pressed just to see her face and check if she has gained or lost weight, but he cannot bear any sustained contact, since for him the webcam is never going to substitute for her actual presence and would only increase the misery of her absence.

So, despite the heightened visual cues, interactivity and simultaneity, webcam is not a simple replication of a greater reality or veracity. People can still see only what they choose to acknowledge. For example, the children might hope a webcam forces their parents to acknowledge how much they have grown up, and for some such as Donna this is the case. But Jason recalls a webcam conversation when present at his parents' party, where they and their friends looked terribly sophisticated and intimidating in their metropolitan setting. Nevertheless the dominant response was highly positive in comparison to the constraints of previous media.

Webcam was also used to break away from dyadic communication to recreate something more like family gatherings. No longer does the phone have to be passed from one sibling to the other in a highly artificial sequencing of conversation. The siblings are now gathered together in a sometimes informal or sometimes more formal presence, depending upon the nature of the family. Children may play and quarrel; parents can admonish a younger sibling for failing to respect the control of the older sibling in front of both of them together. As well as slightly artificial periodic family gatherings, held perhaps weekly, the webcam allows for the reinstitution of significant family gatherings, of which the most important tended to be birthdays and Christmas, though Christmas meals are notorious in their potential for awkward family encounters (Lofgren, 1993). Zoilo described a four-hour webcam session when the family were all getting ready to go to their uncles for Christmas. This informal period of helping each other with clothes and wrapping amidst chat and banter was highly effective at allowing absent family members to feel included in the event. However, webcam because of its lack of mobility, was less effective when it came to the other event which may dominate Filipino discussion of significant moments of parental absence, that is graduation ceremonies.

For Donna long webcam sessions are not the preserve of special occasions, but what she routinely does on her day off. On Saturday mornings she webcams her mother's house where all her extended family has gathered in the late afternoon. They often leave the camera on for eight hours until her children have gone to bed and the *barkada* (group of friends) has dispersed. Greta is only able to use webcam during her children's school holidays when they stay with her brother, who has internet access at home. Although initially webcam was an opportunity to admire her children and realise how fast they are growing, gradually she found out that she could use the medium to help them with practical things such as their remedial classes.

The final extension of webcam is that of a constant co-presence when access to broadband at both ends allows for an 'always on' webcam presence. Some families tried eating meals together, though the difference in time zone might mean that it was often a different meal at each end. In one case a mother in London who might otherwise have been in bed asleep felt she had to get up and dress properly to meet and greet her relatives in the Philippines.

Despite its enhanced visual cues, simultaneity and interactivity, communication via webcam does not always generate the emotional depth of voice calls. Some of our participants found that there can be many distractions in webcam, unlike phone calls when one concentrates on the voice. This may also be related to the typically less private nature of webcam, compensated with the increased realism of the medium.

Conclusion

This chapter has conveyed the detail and nature of our evidence, illustrating also many of the key points that emerged in previous chapters. Webcam seems the obvious end of a trajectory that starts with the much more constrained and limited possibilities of letters and cassettes and leads to a situation that everyone regards as far closer to the experience of co-presence that preceded migration.

This would imply that, for example, parents who want to legitimate a continued absence on the grounds that they can remain effective as parents, even when living abroad, have much more plausible evidence following this potential for visual co-presence than was represented by cheap phone calls. We also have several examples of the basic ambivalence that is characteristic of the children's response to parental absence. They can come much closer to their parents, who can seem much more like real persons with whom they chat about clothing and shopping while surfing together, and be virtually present in family gatherings and not just dyadic and sequential calling. For those with easy access to the internet, since the expense is shunted onto the provision of the computer and connection costs, there is also no longer a consciousness of the communication event as a cost relative to duration. Equally important, communication can take place within a general background of inconsequential chat, everyday remarks about how one's hair has grown longer or the spot that is starting to look unsightly and how the room needs repainting. This adds considerable naturalism to the encounter. But at the same time there are still more possibilities of surveillance and intrusion that bring back many of the more problematic aspects of parent–teenager relationships. And above all, the more effective the new media, the more they can still be an unbearable reminder of an actual absence, which becomes the main consequence of the realism of 'connected presence' (Licoppe, 2004).

Having looked at each of the media that mothers and children use to keep in touch in the context of separation, it becomes clear that today almost all of the relationships we study use a combination of new media. The more complex and sustained relationships are often reflected in increasingly complex complementarity between media as users exploit their different functionalities and affordances (see also Haythornthwaite, 2005). As we showed in its simplest form with respect to letters and cassettes, the significance of one medium is constructed in large measure from its differences with another. In this chapter we have given attention to the affordances and usages of each discrete medium in turn. In the following chapter we will shift our attention to understanding all these new media as part of a communicative environment which we call polymedia. The affordances we have just described provide the internal structure of polymedia.

Taking temporality and using the illustrations from our analysis as examples, letters which often took a month or more contrast with the immediacy of texting or IM. With voice-based media, the phone has immediacy while cassettes suffered delay comparable to letters. Social networking may not require simultaneous co-presence as chat, but can 'freeze' interactions that can subsequently be revisited and relived.

Similar arguments could be made for any of the affordances highlighted in this chapter, such as interactivity, storage capacity, persistence of content, reach and visibility, private/public nature, materiality, replicability, searchability, mobility, social cues and informational capacity. A summary of the ways in which affordances have corresponded to different media in our present analysis can be found in Table 7.1. This shows how new media form a wider structure of affordances which individuals tailor to their own interpersonal relationship needs. So rather than treat them in isolation, as tends to be the case within the existing literature, we shall examine them in the next chapter within the more holistic environment of polymedia.

TABLE 7.1 Affordances and costs associated with discrete media and types of communication

	Interactivity	Temporality	Storage	Persistence (of content/durability)	Replicability	Searchability	Reach and visibility	Mobility	Cues	Private	Public	Cost*	Informational capacity
VOICE-BASED COMMUNICATION													
Voice calls: mobile phone to mobile phone	High	Synchronous	No	No	No	No	Low	Yes	High	Yes	No	Very high	Medium/High
International card/mobile phone	High	Synchronous	No	No	No	No	Low	Yes	High	Yes	No	High	Medium/High
International card/landline	High	Synchronous	No	No	No	No	Low	No	High	No	Yes	Medium	Medium/High
VOIP call PC-to-PC	High	Synchronous	No	No	No	No	Low	Yes	High	No	Yes	Minimal	Medium/High
VOIP call PC/mobile phone	High	Synchronous	No	No	No	No	Low	Yes	High	Yes	No	Medium	Low
Audio-recorded cassette tape	Very low	Asynchronous (but durable)	Yes	Yes	No	Yes	Low	No	Medium	No	Yes	Low	Low
TEXT-BASED COMMUNICATION													
Email	Intermediate	Asynchronous (but durable – see persistence)	Yes	Yes	Yes	Yes	Low	**	Low	Yes	No	Minimal	High
Chat (IM)	High	Synchronous (but possible time delay)	Yes (unusual)	Yes	Yes	Yes	Low	No **	Low	Yes	No	Minimal	Medium/High
Text (SMS)	Intermediate	Asynchronous (but durable)	Yes	Yes	Yes	Yes	Low	Yes	Low	Yes	No	Low	Medium
Letters	Very low	Asynchronous (but durable)	Yes	Yes	Yes (unusual)	Yes	Low	Yes	Low	Yes	No	Low	High
MULTIMEDIA COMMUNICATION													
Text and image (e.g. social networking sites, blogging)	Intermediate	Asynchronous (but durable – see persistence)	Yes	Yes	Yes (ambiguous)	Yes	High	**	High	No	Yes (ambiguous)	Minimal	Medium
Voice and image (e.g. webcam, Skype, etc.)	High	Synchronous	Difficult and unusual	No	No	No	Low	No	High	No	Yes	Minimal	Medium/High

* once installation and connection charges are met.

** of course, email and SNS can be checked through internet-enabled mobile phones, but this was not readily available amongst our participants at the time of our fieldwork.

POLYMEDIA

Various forms of communication
Poly - many/multi media

It was always the intention of this research to consider the example of extended separation represented by Filipino transnational parenting, not only to challenge our assumptions as to the nature of parenting, but also as a means to think more deeply about the consequences of new communication technologies. As it happens, this research aim has coincided with a radical and unprecedented transformation of media such that it is perhaps only in the past two or three years that we are finally reaching the situation we propose to term 'polymedia', which we would argue demands a very different kind of theorisation from that of earlier periods of communication. One trend in recent theories of new media has been the focus on the vertical dimension, investigating changes in media over time. A clear example would be the theory of remediation (Bolter and Grusin, 2000; see also Marvin, 1988), which is concerned with how one medium comes to influence the next. Our aim is to look at the more horizontal dimension, alongside recent work such as Baym (2010) and Gershon (2010), that is, how each medium finds a niche in relation to the properties of co-existing other media. In the previous chapter we examined in some detail the affordances and usage of each individual medium for long-distance communication. However, through our analysis it also became clear that few people would rely on only a single medium for communicating, while the trend was increasingly towards using, and choosing between, a plethora of different media. Therefore, although it is important to understand the functionalities of any particular medium, it is no longer possible to assume that its affordances might frame a long-distance relationship in a particular way. In order to understand the process of mediation, we need to look at the entire range of media as a communicative environment.

Apart from being a new theoretical approach to understanding the uses of new and constantly proliferating communicative opportunities, 'polymedia' is also proposed here as a term to refer to these various, constantly changing media and the

[handwritten margin note at top: several different ever-changing media]

need for each relationship to create a configuration of usage generally employing several different media. The need for a new term became apparent as soon as we started analysing our data and writing this book. We recognised that while analytically there were prior distinctions between application, platform, medium and technology, these have been superseded by media convergence which conflates them. Instead we need a term to refer to all these new communicative opportunities. For this reason we will introduce polymedia through continuing the analysis of our material and then consider the concept's larger consequences.

[handwritten margin note: a term to refer to new communicative opportunities]

We argue that the term 'polymedia' is more appropriate than alternatives. There has been some previous discussion around the term 'media ecology' (e.g. Slater and Tacchi, 2004) which tends to signify more the niche occupied by each medium not only relative to each other, but also to wider systems of communication such as transport, or issues of usage such as politics and health. We felt we needed instead a term which placed the clear focus upon the unprecedented plurality and proliferation of media. 'Multimedia' is a much-used term that might have had such a connotation, but it has now a very well established, but very different meaning referring to a situation where several different forms of media are being used simultaneously and in direct relationship to each other, for instance giving a lecture combining several different media, such as video, images and typed-handouts all at once. It would obviously be confusing to use that term for our purposes. 'Multi-channel', or 'multi-platform' might be closer to what we wish to describe, but the problem with choosing either term, is that it would force us to prioritise either 'platform' or 'channel' when in fact our findings in the previous chapter demonstrated that such technological hierarchies are not particularly meaningful in the context of convergence as reflected in the users' disregard for such semantic distinctions. They simply see a variety of media through which they can accomplish specific forms of communication with particular consequences. Given that 'polymedia' lacks an established meaning in the academic context (we found only one reference, see Alm and Ferrell Lowe, 2001), the term, drawing from the Greek word *poly* meaning many or several, seemed entirely appropriate to emphasise the proliferating nature of new media as part of an integrated environment.[1]

In this chapter, we wish to show that the term 'polymedia' has far more significance than merely an acknowledgment of the contemporary alternatives in communication. The main point we will make is that the very nature of each individual medium is radically changed by the wider environment of polymedia, since it now exists in a state of contrast, but also synergy, with all others. To take this a stage further, we shall see that the importance of this contrast is not simply the technical differences and affordances of each medium. Rather it is the finding that in a given cultural and personal context these contrasts become the idiom through which people express distinctions in the form and purpose of communication itself. This is why our discussion of polymedia will not follow the previous chapter in simply dissecting the affordances of each available medium and platform; we have already done this. Instead we use polymedia to explore significant differences that are exploited to enact and control the expression of emotions themselves, because for us that is the more important consequence of polymedia. Media are not simply the means of transmission for content; rather they become the idiom of expressive intent. This starts us on a journey of transcending the dualism between media and relationships that leads on to the theorisation of mediated relationships in our final chapter.

Although this point is most fully realised with polymedia, it is consistent with our treatment of media since the discussion of letters and cassettes as a simple yet integrated communicative environment in Chapter 4. What that chapter explored was not simply the technical contrasts, but the significance those distinctions acquired when exploited by our informants: the way the differences between hand-written letters and voice-recorded cassette-tapes gave rise to hugely important differences of interest, emotion and often unintended information that could be gleaned from the way something was composed, or the care that went into it.

For this reason, we will concentrate on why a discussion of each medium's qualities cannot provide a complete answer to why people choose a particular medium over another. Neither can a technical analysis on its own predict the consequences of a particular medium. The comparative analysis of the media's affordances in Chapter 7 needs to be accompanied by an understanding of the sociality in which the relationships are enacted (including the roles and normative expectations within the relationships). The cultural context is also relevant, as are the relationships themselves. All these are, of course, embedded in structures of power which also contribute to the shaping of the experience of polymedia. Finally, all the above parameters have a marked emotional dimension which needs to be examined not only as a driving force, but also as a consequence.

To achieve a state of polymedia requires three changes in the conditions of communication. The first is that an individual has ready access to a wide range of at least half a dozen communication media. This means that the household has the ability to pay for the hardware (mobile phones *and* personal computer) as well as for internet connection and phone use. The second criterion is media literacy: having access but also being able to analyse, evaluate and produce digital media content (Livingstone, 2004). The third criterion is that the expense is now largely shifted to infrastructure rather than the cost of any particular act of communication. Once these three criteria (that are concerned with both first and second levels of digital divides, see Hargittai, 2002; Hargittai and Welejko, 2007; Hargittai and Hinnant, 2008) have been met, the crucial point here is that when users are engaged in any specific act of communication it appears in that instance as costless. For example, it makes no difference if one sends 10 or 100 emails. The implication is that prior to polymedia the choice of any given medium was, or at least was legitimated as, an issue of availability, technical knowledge, or cost. The situation of polymedia arises when parameters of cost move from the foreground to the background and therefore both the choice and the legitimation of medium is transparently that of the user, and them alone, which means that they can be held responsible for choosing one medium as opposed to another.

Given this definition, we should be clear that polymedia was only an emergent condition in relation to our actual fieldwork. In practice, very few of our informants have experienced communication as a kind of entirely free choice from a menu of possibilities. And we can count even fewer cases where both mothers and children were equally immersed in an environment of polymedia, which presupposes a robust and evolving media literacy (Livingstone, 2004). So for, example, we have examples of children who are very conversant in digital media, but whose mothers are not yet entirely comfortable with new communication technologies. Or, conversely, we have examples of mothers, like Greta, who have invested in a new laptop after having attended IT classes at the Centre for Filipinos, but whose children still live in areas without landlines, let alone broadband connection. So we are still at a point in the evolution to polymedia, which is not yet fully realised. The literature on the first-level digital divide (involving questions of access and availability) remains highly pertinent to the Philippines given the still low internet rates discussed in Chapter 2. Equally relevant is the second-level digital divide (Hargittai, 2002; Hargittai and Hinnant, 2008) which concerns the skills that users employ in their use of the internet. Nevertheless we are already far enough down this road to polymedia that it seems important to engage with it theoretically as well as descriptively grounding our discussion on those participants from within our wider sample who are already immersed in the world of polymedia. Even now, at the time of writing, the situation has changed considerably since the period of our fieldwork, though our participants would obviously tend to be in advance of other Filipinos given their transnational connections and greater dependence on new media. As we pointed out earlier, given that we are unlikely to retreat to a simpler situation of letter writing, the need to address the consequences of polymedia is very present.

The bridge between the previous chapter and this chapter comes with our discussion of affordances. Although the previous chapter was structured by the sequential consideration of each medium, we also noted that there was the potential to abstract various aspects of usage which become the basis for comparison between media, for example, temporality, replicability, or cues. To call these affordances meant that a given medium seems to lend itself to that usage, but this is only a propensity, as we then have to include social and other factors to see if this becomes a norm of usage. For example, voice calls provide a high number of cues, mainly as voice seems to convey emotions and a sense of the person. However, we can then start to tease out usage in relation to the perception of users. For example, mothers largely prefer voice calls to all other media precisely because of the interactivity, immediacy, simultaneity and high number of cues involved. But we also found that such propensities should not be assumed to be a predictive factor for how the media are actually going to be used. Some left-behind children detested phone calls. In the case of Ricardo, it was precisely those technological features that his mother valued, that turned him off from this kind of communication. Ricardo in contrast preferred the reduced interactivity of emails and their lack of simultaneity. He preferred to be able to reply at a time of his own choosing, often a week after receiving an email from his parents. The lack of cues was a boon for this particular son, who wanted to share as little information as possible with his parents. These issues lead us to polymedia, in which the focus is less on the affordances of each particular medium and more on how users exploit the contrasts between media as an integrated environment in order to meet their relationship and emotional needs. What emerges as crucial in this context is the morality of choice as perceived by users, as well as the wider context of power.

In terms of how our participants talked about media, the most common analogy to affordances tended to be conversations about functionality, which reflect many of the examples from the previous chapter. So typically, we might be informed that an email allows for a long exposition that can be easily stored and referred to (searchability and persistence of content). But sequential texting, which is more interactive, allows one to negotiate exactly how the contents of a *balikbayan* box can be dispersed, and ensures that the correspondent has understood and agreed to these instructions, in a way that is much harder to achieve in an email. Voice calls offer immediacy, cues and authority, but cannot be stored and cannot be referred to subsequently as evidence. Texting is replicable and reproducible, while voice tends to be immediate, immaterial and dyadic. Often in the discussion of these practical issues of communication, the advantages and problems of any particular medium become part of explicit comparison. For example:

> With texting, it's more of – for me – the random stuff, like something that immediately came up. But for important matters – like if we're going to pay taxes or register something – I would email it instead to my dad because I can compose it, think about it, the details. I'm not really time-pressured versus phone calls or webcam or chatting.

These all demonstrate the importance of affordances, but we have already suggested that the principle impact of polymedia is the way this begins to shift the balance from the emphasis on technology or functionality or indeed affordances, and move us further down the road towards social and moral issues. So for the remainder of this chapter it is the latter we want to emphasise, examining in turn the way polymedia are embraced in the context of different social relationships and socialities, the impact of power and the expression of emotions. As we shall see, each of these also relates to different levels of generalisation.

Sociality

How people navigate the realm of polymedia becomes evident if we look at the different relationships that they are in. What works in the context of one set of relationships may not work so well in a different context. So when we write that mothers overwhelmingly prefer voice calls for communicating with their children, this should not be considered to be an overarching preference that these particular women display for that particular medium, although there are some cases of participants who have developed a long-standing relationship to a particular medium and seem to be wedded to that. But, increasingly, we see people willing to switch between media for different purposes. It is interesting that some of the same women who would consciously use the phone in the context of their intensive mothering at a distance (Chapter 5), would also tell us that they often prefer texting, or email when communicating with their husbands, or other relatives.

Nelia is a case in point. Although she makes at least two short calls to her nine-year old son in Manila every day, she prefers to text her husband, who lives in one of the Northern provinces taking care of the family business. She finds that texting allows her to better express romantic love and even to continue flirting, which she thinks is essential in their long-distance relationship. Recall that texting is widely used for flirting in the Philippines (Pertierra *et al.*, 2002), so here we can also detect a cultural idiom at play. Unless there is something urgent, Nelia will talk with her husband only when he visits their son in Manila during weekends. But otherwise, the couple send several SMS each day, which they normally save on their phones. Nelia also saves the texts that she sends to her husband and often re-reads them together with his replies after she finishes work, or when she is on the bus. She finds emotional reassurance in the storage capacity and retrievability of texts, which is very important in the maintenance of her relationship to her husband Raul.

Eduarda, in turn, will use mainly email with her husband. She checks her inbox first thing every morning and expects to find a message, even a short one, from him and cannot hide her disappointment if there is none. Greta will send emails to her in-laws, who are looking after their children. These emails mainly contain instructions and advice, which are better conveyed in writing. Vicky, in turn, will send several emails a week to her various relatives who are scattered across the world. She emails her cousins in Australia and in New York as well as her nephews in San Diego. She feels that email has allowed her to reconstitute her extended family after 30 years in the UK and this is something that gives her much fulfilment.

Sociality is as important in determining the choice of medium as are the medium's own properties and affordances. Of course, the other parameter here is culture, as these social relationships are part of a set of cultural idioms and practices. Take, for example, the distinction between a landline and a mobile phone. As noted in Horst and Miller (2006), the mobile phone transforms relationships because of its fit with the unusual stress on individuality in Jamaican society. Landlines almost inevitably created quarrels within the household when it came to payments as to which individual had been responsible for which call. Landlines were also disliked because of the absence of privacy, the lack of a sense of individual ownership and their importance in crafting dyadic relationships. Some of these things would also hold for the Philippines, especially with the rise of texting as the primary means of flirtatious banter between the sexes. But in other respects Filipinos value a communal sense of family to about the same degree that Jamaicans value individuality. Previously, letters had tended to be seen as family ventures often read out publically and composed collectively.

So when we think about how the mobile phone works in a society, it is not just the technical differences in types of phones that are important. It is also the cultural differences between and within society and the fit between the affordances of the technology and the propensity of cultural tradition, as to what kind of sociality people value, and how the phone can be used to facilitate that form of interactivity. Even with the mobile phone, we found evidence that when the person caring for a child (especially an elder sibling looking after a younger sibling) had a problem or complaint they wished to discuss with the absent parent, it seemed appropriate and natural to do so in the presence, rather than the absence, of the sibling they are talking about, though not in every case.

Power

A leitmotif throughout this volume has been the evidence that while polymedia gives the appearance of free and unfettered communication between parents and children, for a variety of reasons it may do little to assuage the basic asymmetry in power that exists across such conversations and may indeed in several ways exacerbate this asymmetry. In general it seemed as though letters and cassettes were more equal in the way they expressed relationships (although that was often illusory, given the suppression of problems and bad news). But at least once the children had grown up, letters sometimes became a more genuine expression of themselves compared to their childhoods when letters were a kind of school exercise they were dragooned into doing by their carers. It is the phone that is seen as leading to a deterioration in this equality within the relationship. This was particularly the case given the differences in the ability of children and parents to pay for phone calls, making the children in effect the passive recipients and rarely the initiator of communication. At best they could send a text to a roaming phone or make a missed call to a UK number, in effect informing their parents that they would like to speak. Previously also the child could determine the time of the communication, e.g. reading a letter when they chose, but a phone call pins them down, locates them, finds them out, and may intrude. Likewise the mothers also experience an intrusion and burden from the frequent texts – usually sent by their relatives, but also their own children – requesting money, goods or general advice and help.

The main issue with regard to power asymmetry was not, however, simply the difference in resources and therefore control over the medium itself, but the way in which more advanced communication brought back the ability of the parent to control and discipline the child, as well as far more effective devices of surveillance. Recalling their lives as teenagers, participants remembered how the phone makes the parent present in the form of an argument or quarrel they would seek to avoid. Or they may come to see the phone simply as a demand they have to fulfil.

In general, children might prefer computer-based to phone-based media since they tended to have greater technical proficiency, and the parent therefore has to cede authority to them at least in the matter of how to use and organise their communications. Parents, and even more the *lolas*, who were commonly the designated childcarer, could easily be embarrassed or even humiliated by this reversal of authority. An elderly man hated the way his slow typing speed was reflected in any IM correspondence. He wants to keep in touch with all the details of what his children or grandchildren are getting up to. But the younger generation just type so quickly in chat he feels he cannot keep up. So for him email is a more relaxed, a slightly less humiliating, way of exchanging news. This of course is even more of a problem for a few of the older mothers in London who simply never learnt to type. For them the rise of all these text-based media, as opposed to letter writing, is a challenge. In one case, Nora has asked a friend to type the emails for her, twice a week, and to print out the replies for her.

Power tends to refer mostly to particular periods within the history of these relationships, and is often less important in the relationships when the children are more grown up and there is a mutual sense of maturity in how parents and children have come to understand each other. But it is still generally the case that mothers talk at some length about their use of different media in terms of trying to retain some sense of discipline and control over the children when they were still at school, for example checking on homework or whether they stay out too late at night. The children, on the other hand, talk at length about the way they manipulate different forms of media in trying to escape surveillance and control during their teenage years. A typical example of the latter would be Ricardo who states: 'They never really found a way to get close to me because I always found a way to shield myself from them. Like with emails, what I do is I take a long time to reply. Like, I've read the email today but I'll reply next week. Usually, my dad would pester me like, "You're not updating. Are we still your parents?"' Another son for similar reasons insisted that communication centred upon email alone, and then took weeks before replying, a delay whose significance was certainly not lost on his father.

Power is evident not only in the asymmetrical relationships of children and parents. It is also present in the material and work conditions of all of our participants. We have already addressed the structural limitations pertaining to access and literacy in this and in previous chapters. But practical constraints are faced even by those who are already at ease with these technologies. Sandra is one of the mothers who, like Donna and Greta, are already further along the path to polymedia. Sandra has her own laptop and is able to use more than half-a-dozen platforms, including email, IM, webcam and social networking. As is typical with our informants, Sandra also has two mobile phones, one for roaming and one for texting. Sandra's switching between different media is not determined by cost, but either by her work constraints or as we shall see in the following section, by her emotional state. Like other domestics, Sandra has an unpredictable schedule and is not always available when her daughter wants to have a long chat. 'Sometimes they want to speak to me long, but I don't have a chance because it's Sunday. Sometimes she gets mad at me. So what I do is send an email and try to explain my routine here.'

Emotions

One of the most significant results of polymedia is the way it gives people the ability to reconfigure the relationship between persons and media as a means to create different emotional repertoires and registers. Of all the potential technical distinctions that could have been exploited, it was already apparent in the previous chapter that the most significant distinction seems to be that between voice and text. This is not surprising given the precedent in Chapter 4, where it became clear that the primary concern with the distinction between letters and cassettes related to their difference in registering the emotional dimension of the relationship. One of the key attractions of email was often simply that it was not voice, so that it could be resorted to in cases where voice would cause embarrassment. For example, Bea readily admits that one of the main things they were concerned with as children was to ask for things they would like purchased for them, or even more embarrassingly to directly ask for money. She, along with several others, noted that this became one of the main reasons why children might prefer to use texting rather than voice. Others avoid voice for any particularly bad news, or at a time when they are quarrelling and they know a conversation is likely to turn into an argument. In all such cases texting might also be a preferred medium since it allows the substance to be communicated, but without having to hear a riposte that may be negative and stressful.

Sandra, a mother of two, will consciously choose email when she wants to be more in control of her own emotions:

> Because as I said, especially when I get upset, I don't want to let [my children] know. Sometimes I would like to cry, but I don't want them to feel that, because I want them to be strong. So much better to write this in email, to explain whatever I would like to say. Because when we talk sometimes my daughter asks questions, 'Why is it like this'? [...] So I write an email. And then she wrote back to me a very long [one], much longer than the one I sent to her.

Similarly, Donna prefers typed chat or texting when she feels particularly upset. Although chat with webcam is her favourite medium for communicating with her children, she does not want them to see her crying – which she often feels like doing especially when she sees her eight-month-old daughter. We saw in Chapter 5 how she was overcome with emotion during her daughter's first birthday which she witnessed on Skype, leading her to abandon the call. However, we have also noticed a change recently in how she expresses emotions in her Facebook status updates. She often writes of her 'loneliness and sadness', or her 'mixed emotions': happiness she found a new contract but sadness at the prolongation of separation. She takes strength from the comments left on her 'wall' by her husband, sisters, friends and children. Recently, we also saw her complaining about the lack of acknowledgements following the sending of a *balikbayan* box full of gifts, which prompted an outpouring of messages on her wall by all the embarrassed relatives. Perhaps because the typed status updates of Facebook allow for some distance compared with the interactive, direct nature of webcam, Donna finds it a more appropriate medium for the expression of some emotions. It is possible that this example may even signal a deeper transformation of emotional expression that is also shaped by the medium of social networking coupled with the experience of migration.

In Vicente's family, email is constantly used as a way of avoiding confrontation. This is the reason his mother contacts him through email when she is angry. Behind this preference for email lies the history of their phone calls, during which Vincente's brother has a tendency to make more and more demands for money, claiming he needs it for transport and such like. At such times their mother, who knows perfectly well how money sent previously has actually been used for drink, just gets angrier and angrier. Email feels like a blessing for people who have a real fear and loathing for such confrontations. As one person put it: 'Nobody can shout in an email' – though some try by using capital letters. It is one of the most common clichés about Filipino society in general that people are expected to avoid confrontation. It appears prominently even in tourist guide books such as the *Rough Guide* or *Lonely Planet* as something outsiders should be aware of as a matter of cultural sensitivity. Such stereotypes are always overgeneralised and we have plenty of examples of actual quarrelling and exposures; nevertheless this does correspond to an established issue that was previously described in terms of *walang hiya*, that is being without shame, as one of the worst things one Filipino can say about another. So it seems fair to say that the avoidance of any emotion that might give rise to shame is conventional etiquette.

In our own fieldwork we quickly found that our tendency to phone people up was felt to be quite inappropriate other than when we were contacting a university trained elite. People could become quite agitated and surprised to be called. The etiquette was first to text to say that one was going to make a voice call and only then to do so. The reason usually given was that voice is so expensive relative to texting that it implies some kind of emergency. This seems to be the case, but it may also mask this other concern with the potential for confrontation and uncontrolled emotion. In the past, letters were often preferred for communication for similar reasons, and still today when it comes to highly significant acts of communication, as when a nurse working in London decided to tell his father that he was gay, it was a letter that was the preferred medium.

These things can also work in reverse, however. Some people suggested that the lack of cues in emails and the difficulty of interpreting them can lead to ambiguity. This results in misunderstandings and may possibly turn into conflict, which might not have been the case with voice, where content can be couched in various ways that make clear the sensitivity of the speaker to the issues raised. Sometimes people at the two ends of the conversation have different interpretations of the implications of the medium used (Gershon, 2010: 16–49). Some parents at first felt dispirited by the fact that their children merely texted them to wish them happy birthday or to ask for things they wanted sent, especially since texting seemed a particularly terse medium that reduced things to a rather naked and mercenary relationship. But later they came to be at least partly reconciled to these when they appreciated that for young people within the Philippines texting was in fact the core emotional and intimate mode of communication. So, for example, when one mother broke up with her relationship with an Englishman, her daughter responded by texting and the mother responded by saying something like, 'You probably feel what I'm feeling right now. That's why you texted me.'

Both mothers and children noted that they sometimes found it easier to say 'I love you' in phone calls, or text-based media such as texting, email, or IM than in person. The temporality of texting and email means that although you lose the immediacy and sense of connection in voice, you gain the pause between message and response. As we have seen in previous chapters, the mediated distance of text-based communication in some cases offers the ideal balance between autonomy and proximity for emotions to be expressed.

In another case it was argued that email works well for affective communication, providing one utilises its potential. The ideal email starts with various inconsequential pieces of news, the phatic communication discussed in the previous chapters. Then you can start to hint at the problem. Gradually one moves on to convey the emotional issues at stake and confess to how much one is troubled. Andrea's sister, for example, admits she is not very fond of college and is homesick and feels tired. With email there is the scope to allow emotions to work their way up to the surface and be expressive. Similarly in the response, in this case her mother writes back with messages to boost her confidence, tells her to pray, but again surrounds this missive with stories of her own life to make the emotional aspect easier to package without seeming too naked or sharp.

For others the only appropriate medium for conveying and capturing emotion is voice. As noted in the discussion of cassettes, the experience of listening to the voice of one's left-behind child can be a singularly moving experience. Voice-based media also seem to be particularly successful as a means of gauging the feelings of the other party. By the same token, when communication between mothers and children is fraught, then voice media, such as the telephone, can be experienced as disturbance, surveillance and rupture. The immediacy of the telephone cannot allow the masking or delaying of communication or emotions, but forces the interlocutors into confrontation. We saw in Chapter 5 that for some mothers, such confrontation was at times accepted as a more 'real' experience of mothering, which they preferred to the past situation when all conflict was suppressed, usually leaving them feeling deceived if and when they eventually found out about problems.

The level of realism is still greater with webcam, which creates a combination of sound and vision and sometimes also simultaneous typed chat. Webcam is not only interactive (which is linked to its temporality), but also provides strong visual cues (facial expressions, tone of voice, pauses, gestures) that contextualise communication. The combination of more senses in the communication process works better in some contexts than others. For example, voice allows the concentration on two parameters (listening and speaking) and this concentration may partly explain the depth of feeling that is reported in connection to voice calls. Likewise, while Skype is appreciated for facilitating a sense of co-presence and conveying realism, it is not usually described as a medium that has depth of feeling. By contrast, blogging has none of the immediate interactivity of webcams, or even the expressive possibilities of voice, yet blogging may be the place for expressing extremes of emotion because in this case it resonates with the older tradition of confessional diary writing, only that in this context it is transposed in a public setting.

It should not be thought that polymedia necessarily resolve the issues of separation. Clearly as seen in Chapter 6, for many of the children the more immediate and effective the media, the more negative the impact on those who see all this as simply further reminders of actual absence. This was not only the case with young children. A particularly poignant example of this logic came with Vicente and his wife Corrie. Corrie was an older woman who migrated out of desperation to help a child with a rare health condition which required expensive treatment. She always remained in close conversation with her daughter, and was able to continue this relationship through a combination of media including a 40-minute phone card used weekly, some YM, some Skype that amounted in combination to daily correspondence. By contrast, Corrie rarely speaks to her husband with whom she has been together for 27 years, this being the first time they had ever been apart. It seems likely that, as often happens in couple relationships, their closeness is taken for granted and not based on long conversations. As a result none of these new media really help, as they cannot replace that sense of closeness in terms of mere presence. Following Corrie's migration, Vicente went into depression and ended up being hospitalised. In a situation where communication had become effectively the silent medium of co-presence, not even polymedia could compensate for this absence of emotional bonding.

A theory of polymedia

The concept of polymedia arose during the course of our analysis of the material from this particular project. But it resonates with many other studies and its implications are obviously global. Even though we recognise that most of our informants are still some distance from what may be termed true polymedia, the implications are becoming evident of a situation where the cost of any individual communication has migrated from foreground to background and half a dozen modes of communication are immediately available and within a person's digital literacy.

It was noted at the start of this chapter that the concept of polymedia builds on several prior academic traditions, especially in media studies, and we are not suggesting that it makes these redundant. On the contrary, it complements them in particular ways. For example, the idea of 'communicative ecologies' is likely to remain particularly important in development studies (see Tacchi, Slater and Hearn, 2003) since there the concern is not just the internal relationship between media or their socialisation, but the way, in combination with other facilities such as transport or government information, people gain certain capabilities with respect to areas such as health and education. Similarly there is a clear overlap with Baym's (2010) discussion of key concepts for understanding computer-mediated personal relationships, which we referred to in our earlier discussion of affordances (Chapter 7). Baym notes that as interpersonal relationships become richer and more complex, so do the media on which they depend (Baym, 2010: 132). She echoes Haythornthwaite's (2005) concept of 'media multiplexity', which she developed to describe the finding that the number of media used depends on the strength of the relationship bond. The 'social shaping of technologies' approach (MacKenzie and Wajcman, 1999) on which the concept of affordances (Hutchby, 2001) is based, also provides some of the theoretical foundation for Baym's (2010) analysis. Although we acknowledge the mutual shaping of technology and society and thus the importance of a degree of 'soft determinism' (MacKenzie and Wajcman, 1999: 3–4) especially in the context of mediated communication, in situations of polymedia the emphasis shifts more towards the 'domestication' of the various media (see Berker *et al.*, 2006; Silverstone and Hirsch, 1992). The approach that is most compatible with polymedia is that of mediation (Couldry, 2008 and 2012; Madianou, 2005, 2012b; Livingstone, 2009b; Silverstone, 2005), which represents a holistic approach to understanding the mutual shaping of media and social processes. Such an example is the work of Livingstone (2002, 2009a), who has extensively examined new media within the family context and with particular reference to the usage by children and young adults.

One of the other literatures that precedes polymedia is the work carried out under the auspices of the communication industry with a focus upon new product design. Much of this comes under the heading of 'convergence', which derived from the recognition that media that originally had quite different functionalities started to intersect and hybridise, thus appearing as alternative forms of communication (see also Jenkins, 2006). Of particular interest are studies that concentrate on how convergence has impacted upon families and studies of communication within families (e.g. Little *et al.*, 2009). Another example is the very extensive ethnographic study of communication carried out in Swiss families over several years by Broadbent and colleagues (Broadbent, 2011). For example, they identify a clear gradation between communication that pertains to a person as a member of a household and increasingly intimate and dyadic communications. The landline is the foundation for the household, while people move from that to the mobile phone, to text and finally to IM, where each is seen as successively more intimate than the last. Furthermore, each of these media is seen as having shifted in its usage and connotations, not necessarily because of any change in its technology but often because of a shift in some other technology that represents an alternative (Broadbent, 2011: 25). Media convergence remains highly significant also in the more technical sense of, for example, social networking migrating from computing to smart phones, something already prominent in Trinidad (Miller, 2011), but not yet in the Philippines.

All of these precedents are useful foundations but we believe that the material presented in this book leads us to a situation where we require something that transcends them. This is the concept of polymedia and we want to conclude by making clear what this now refers to and its further consequences for the understanding of media today. As noted in the introduction, this is an emerging condition that would be far more true of the US students discussed by Gershon (2010), or even Trinidad (Miller, 2011) than our Filipino participants described here, but the previous two chapters have shown that there is a sufficiency in the trajectory towards polymedia to make it imperative to clearly theorise this state.

To summarise: the first condition for the emergence of polymedia is the availability of a plethora of media choices, when a user has at least half-a-dozen media at their disposal that their household can readily afford. Secondly, users must have the skills and confidence to use these digital media. The third condition is that the main costs are infrastructural, such as paying for the hardware and the internet connection cost, rather than the cost of individual acts of communication.

Turning to the theorisation of polymedia, the first stage is to recognise that the understanding of media as an integrated environment within which each medium is defined relationally corresponds to some of the basic ideas of anthropological structuralism as constructed by Levi-Strauss (1963). Structuralism radically altered our understanding of the world, from a common-sense perception of the things around us seen in and of themselves, to a relativist perception in which any given thing was experienced in terms of the other things it was not. An email is not just an email; it is its differences from a voice call or a text that partly make it what it is. Polymedia is a form of structuralism in which the understanding we have of any one medium becomes less its properties, or affordances, and more its alternative status as against the other media that could equally be employed for that message. Media are thereby increasingly to be defined as relational within the structure of polymedia.

Structuralism, however, refers only to the internal relationship between the media. The next state is to recognise that polymedia actually shifts the core relationship between society and media. The reasons why people choose one medium rather than another, even the affordances they perceive a particular medium as possessing, come much more from the wider social context of their communication rather than the narrower issues of technology and function. This is exactly what the evidence of this chapter demonstrates. To take just one aspect of our discussion, that of power, we can now see that power refers not only to the asymmetrical relationships between persons, but also to the changes in the relationships between persons and things. Following the work of Gell (1998), Latour (1993) and others, we are used to thinking of objects also as agents, especially when it seems to be the objects and technologies rather than the persons who use them that lead to a particular consequence. One of the key attributes of polymedia is that it shifts the power relationship from one in which the agency of the technology is often paramount towards one in which people have regained much of their control over the technologies, because they now have alternatives. One of the reasons the very term 'affordances' starts to become less relevant as we proceed with this chapter as opposed to the previous one is because with the proliferation of media an individual can shift to a different medium, or ignore what appears to be the evident propensity of a given medium. At one level, polymedia almost paradoxically implies that the more communication technologies proliferate, the less prominent they become as a perceived causative aspect of any relationship. This can also be described as a re-socialisation of media, since in a situation of polymedia there are new possibilities of alignment between media and cultural, moral, social and individual ways of conducting relationships. This chapter mainly consists of examples of how media are now reconfigured by the demands of Filipino culture and particular kinds of relationships. The next stage recognizes that this is not just a re-socialisation of the media, but also a radical shift in the moral context of communication. With polymedia it is the user, rather than external factors, that is held responsible for the selection of any particular medium. In a situation where it is no longer easy for an individual to legitimate their choice of media on the grounds that this one was cheaper, or that the other was more accessible, the choice of medium invites a moral judgement about its appropriateness. This can be best explored through a comparison of our material with perhaps the fullest treatment of polymedia to date (though she does not use this term) by Gershon (2010). Her book is concerned with the way that young people who dump their boyfriends or girlfriends are increasingly held responsible for (not) choosing the appropriate media when taking this action. In Gershon's case this is a true situation of polymedia since accessibility and cost for these US students is simply not an issue. Gershon develops her own terminology around 'idioms of practice' based on 'media ideologies'. Her informants can be outraged almost as much by someone dumping them through what they see as an inappropriate or even inhuman medium, as by the fact that they are being dumped. A woman feels almost glad her boyfriend dumped her because to have done it using a text message shows how worthless he really is. The implications are that in conditions of polymedia the selection of media is viewed as a moral act to be judged.

This is an important element in our study, but here the question of morality tends more to be subsumed within issues of, for example, power and shame and emotionality because of the very different situation we describe. Gershon provides considerable evidence for the lack of standardisation being relevant to the degree to which people mistakenly presume what others intend by such choices, because they retain particular ideologies of what the use of a particular medium implies, from which follow various misunderstandings. Chapter 3 of her book is a particularly good example of this perspective. By contrast, one of the things that can fascinate in our ethnographic study of polymedia is the speed at which normative and relatively standardised expectations arise as how to use new media and their consequences. While we have encountered some degree of individual idiosyncrasy, there is a much stronger sense in this chapter of how Filipinos more generally may feel about particular media and etiquettes of communication. Part of this is just a result of the method of comparative research. As more studies become available including our own in Trinidad,[2] we may be able to more readily generalise about differences between Filipino and Caribbean usage (see Madianou and Miller, in preparation). But in addition there may be an expectation that US students put more premium on individual difference and responsibility, while Filipinos tend more to the consensual and collective (see also Jocano, 2001), in which case we would expect that the normative would be more quickly reestablished in the Philippines than in US colleges.

We can now see the analytical progress that we can make using the descriptive material of this and the previous chapter. Instead of simply studying the impact of one particular medium on the relationship between mothers and children, we can see that each medium makes sense only within a wider environment within which it finds its niche and is defined relationally. This environment includes the relationships between the various media as analysed through the various affordances which emerge through the media's functionalities and the conditions of their consumption. Navigating this integrated environment that is polymedia is not a free-floating process but rather is dependent on cultural genres of sociality and emotional registers and struggles over power. In this process the emphasis of our analysis gradually shifts from the technological to the social and moral implications of media use, such that an individual is now judged according to which media they selected when this choice can no longer be hidden behind grounds such as price or accessibility. This acknowledges something that is found throughout this book, which is that the medium does far more than carry communication. The choice of media and the combination of various media that is found in the development of any given relationships is itself a major communicative act.

So although when we began Chapter 7 we suggested that we were moving from a concern primarily with social relations to a more explicit focus upon the media, this was only partly true. Actually we find that the two remain inseparable and that one of the main changes has been this re-socialising of media. This is why our final chapter will be focused on the further theorisation of media and relationships. While we have focused here on our material from the Philippines, actually the arguments we have made are likely to be still more true of countries with higher income levels and higher levels of media literacy. This is why we believe that polymedia is going to become an inescapable topic for almost all and any media research in the future. We anticipate that there will be many different interpretations of it as a phenomenon and arguments over its consequences and significance, which may well contradict each and every proposition that we have put forward in this chapter. But to even begin such a discussion we first need a name for this new situation, and for that purpose we propose the word – polymedia.

9

A THEORY OF MEDIATED RELATIONSHIPS

When we began this research it seemed obvious to us that what we would be studying was the way media mediated relationships. We assumed that this is what is implied simply by juxtaposing the two words 'mediated' and 'relationships'. The relationship itself was both given and paramount, in this case, the desire for mothers to be mothers to their children and for children to still have mothers. The question we wanted to investigate was how far this had been constrained by the previous lack of media, and how far it was now facilitated by the extraordinary transformation in the past few years towards more diverse and affordable polymedia. But the theory that will be presented in this concluding chapter comes from our gradual appreciation that the situation is more complex than what we had originally anticipated.

The task in this chapter is to bring together two perspectives that so far have been examined largely in their own right. Chapters 2, 3, 5 and 6 were concerned mainly with mothers and their children and the relationship between them, including the reasons for and consequences of overseas migration. Chapters 4, 7 and 8 concentrated upon the communication technologies and how these are exploited in such relationships. Here we aim to bring together the conclusions of those respective discussions. We will illustrate our key typologies of mediated relationships under conditions of polymedia by revisiting some of the actual pairs of mothers and left-behind children that we have worked with.

Chapter 6, which was mainly devoted to the problem of relationships, ended with some initial theorisation about the nature of mother–child relationships. It was suggested in its conclusion that what we call a relationship is actually a kind of theoretical triangle. The foundation, or baseline of this triangle, comes from a normative understanding of what a mother or a child is supposed to be and the subsequent expectations and obligations each has for the other. For some of these children the image of what mothers are supposed to be, and their desire to have someone who accords with that representation, was powerful, to the point of being obsessive. Recall the case of Andres, the young man who was prepared to get into debt himself in order to raise money for someone who had never behaved as a proper mother. But by seeing himself in debt to *her* he could nevertheless reconstitute her as a 'real' mother, almost irrespective of how she actually behaved, partly because there is a powerful Filipino concept of debt known as *utang na loob* that is supposed to pertain to the normative relationship between all children and all parents. Similarly, we have seen that the fundamental legitimation that allows several mothers to migrate in the first place, need not derive from any knowledge of their actual child, who could even be a newborn, but from what is projected as the obligations of debt and love that exist merely by virtue of the existence of that individual as their child.

So the baseline of the triangle is the normative projection of what a child or a mother represents by their presence in the world. The second side of this triangle, which emerges over time, is the increasing evidence for the actual person who occupies that position. Given the situation of separation, evidence for this comes primarily through the conversations between the mother and the child through whatever media are available to them both. Inevitably, in this triangle the normative ideal goes in one direction and the evidence for the actual person moves at an angle to that norm. This provides the basis for a third line which has to be drawn between the other two, which represents the discrepancy between them and which makes this a triangle. The length of that line is the degree to which an actual mother or child deviates from the normative ideal. All of this suggests that a relationship is intrinsically a mediated entity. A mother works for a child on the premise that her actual child should deserve a private education and should grasp the opportunities that such schooling represents. A child who acts differently, is not acting as a proper child, and should and must be cajoled into becoming more like a proper child. Similarly a child needs a mother, someone who is highly attuned and sensitive to their needs and not one who buys presents that are appropriate for someone considerably younger than they actually are. Our study has shown how communication is not just a revelation of the actual mother and child, it is equally a revelation of the discrepancy between the actual and the normative. Furthermore, we have also shown how this same communication is the main means by which our informants hope to bring their actual mother or child back into alignment with what a proper mother or child should be without needing to be told.

So the first part of our theory states that any relationship is intrinsically a mediated form and that while this is true of all relationships, it is particularly clear in the relationships that we have analysed in this book, because of the condition of prolonged separation. This understanding of mediation as the 'activity which expresses the relationship of otherwise separated experiences' quite irrespective of the technological mediation of the media echoes the writings of Williams (1977: 172). However, the fact that the relationships studied in this book depend, often entirely, on communication technologies reminds us that our task in this final chapter is to also understand the ways in which relationships and media are mutually constituted. In order to do so we draw on our conclusions from previous chapters

The ideal vs. the real vs. the discrepancy between

ALL RELATIONSHIPS ARE MEDIATED

as well as the theory of mediation (Couldry, 2000, 2008 and 2012; Livingstone, 2009b; Madianou, 2005; Silverstone, 2005).

Mediation is a fundamentally dialectical notion (Silverstone, 2005) which aims to capture and describe the heterogeneity of transformations to which media give rise within our complex societies. Its advantage is that it understands communication as a holistic and non-linear process and in that sense, as Couldry has argued, mediation is a much more nuanced term compared to the proposed alternative of mediatisation which, at least in some of its versions (Hjarvard, 2008), 'implies a single media logic transforming a whole social space at once' (Couldry, 2008: 375). While those versions of mediatisation might be useful for assessing the ways in which one medium may transform a specific institution or field (such as election campaigning), it is hard to see how it can explain the role of the ever-proliferating media in our contemporary societies without resorting to some level of technological determinism (Couldry, 2008: 378). Moreover, the singular 'logic of the medium' that some, though not all (for exceptions see Hepp, 2009; Krotz, 2009), proponents of mediatisation (Hjarvard, 2008) emphasise is incompatible with the plural notion of polymedia.[1] A meditational perspective recognises the mutual shaping of technology and society (MacKenzie and Wajcman, 1999; Wajcman, 2002). Technologies are socially shaped and 'domesticated' through consumption (Berker et al., 2006; Silverstone and Hirsch, 1992), but they, in turn, contribute to the shaping of social interactions. As Livingstone has observed, mediation does not add another layer, it changes the whole process (Livingstone, 2009b). For example, writing on television, Madianou has argued that mediation transforms emotional registers and amplifies negative emotions such as shame in situations of unwanted mediated exposure in news media (Madianou, 2012b). Whilst initially developed with regard to mainstream, one-to-many media, mediation can equally be applied to the environment of new communication technologies (see Couldry, 2008 for a persuasive account). Applied to our current concerns of interpersonal communication, mediation provides for a more dialectical sense of the tension between the technical and the emotional.

A parallel set of debates about mediation in anthropology has recently focused on the relationship between media and religion (Eisenlohr, 2011; Engelke, 2007, 2010; Miller, in press), because as in the history of Protestantism there have been huge ideological conflicts over whether the relationship of humanity to the deity is, or should be mediated. The value of this approach is that we have a tendency to see any new media as mediated, leading to a nostalgic simplification of the previous media we had become used to as less mediated (for an example of this, see Turkle, 2011). But for anthropologists there is no stage prior to objectification; in other words, as we have argued here, the relationship is intrinsically mediated and always has been.

Media constituting relationships

About half of the mothers in our sample emigrated when their children were young, often babies or toddlers. Even though Philippine migration is routinely referred to as short-term (Castles and Miller, 2009), in fact most mothers remain separated from their children even now that these may have grown up into adulthood. For some of our participants there were significant constraints that prevented regular visits, although on average mothers visited every 1.6 years. Most of these women migrated before the mid-1990s when communication was infrequent or expensive. So many of these mothers and their children had known extensive periods of time, often several years, during which they had not seen each other. On reflection this was always likely to mean that these participants' relationships were less likely to be determined by the personality and character of the child, or the mother as specific individuals, and rather more by the projection upon them of the same aspirations and obligations that legitimated the act of migration in the first place.

This would seem at first to be an extreme case, a rather bizarre aberration. Surely in most other cases, where the persons are present to each other, we have a simple relationship between two actual people. But there is another possibility which we would like to propose. Sometimes an extreme case is of interest not because of how extraordinary it is in its own right; but rather more because it clarifies a property of ordinary relationships that had been obscured, or denied. To explore this possibility we need to consider a mother–child relationship that exists in the situation of ordinary co-presence, whether in Manila or in London. We would not contest the assertion of many parents that right from birth they feel a strong sense of their particular baby and its personality. But there have been many societies in which babies were brought up at first by wet-nurses and others. The point this makes is that being a parent creates an orientation to the baby simply as an entity, irrespective of those individual characteristics and personality. Not knowing these is no constraint on our ability to project a huge emotional charge. Often immediately from their birth we feel we would happily sacrifice ourselves for them, before we have any experience of them as individuals. We may have decided what school they will go to and even how well they will do at that school. We already know they are going to succeed in becoming all the things that we feel we failed to become in our own life. Furthermore, the woman who gave birth to the baby may suddenly come to realise that two new beings were born at that precise moment: not just the baby, but also a creature called a mother. Up to then she was a young woman, who possibly went to parties and had a career, and most likely had an education she had expected to use in life. But now she is a mother, and seems to be regarded as an altogether different sort of person, whether she likes it or not. She discovers that, just as the baby, she too is newly born into the category 'mother' (Miller, 1997; see also Hollway and Featherstone, 1997; Parker, 2005).

Merely having a baby is sufficient for a mother to feel obliged to go abroad and work for them. The result is the situation described by Aguilar *et al.* (2009) for parents who migrate from a rural *barangay* to Milan, Italy. They work and they work and they work ... for what end? Most of the money that is not required simply to get through life is destined for two purposes in particular. One is a house and the other is a private school. The house may be built irrespective of whether there is anyone to live in it; it objectifies the relationships and obligation one has to others (Aguilar *et al.*, 2009). But then so does the private school. Such feelings of obligation or legitimation are also relevant in a situation of co-present parenting. So in many ways this book simply brings into sharper focus something that is entirely ordinary in the relationship between parents and children, the relationship we generalise as kinship.

If we examine the media in this extreme situation of separation, then there are many grounds for claiming that the media become constitutive of the actual relationships. This was largely the case in the period of letter writing when for years the only sign of the other person was their letters. The person to all intents and purposes was in the letter itself, re-read, placed close to the heart, dissected for unintended contents and intentions. Clear evidence of how letters (and cassette tapes) came to carry a trace of their authors is the almost universal reluctance amongst our participants to discard them. Such deep attachment to the materiality of letters was expressed even when the shortcomings of letter writing were evident, for example the frustration with regard to its temporality and the fact that it often aimed at suppressing, rather than dealing with, actual problems. What letters achieved was to constitute what we have termed the 'actual person' who can then be compared with the normative model people have of that other person. The mother was looking for signs that the child was doing their homework properly. But for the child the letter above all signified that they in fact had a mother, a person who loved them deeply. This would be complemented by other communication, where as McKay (2007) puts it, 'sending dollars shows feeling'. Letters and cassettes were also a major constraint upon the ability for relationships to be expressed and maintained. No one wanted to have these gaps of months within a conversation, but they could not help it because that was all the media they had. In all these ways the media had significant material impacts upon the relationships.

The arrival of digital media does not necessarily solve these relationship problems. As we saw in Chapter 6, three factors impact here: the age of the child when the mother left, the available media and the quality of the pre-existing relationship. When the latter is weak, digital media can even heighten tensions within long-distance relationships. The most extreme such case is that of Andres discussed at the end of Chapter 6. Andres, who had been effectively abandoned by his mother, described the disruptive effect of his encounter with his mother's Friendster profile following her 'friend' request. In this case of extreme absence, the Friendster profile constituted the 'actual' person, which shattered the son's idealised projection of his mother.

Such cases of prolonged absence bring to the fore one critical feature of the internet, and social networking sites in particular, which is the way that they can make the absent other 'tangible'. The visual cues afforded by photographs and the persistence and searchability of content which can be perused again and again come to constitute the other person. In conditions of prolonged separation the lack of any other symbolic or actual cues lends both agency and power to these materials.[1]

Ideal distance and 'pure' relationships

If one extreme concerns how old or infrequent media constitute the actual person in a relationship, at the other extreme we can observe the role of new media (as polymedia) in the emergence of 'pure relationships' (Giddens, 1991). By pure relationship Giddens is trying to define an ideal of relative equality that has emerged within the field of contemporary relationships which are sustained for the rewards that they deliver (Giddens, 1991: 6). Although Giddens initially developed the concept to refer to the transformation of intimacy and the reconfiguration of romantic relationships, we argue that the basic definition can also apply to mothers and children. In that case a pure relationship is one which allows mothers and children to gradually move towards the kind of more equal relationship envisaged as friendship. This may sound paradoxical as mother–children relationships seem to be almost axiomatically asymmetrical. However, as the following example of Nora and Domingo's relationship shows, when children become adults such asymmetries can sometimes be softened.

Domingo was 13 when his mother Nora left and he did not see her for 13 years, by which time he was 26, married and with one child. For years communication was intermittent, based mainly on letters and the occasional phone call. Domingo remembers that writing letters was a chore and as a teenager he never felt that he could fully express himself in them. The consequence was that he lost touch with his mother. The reason his story is so dramatically different from Andres' discussed earlier is because Domingo and Nora began developing a strong bond during Nora's first visit after 13 years, precipitated by Domingo's father's illness and subsequent death. Domingo by that time was a father himself and initially sought his mother's advice and support. But soon mother and son developed a friendship based on what they saw as their similar personalities. Apart from that initial visit and some subsequent ones, this mother–child friendship largely developed and grew through mediated interactions, first phone calls, some emailing, and now webcam. Following a period of intense communication, Domingo even came to London to visit his mother and they travelled together to Scotland, Ireland and Wales. His house in Laguna is full of memorabilia from their UK tour. Nora, who initially had not been able to visit her son because of her irregular status, now has permanent residency in the UK. As discussed in Chapter 5, even though Nora is retired, she does not want to return to the Philippines, as she values her independence and autonomy in England. As she has not been able to build a house of her own, returning to the Philippines would entail her moving in with her son which would mean a throwback to their traditional roles of mother and son, which she resists: 'I don't want to be controlled by anyone, in the Philippines always someone, a man, tries to control you.' Domingo is equally relieved that his mother does not want to return as the financial burden would fall on his shoulders. Continuing their long-distance relationship means they can simply focus on what they enjoy the most about each other: their banter and jokes and the admiration of Domingo's children. In their case webcam makes all the difference as it allows them to enjoy each other and develop a kind of 'pure relationship' in which external criteria have been weakened. Nora does not call out of obligation towards her son, but out of desire to hear their news and spend some time together.

Of course, this is not to say that the normative dimension is not present in Nora and Domingo's relationship. Normative roles are ready to be assumed when necessary and are often expressed in relation to Nora's granddaughters through the sending of gifts. We also encountered this trend towards a 'best-friend' mother–daughter relationship in the cases of Cecilia and Ofelia discussed in Chapter 6. The point is not that we leave the arena of normative relationships, but rather that the pure relationship is itself a shift in that normative ideal. As Giddens (1991) showed, people believe in these pure relationships because they feel this new normative form is closer to the actual personalities of those involved in the relationship.

The situation of migration may accentuate this process. Our evidence suggests that separation and distance can increase the appreciation for the absent other. Mothers routinely told us that they first felt appreciated and valued after their emigration. This is partly due to the sending of remittances and their newfound breadwinning status, but also due to the fact that they are missed rather than being taken for granted. Distance forces people to make time and effort to show they care, as attested by many of our participants who said that they would more readily express love in mediated rather than face-to-face communication. Within this new ideal of equality, mediation can potentially create the 'ideal distance' necessary for a relationship to flourish. This distance not only facilitates the discursive expression of love, but also provides the right balance or 'ideal distance' between autonomy and emotional support that is crucial for teenagers (such as Cecilia, Carlito and Ofelia). Paradoxically, the sense that the relationship has thereby worked well partly through the circumstances of distance and the mediating technologies, can then become the justification for the continuing separation. If Nora can have the best relationship with her son through webcam, then why should she give up her autonomy and sense of personhood that comes with living in the UK to return to the Philippines and a more claustrophobic sense of community and kinship?

This last point highlights the observation that new media and relationships do not just mediate each other; what is also mediated is the whole project of migration, as they contribute to the justifications and rationales for settlement and return. As earlier examples have shown, this applies not only to relationships which have ultimately worked, such as Domingo's and Nora's, but also to those whose relationships are more fraught. So regardless of whether they resolve or exacerbate the problems of separation, new media contribute to the framing of patterns of migration.

Polymedia and emotional management

References to media in the previous section actually implicate polymedia, since it is the management of this constellation of different media that is now the instrument for attempting to resolve discrepancies between actual and normative aspects of a relationship, or the struggle towards pure relationships. For years Lisa, whose mother Janice left when she was five years old, wanted to punish her mother for not telling her the truth when she was about to emigrate:

> I hate promises. I don't like you saying, 'I'll be back and then I'm going to bring your favourite snack.' [...] And then she didn't came. It's like, you're waiting for such a long time and no one came. I really hate that. And the other thing is: she never really showed her pain. So I never really understood what she was trying to do for us, what she has been suffering from, what she has been doing. I don't even know what's happening to her. She didn't have the time to tell me. Also my mind was suddenly closed. So basically, I was always the one who made her cry. Even at a young age.

What Lisa did not know is that Janice had suffered abuse in her relationship and had been humiliated by her husband's affairs. Leaving the country secretly seemed to be the only way out for her. Lisa only sensed her mother's humiliation as a teenager when her father brought home his girlfriend when he was supposed to be reunited with Janice. Now at the age of 21, Lisa is beginning to understand what drove her mother away. Lisa has been making collages using photos, letters and images from her childhood. She scans the photos and the collages and sends them to her mother, effectively rewriting the family history through visual media. This is cathartic for Lisa, but it is also important for her relationship with Janice, who displays her daughter's images in her bedsit. Lisa has not explicitly told her mother that she understands, but the sheer fact that she now writes longer emails and sends pictures is perceived by her mother as a positive signal.

For Lisa and for Janice, new media provide the idioms of expressive intent – writing a long email matters as much, if not more, than what is actually said in the email. Media are also the tools for the management of complex emotions and the negotiation of the fundamental ambivalence that both Lisa and Janice recognise and share. Being in an environment of polymedia matters because polymedia allows the choice of medium or combination of media that best conveys one's feelings and intentions. However, Janice's choices are not always approved by Lisa. For example, Janice prefers voice calls (partly because she does not own her own laptop), while Lisa prefers emails which often results in a power struggle and Lisa feeling frustrated when her mother takes so long to respond to her emails, which has sometimes led to misunderstandings between them. So although new media provide the tools for the negotiation for emotions, Lisa can only explore the whole range of polymedia with her father, currently also an OFW in Canada with his new partner. Lisa will text her father provocative messages such as 'I am drunk' in order to grab his attention, while she will seek advice on any difficulties she faces in an email. IM chat is preserved for debating issues of common interest and making plans for the future. It helps that Lisa's father shares his daughter's ease with new media and also, crucially, understands her codes.

We know from earlier examples that mediated communication can often amplify emotions. Conflict, for instance, can be heightened because of the reduced social cues that lead to ambiguities. Mediation can also accelerate idealisation and love. All this echoes arguments about the amplification of mediated emotions in the context of traditional one-to-many communication (see Madianou, 2012b). In situations of polymedia our evidence begins to suggest that we may be witnessing potentially the opposite, as people use one medium to overcome the limitations of another in order to deal with the tensions within relationships. So Lisa's provocative texts do not lead to quarrels, but are read as invitations for an IM or webcam session.

As we have noted, with polymedia the foreground is taken by the issues of power and moral responsibility within relationships, or the desire to either engage with or avoid certain forms of emotionality. These lead people to excavate and exploit particular qualities that create contrasts within the field of media that are now available to them; to choose the immediacy of phone or the delay of email, the emotional charge of voice or the playful banter of texting. Polymedia is not a range of technical potentials, it is a series of cultural genres or emotional registers that make these contrasts into significant differences in communication by exploiting them for various tasks within relationships. As polymedia becomes more present and taken for granted, the range of encounters, including very direct webcam conversation, may approach the nuance of traditional co-presence in which the 'actual person' is confronted more directly. Once the media seemed to be creating a kind of vicarious alternative to the actual person one would have been living with. Today when mothers may text, phone and peruse social networks many times in a day, it emerges more as another type of co-presence.

All of this can be accounted for by our theory of mediated relationships. We noted in the previous chapter that polymedia corresponds to a more general re-socialising of media. The focus moves from an awareness of the media themselves, their constraints and affordances, to the moral and social issues that have always been central to that third line drawn between the normative and the actual in all relationships. Every conversation has an element that is far more than just report-age. Either through forms of support or of discipline there is the attempt to make the person at the other end more cognisant of how the person at this end would like them to be and how they should really want this for themselves. In reading the sections on power and emotion in the previous chapter it is clear that there is always a desire to shift the relationship itself, and make it more how one would wish it to be.

So when we came to explore the detailed linkages between media and rela-tionships in the previous chapter, we found that the situation of polymedia is one in which the media are mediated by the relationship as well as the other way around. A phone is not just a phone, it is that which an individual girl hates, that which can change the balance of power between mother and daughter, that which may be seen as more shallow since there is no time to consider, or more deep for the very same reason.

We do not want to imply that this is necessarily experienced as a positive trajectory. In Chapter 4 we saw that letters and cassettes seem to have often been quite effective, if somewhat frustrating, media of communication. This may be because they were relatively compatible with the idealised absent mother, giving free range to the children to construct and project for themselves what they needed their mother to be. What is intensely irritating about this more constant presence of an actual mother that comes with cheap new polymedia is that she is much less under control. For those children who had negative responses to the impacts of new media, this mother is always saying the wrong thing, doing the wrong thing, not actually being there when needed, while effectively disrupting the ability of the child to construct and project the mother they need at that time. This actual mother may therefore become less like one's normative ideal, rather than more.

Similarly as anthropological writing on mediation suggests, one of the dangers of a focus on media per se is that it can lead us to simplify and romanticise unmediated co-presence. We might then associate all the problematic aspects of these relationships with absence and the issue of how that absence is mediated, which would be quite misleading. After all, much of this book has consisted of discussions about relationships between mothers and their teenage children. It does not take much self-reflection to appreciate that these particular relationships are highly charged even where there is as much co-presence as either would want, indeed in typical scenarios it is co-presence that the teenagers find to be the biggest problem. Wolf's (1997) work on attempted suicide amongst second-generation Filipina girls in California is salutary here. We have several examples of children saying their relationship to their parents improved only when the parents migrated. So our material is rich in examples of absence that exacerbates conflict with parents and equally rich in examples of absence that helps resolve conflicts with parents.

This is not just a theoretical point. Our informants may also imagine that the root of their problems lies in absence and that these will be simply resolved in a situation of cheap polymedia. This is made very clear by Ricardo who reflected on the way that once a computer and its associated communication plan is paid for, there is an apparently free package of voice, chat and image that can simply become part of the routines of daily life. But his concern is with what this still fails to deliver:

> I guess it also improved the quality of communication because we got to talk about things that were going on in our life more than we did before. But in all forms of communication there are also things that we leave in and things that we leave out. In the interest of keeping things pleasant, sometimes when there are bad things going on in your life – and the same goes with her – you don't really talk about it. So there's still that wall.

The key point here is that for Ricardo the significant differences come not from differences between the media, but differences that would almost certainly have been present even when the two correspondents were co-present living in the same house. As we might expect, polymedia merely brings us into more complete confrontation with the problems of relationships that have always been part of co-presence.

Conclusion

We can now see why theories of mediation need to start from a premise, which is that communication technologies and relationships are mutually constitutive. Relationships are transformed because of the tangibility of the internet, which can objectify and constitute one's relationship to one's mother or child. Relationships are also transformed because the media allow, but they also crucially sustain, what for some is the ideal distance for the development of pure relationships. This leads to the mediation and transformation not only of relationships, but of the process of migration more generally. Finally, new media can provide the tools for the management of emotions. This is particularly effective in the case of polymedia, which can cater for different emotional registers. Relationships in turn shape technologies by driving the choices about which medium to use and to what desired effect.

Ultimately if we combine the theorisation of mediation in this chapter with that of polymedia within the previous chapter, they amount to a more general argument with respect to the place of media studies within social science. The value of the kind of social science exemplified by ethnography is that it shows how communicative media have always been highly socialised and mediated by the relationships within which media are employed. As it happens, we would also argue that one of the main effects of polymedia is that for the people we study, and not just for academics, it has also become more apparent that the choices they make today as to media usage cannot be blamed so much on issues of access and affordability, which thereby exposes the social and moral basis for those choices.

This concludes the discussion of media, using the evidence mainly from the latter chapters of this book. But as a final conclusion we also need to reconsider the material from our first three chapters in the light of these theoretical discussions. The starting point for our theoretical triangle was the given nature of the normative. But that rather begs the question of where those normative expectations actually derive from in the first place. To answer this question we need to recall the macro factors of political economy and kinship ideology that were the context for this research. The literature we surveyed reveals a wide spectrum of alternative sources for normativity. These ranged from Parreñas (2008) who explicitly takes her stance from US-dominated academic debates on gender, feminism and global care chains, through to ethnographers who take their point of departure from regional idioms and models of behaviour that may be very different from these more universal aspirations and indeed may vary considerably from one region of the Philippines to another. A case in point would be the detailed analysis of competing models of masculinity found in Pingol (2001), but also in Johnson (1997).

But this is not just the stuff of academic debate. We also suggested from our evidence that the Filipino people we worked with were well aware that they were exposed to a wide range of normative influences. They are increasingly knowledgeable about feminism, especially if they migrate, and of the kinds of mothering ideals portrayed in films such as *Anak*. But we also found they could discuss in depth their sense of *utang na loob* or *walang hiya*, and the impact these still had upon their lives.

To give an example of this more conflicted and nuanced sense of the position of Filipina migrants, Johnson (1998) discusses a contrast between two local terms, *adat* and *istyle*, amongst Muslim migrant women from the south of the Philippines. On the one hand, they are very aware of their responsibility for cultural reproduction and the importance of *adat*, which means both 'traditional' and 'customary'. At the same time, they wanted to appear accomplished at *istyle*, the incorporated modern look that shows they have staked a place in the wider world, and which emerges in part as to whether they invest their money in gold or in consumption. Through such mediation, they construct something neither simply feminist nor traditional, ultimately irreducible to either *adat* or *istyle*. A similar point could be said about the relationship between the materials discussed in Chapters 2 and 3 of this volume. In Chapter 2 we examined wider issues of political economy such as the stance of the Philippine state towards overseas workers. While this sets the parameters for migration, by Chapter 3 we saw that even if we add further pressures such as the demands of family, or the desire to see the world, still these women cannot be reduced to a list of factors. Chapter 3 attempted to convey through stories and examples how all such influences become enmeshed in personal discourses and narratives that can only be fully ascertained through deep engagement with the women themselves.

The various academic debates represented by the initial literature review represent more than just an abstract discussion of the impact of power and struggle upon the situation in which the Philippines government sees migration as an instrument of economic development. The discussion is more than the theorisation of global care chains and the use of the Philippines as a case study to exemplify this phenomenon. Most of all it is more than just an 'extreme case' that helps us create academic theory about the nature of polymedia or of mediation.

This is a book about people, real people whose lives have often been full of suffering and struggle, and who come back to us as we write, in their full humanity as individuals and characters and stories. The reason our ethnographic approach tries to deal with such a huge constellation of different factors is because that corresponds to the natural holism of all these individuals. They in their lives have to deal with all these things at once. They cannot separate out the influence of their state, the needs of their children, their sense of personal autonomy, the issues of debt, and the ways they use new media to negotiate some of the above into separate compartments. In their lives all these things come together.

It may then appear reprehensible to end the book with a chapter on theory, since this might seem to only add to the dehumanising objectification that takes them from their individuality as persons to this level of abstraction. But when theory is used appropriately, it can be respected as an essential component to understanding and comprehension. Its value lies in its ability to advance us from a condition in which we incorrectly assumed that we understood what it is we have observed. Our theoretical propositions were not some ideological premise. They emerged only at the end of our attempts to analyse the vast body of materials that arose from interviews and observations and simply our experience of coming to know the people whose stories populate this volume. It was those people who forced us to appreciate how much of that apparent understanding was based on faulty presumptions and opinions, often projected onto the material, which in many respects is very different from what we had initially anticipated. This is why it is fitting for theory to be the end result of this project, not its initial hypothesis. It should not represent merely the fitting of our observations into some given theoretical debate within media theory, migration theory, or feminism. It should rather be a humble acknowledgement that these same people, these Filipina mothers and their children, have taught us much that we previously did not face up to, or comprehend.

APPENDIX

A note on method

This book is based on a long-term (2007–2010) ethnography with Filipino transnational families in the UK and the Philippines. The research was funded by the ESRC as part of the award on 'Migration, ICTs and the transformation of transnational family life' (RES-000-22-2266).

Our research was comparative in nature. One dimension was transnational, comparing the perspectives between migrant parents and left-behind children. This way we were able to capture the dynamic nature of transnationalism as web of relationships, moving beyond categories such as identity and the nation (Wimmer and Glick-Schiller, 2002; Beck, 2007). The other dimension was diachronic, as we were comparing people's experiences of interactive, frequent and cheaper communication made possible through developments in new media to their accounts of the past situation when keeping in touch depended on infrequent letters and very expensive phone calls. Finally, our comparisons also involved the different technologies and media available to people.

Our research took place between 2007 and 2010 and consisted of three phases. The first period of research was UK-based and began in the summer of 2007 and continued throughout 2008. During this time we developed links with Filipino networks and associations such as the Filipino community in Cambridge and the Centre for Filipinos in London where we spent several Sundays. Cambridge has a large population of Filipino nurses following the systematic recruitment by the University Hospital, Addenbrookes. The East Anglia NHS Trusts (which include Addenbrookes, Cambridge) have the largest concentration of nurses from the Philippines across the UK (estimated between 3,000 to 4,000, see *Guardian*, 2006), which is the reason why we chose Cambridge as one of our fieldwork sites. Not counted in this figure is a significant population of care-home workers on 'student' visa schemes (explained in Chapter 2) many of whom are also based in Cambridgeshire. The Centre for Filipinos in West London – chosen because it is the only Centre of its kind serving the Filipino community in the capital – proved a key site for our research as it was heavily frequented by migrants, especially domestic workers, for its legal surgeries, consultancy services and social events. Given that we were researching an often hidden population of domestic workers and undocumented migrants, the Centre was essential for enabling us to meet what is otherwise an elusive population. The Centre also offers Sunday IT and English language classes which gave us an opportunity to witness the acquisition and development of digital literacy among some of our informants over a period of over two years. During this time we also attended several festivals in South and West London, such as those for the Philippine Independence Day and the *Barrio Fiestas* where we also met some of our participants.

Apart from these more ethnographic encounters during this initial phase, we also conducted 53 in-depth interviews with Filipina domestic workers and nurses in London and Cambridge, most of whom are mothers with children in the Philippines and most of whom arrived in the UK following stints in the Middle East or Hong Kong. Twenty-eight of these participants arrived in the UK between 1973 and the mid-1990s, while the rest came after 2000. The majority of participants were documented, although several had experienced visa problems at some point during their migration. We tried to keep a balance between health workers and domestics, and we also interviewed some self-employed entrepreneurs, office staff and retired women (many of whom had arrived as domestics). The average number of children per mother was 2.43 (a considerable drop from the average number of siblings per participant, which was 6.04) and the average period of separation was 15.65 years. On average our participants visited their left-behind families every 1.6 years, while the average period between initial migration and first return visit was 2.6 years.

This first research phase was followed by fieldwork in the Philippines during 2008/9 where we interviewed the (now young adult) children of some of these mothers as well as other left-behind children. In total we conducted 53 in-depth interviews during this period, and we met several others as part of our ethnographic encounter. Approximately half of our participants had been separated from their mothers in early childhood when communication was scarce and expensive. The other half of our sample had experienced separation more recently after the introduction of mobile phones and internet-based communication. Most of these participants had been older (over the age of 10) at the time of their mother's migration. The families we worked with were based in Metropolitan Manila and four of the surrounding provinces (Batangas, Bulacan, Cavite and Laguna). Additionally, while in the Philippines we also interviewed representatives from government agencies and regulatory bodies dealing with migration as well as officials from migration agencies, advocacy groups and telecommunications companies. We also attended the mandatory Pre-Departure Orientation Seminars organised by the Philippine Overseas Employment Agency for migrants prior to their deployment to the UK.

On returning from the Philippines, we re-interviewed and maintained contact with 12 of our initial informants. By that stage we had established a very strong rapport with these participants, having met their families back home and having carried their gifts and messages across continents, and this level of trust is reflected in these interviews. The longitudinal dimension in this study has also been crucial, as it was during the actual research fieldwork that several of our participants (though not all) adopted new media and began to use them for communicating with their children.

In total we interviewed 106 participants (several of whom we interviewed more than once) and were able to pair 20 mothers and children. Although we offered all participants the option of having the interview in Tagalog, only four opted for that, and all other interviews were in English, reflecting its status as official language. All interviews followed a semi-structured topic guide that included questions about life history, key relationships, an account of the precedents of migration within the family and a history of media consumption for interpersonal communication. Mothers were asked about their trajectories of migration, their motivations for migrating and (not) returning, as well as their plans for their future. Left-behind children were asked about their memories of separation and family reunion as well as current circumstances and future plans. All were asked about their experience of long-distance communication and the range of different media that are used to sustain it. Although we broadly followed this topic guide, we also allowed the interview to flow, an approach which often lead to welcome surprises. All interviews were recorded, transcribed, anonymised and analysed thematically. In addition to such formal interviewing, the long-term nature of our project allowed for a substratum of ethnographic participation as we got to understand the conditions of work and living both in England and in the Philippines, where we also developed a close understanding of the institutions of migration. We also asked our participants, both in England and the Philippines, to share their actual correspondences, including letters, cassette tapes, photographs, text messages, emails and IM transcripts. Although we did not formally analyse all of these, being able to access them proved an invaluable source of information. Finally we 'friended' some of our participants on social media such as Facebook, which was crucial in complementing the more traditional participant observation as we hung-out with our friends at the Centre for Filipinos, got invited to their places for meals and *meriendas*, went with them to *Barrio Fiestas* and restaurants, formed opinions as to whose *palitaw*, *halo halo* and *pancit* tasted best, came to know their children and in general developed the natural friendships of fieldwork.

NOTES

Chapter 1: Introduction

1 We follow here Livingstone's definition of media literacy as the 'ability to access, analyze, evaluate, and create messages in a variety of forms' (Livingstone, 2004, drawing on Aufderheide, 1993). Access is an integral part of what constitutes media literacy. According to Livingstone's approach, media literacy is an ongoing process given that technologies constantly evolve. Media literacy then can only momentarily be established as it needs to continually evolve in parallel with changing technologies.

2 In our sample the average period between visits was 1.6 years; see Appendix for a discussion of the study's method.

Chapter 2: The Philippines and globalisation

1 Precisely, 8,187,710 in December 2008 (POEA, 2009).

2 See *Guardian* (2011), www.guardian.co.uk/world/2011/feb/23/nursing-dream-filipinos-uk-jobs?INTCMP=SRCH.

3 Data for internet users are not readily available. The latest government figures for subscriptions to registered internet service providers are from 2004 when there were 1.2 million subscribers (NTC, 2006). According to the World Bank, in 2008 there were 5.6 million subscribers, that is 6.2 per cent of the population (World Bank, 2010: data.worldbank.org/indicator/IT.NET.USER). However, according to media reports, the industry estimates users between 24 and 35 million, that is anything between 30 and 44 per cent of the population. According to research by A. C. Nielsen most users (70%) access the internet from internet cafes: www.mb.com.ph/articles/250369/philippine-internet-numbers. Pertierra (2010: 4) gives overall figures of 25 per cent internet access and 80 per cent mobile phone possession by 2009.

4 For example, in early 2009 a dongle cost 2,800 PHP (30 GBP) while the cost of accessing the internet was an additional considerable expense. At that time a teacher's monthly salary was around 8,000 PHP (88 GBP).

5 Although, as already indicated, this initial cost is significant (and may often not even be an option).

6 According to the International Telecommunications Union, see: www.itu.int/ITU-D/ict/newslog/Mobile+Penetration+Rate+Reaches+The+Mark+Of+75+At+2008end+Philippines.aspx.

7 For recent discussions of Filipino transnational communications, see Aguilar *et al.*, 2009: 204–221 and Pertierra, 2010: 26–27, 124–148, 184–186.

Chapter 3: Why they go – and why they stay

1 A convenience store, from the Tagalog word *sari sari*, meaning variety.
2 The Filipino festivals that take place in London parks during the summer months such as that to celebrate Philippine Independence Day on 12 June.
3 Note that 'middle class' in the Philippines is not a comfortable category but one characterised by insecurities and uncertainties (see Parreñas, 2001).
4 The option is to have the marriage annulled.
5 At least until the 2008 economic crisis which saw the pound devalue by about 20 per cent.
6 Pilar is one of the few who told us that it was not worth it, but now that she has come over she is trapped in this situation and because of her bad health she has no choice – she could not afford private healthcare in the Philippines. But hers is an exceptional story given her several traumatic experiences during previous stages in her migration (including rape and abuse).

Chapter 5: The mothers' perspective

1 An additional explanation is the value and recognition that imported goods enjoy in the Philippines, as participants often told us spaghetti or spam from London tastes better than the local version. We even saw some *balikbayan* gifts – ordinary groceries such as olive oil or pasta – displayed in glass cabinets in our participants' homes.
2 Multiply at the time of fieldwork was very popular in the Philippines and was initially designed with families as one of its target groups of users.

Chapter 7: The technology of relationships

1 The recent expansion of mobile internet is a welcome development, but remains an expensive option for most of our participants' families, and those who used it were not always been satisfied by its performance. For a full discussion of internet availability see Chapter 2.
2 Several approaches have linked social cues with emotional communication (for a discussion see Baym, 2010: 53–54).
3 Such entrepreneurial activities associated with mobile phones are also reported in the wider literature on ICTs in developing countries (see Castells *et al.*, 2006).
4 A local idiom that combines Tagalog (the national language) with English terms (see Rafael, 1995).
5 The recent popularisation of Facebook among low-income Filipinos has been described through the derogatory term *Jejemon*, which refers to a particular usage of English and text-speak that is grammatically incorrect (see Ong and Cabanes, 2011).
6 This pattern was different in London where class distinctions were, if anything, accentuated compared to the situation described at the start of the section. While in the Philippines it is almost unthinkable to refuse a friend's request, in London we can see a separation emerging between the health service workers and the domestic workers where the former refuse friends' requests from the latter.
7 Florencia was unable to join her brother as she was already 18 and therefore not eligible for a visa as a dependent.
8 Komito (2011 in press) notes from his work with Filipinos in Ireland that social networking seems to suit diaspora groups whose orientation is more towards their own community than towards the host community, as it facilitates a kind of bonding through

low-level mutual awareness amongst the dispersed community. It also leads to a wider exchange across kin rather than merely through dyadic relationships (McKay, 2011).

9 Although boyd (2010) uses the term 'scalability' to refer to the potential visibility of content on SNS.

10 Although it has become very fashionable and popular since 2009.

Chapter 8: Polymedia

1 Couldry's recent (2011) development of the notion of the 'media manifold' to describe the complex web of delivery platforms also hints towards the same direction as polymedia.

2 The research reported in this book is part of a wider comparative publicly funded study on migration and transnational communication among Philippine and Caribbean migrant families.

Chapter 9: A theory of mediated relationships

1 Couldry (2012) points out the increasing convergence between approaches to mediation as discussed in this volume (Couldry, 2008, Livingstone, 2009b and Silverstone, 2005) and mediatisation (Hepp, 2009; Krotz, 2009) which agree on the holistic understanding of communication without share the more technological determinist notions of 'the logic of the medium' (see Hjavard, 2008). Couldry in recent writings even prefers the notion of mediatisation following the emerging linguistic consensus (for a discussion see Couldry, 2012: Chapter 6).

2 This agency of digital photos and SNS profiles becomes evident in the case of the death of the account owner, when the profile continues to carry the sense of the person.

REFERENCES

Abu-Lughod, L. (1989) 'Bedouins, cassettes and technologies of public culture', *Middle East Reports* 159: 7–11.

Acacio, K. (2008) 'Managing labor migration: Philippine state policy and intenational migration flows, 1969–2000', *Asian and Pacific Migration Journal* 17: 103–132.

Aguilar, F. (1996) 'The dialectics of transnational shame and national identity', *Philippine Sociological Review* 44(1–4): 101–136.

Aguilar, F. (2002a) 'Beyond stereotypes: human subjectivity of the structuring of global migrations', in Aguilar, F. (ed.), *Filipinos in Global Migrations: at home in the world?*, Quezon City: Philippine Social Science Council, pp. 1–36.

Aguilar, F. (2002b) 'Ritual passage and the reconciliation of selfhood', in Aguilar, F. (ed.), *Filipinos in Global Migrations: at home in the world?*, Quezon City: Philippine Social Science Council.

Aguilar, F. (2005) 'Tracing origins: Ilustrado nationalism and the racial science of migration waves', *Journal of Asian Studies* 64(3): 605–637.

Aguilar, F. with Penalosa, J., Liwana, T., Cruz, I. and Melendrez, J. (2009) *Maalwang Buhay: family, overseas migration, and cultures in relatedness in barangay Paraiso*, Manila: Ateneo de Manila University Press.

Alm, A. and Ferrell Lowe, G. (2001) 'Managing transformation in the public polymedia enterprise: amalgamation and synergy in Finnish public broadcasting', *Journal of Broadcasting and Electronic Media* 45(3): 367–390.

Amrith, M. (2010) 'They think we are just caregivers: the ambivalence of care in the lives of Filipino medical workers in Singapore', *Asia Pacific Journal of Anthropology* 11(3–4): 410–427.

Arellano-Caradang, M. L., Sison, B. A. and Caradang, C. (2007) *Nawala Ang Ilaw Ng Tahanan, Case Studies of Families Left Behind by OFW Mothers*, Manila: Anvil.

Asis, M. M. B. (1995) 'Overseas employment and social transformation in source communities: findings from the Philippines', *Asian and Pacific Migration Journal* 4(2/3): 327–346.

Asis, M. M. B. (2002) 'From the life stories of Filipino women: personal and family agendas in migration', *Asian and Pacific Migration Journal* 11: 67–93.

Asis, M. M. B. (2005) 'Caring for the world: Filipino domestic workers gone global', in S. Huang, B. Yeoh and N. A. Rahman (eds), *Asian Women as Transnational Domestic Workers*, Singapore: Marshall and Cavendish Academic, pp. 21–53.

Asis, M. M. B. (2008) 'The Philippines', *Asian and Pacific Migration Journal* 17(3–4): 349–378.

Asis, M. M. B., Huang, S. and Yeoh, B. (2004) 'When the light of the home is abroad: unskilled female migration and the Filipino family', *Singapore Journal of Tropical Geography* 25(2): 198–215.

Aufderheide, P. (Ed.), (1993). *Media literacy: a report of the national leadership conference on media literacy*, Aspen, CO: Aspen Institute.

Baldassar, L. (2007) 'Transnational families and the provision of moral and emotional support: the relationship between truth and distance', *Identities* 14(4): 285–409.

Barton, D. and Hall, N. (eds) (2000) *Letter Writing as a Social Practice*, Amsterdam: John Benjamins.

Basso, K. (1974) 'The ethnography of writing', in R. Bauman and J. Sherzer (eds), *Explorations in the Ethnography of Speaking*, Cambridge: Cambridge University Press, pp. 452–432.

Baym, N. (2010) *Personal Connections in the Digital Age*, Cambridge: Polity.

Beck, U. (2007) 'The cosmopolitan condition. Why methodological nationalism fails', *Theory, Culture and Society* 24(7–8): 286–290.

Beck-Gernsheim, E. (2002) *Reinventing the Family*, Cambridge: Polity.

Berker, T., Hartmann, M., Punie, Y. and Ward, K. (eds) (2006) *Domestication of Media and Technology*, Open University Press.

Bolter, J. D. and Grusin, R. (2000) *Remediation: understanding new media*, Cambridge, MA: MIT Press.

Borjas, G. (1989) 'Economic theory and international migration', *International Migration Review* 23(3): 457–485.

Bourdieu, P. (1984) *Distinction: a social critique of the judgement of style*, London: Routledge.

Bowlby, J. (2005) *A Secure Base*, London: Routledge.

boyd, d. (2010) 'Social networking sites as networked publics: affordances, dynamics, implications', in Z. Papacharissi (ed.), *A Networked Self*, London and New York: Routledge.

boyd, d. and Ellison, N. (2007) 'Social networking sites: definition, history and scholarship', *Journal of Computer Mediated Communication* 13(1), http://jcmc.indiana.edu/vol13/issue1/boyd.ellison.html, accessed 1 May 2011.

Boyd, M. (1989) 'Family and personal networks in international migration', *International Migration Review* 23(3): 638–670.

Brandewie, E. (1998) 'Maids in Cebuano society', *Philippine Quarterly of Culture and Society* 26: 3–13.

Brinkerhoff, J. (2009) *Digital Diasporas*, Cambridge: Cambridge University Press.

Broadbent, S. (2011) *L'Intimite' au Travail*, Paris: Fyp Editions.

Búriková, Z. and D. Miller (2010) *Au Pair*, Cambridge: Polity.

Cannell, F. (1999) *Power and Intimacy in the Christian Philippines*, Cambridge: University of Cambridge Press.

Carr, N. (2010) *The Shallows: how the internet is changing the way we think, read and remember*, London: Atlantic Books.

Carsten, J. (1997) *The Heat of the Hearth: the process of kinship in a Malay fishing community*, Oxford: Clarendon.

Carstern, J. (ed.) (2000) *Cultures of Relatedness: new approaches to the study of kinship*, Cambridge: Cambridge University Press.

Castells, M., Fernandez-Ardevol, M., Qiu, J. L. and Sey, A. (2006) *Mobile Communication and Society: a global perspective*, Cambridge, MA: MIT Press.

Castles, S. and Miller, M. (2009) *The Age of Migration. International Population Movements in the Modern World*, 4th edn, London: Palgrave.

Chesley, N. (2005) 'Blurring boundaries? Linking technology use, spillover, individual distress, and family satisfaction', *Journal of Marriage and Family* 67: 1237–1248.

Chouliaraki, L. (2006) *The Spectatorship of Suffering*, London: Sage.

Choy, C. (2003) *Empire of Care: nursing and migration in Filipino American history*, Chapel Hill: Duke University Press.

Clarke, E. (1957) *My Mother Who Fathered Me*, London: Allen and Unwin.

Clark, J. (2004) 'Filipino women in Tasmania: negotiating gender ideologies', *Asian and Pacific Migration Journal* 13(3): 363–380.

Constable, N. (1997) 'Sexuality and discipline among Filipina domestic workers in Hong Kong', *American Ethnologist* 24: 539–558.

Constable, N. (1999) 'At home but not at home: Filipina narratives of ambivalent returns', *Cultural Anthropology* 14(2): 203–228.

Constable, N. (2009) 'The commodification of intimacy: marriage, sex, and reproductive labor', *Annual Revue of Anthropology* 38: 49–64.

Couldry, N. (2000) *The Place of Media Power. Pilgrims and Witnesses in a Media Age*, London: Routledge.

Couldry, N. (2008) 'Mediatization or mediation: alternative understandings of the emergent space of digital storytelling', *New Media and Society* 10(3): 373–391.

Couldry, N. (2011) 'The necessary future of the audience … and how to research it', in V. Nightingale (ed.), *Handbook of Media Audiences*, Cambridge, MA: Blackwell, pp. 213–229.

Couldry, N. (2012) *Media, Society, World: Social Theory and Digital Media Practice*, Cambridge: Polity.

Danet, B. (1997) 'Books, letters, documents', *Journal of Material Culture* 2: 5–38.

David, R. (2001) *Reflections on Sociology and Philippine Society*, Manila: University of Philippines Press.

Decker, W. (1998) *Epistolary Practices: letter writing in America before telecommunications*, Chapel Hill: University of North Carolina Press.

DeJong, G. *et al.* (1983) 'International and internal migration decision making: a value expectancy based on analytical framework of intentions to move from a rural Philippine province', *International Migration Review* 17(3): 470–484.

DeJong, G. *et al.* (1986) 'Family reunification and Philippine migration to the United States: the immigrants' perspective, *International Migration Review* 22(3): 598–612.

Dreby, J. (2006) 'Honor and virtue: Mexican parenting in the transnational context', *Gender and Society* 20(1): 32–59.

Earle, R. (ed.) (1999) *Epistolary Selves: letters and Letter-Writers, 1600–1945*, Aldershot: Ashgate.

Edillon, R. (2008) *The Effects of Parents' Migration on the Rights of Children Left Behind*, Manila: Unicef.

Eisenlohr, P. (ed.) (2011) 'What is medium? Theologies, technologies and aspirations', *Social Anthropology* 19: 1.

Ellwood-Clayton, B. (2005) 'Desire and loathing in the cyber Philippines', in R. Harper, L. Palen and A. Taylor (eds), *The Inside Text: social, cultural and design perspectives on SMS*, Springer, pp. 195–219.

Ellwood-Clayton, B. (2006) 'Unfaithful: reflections of enchantment, disenchantment and the mobile phone', in J. Hoflich and M. Hartmann (eds), *Mobile Communication in Everyday Life: ethnographic views, observations and reflections*, Leipzig: Frank and Timme, pp. 123–144.

Engelke, M. (2007) *A Problem of Presence: beyond Scripture in an African church*, Berkeley: University of California Press.

Engelke, M. (2010) 'Religion and the media turn: a review essay', *American Ethnologist* 37: 371–379.

Le Espiritu, Y. (1996) 'Colonial oppression, labour importation, and group formation: Filipinos in the United States', *Ethnic and Racial Studies* 19(1): 29–48.

Le Espiritu, Y. (2002) 'Filipino navy stewards and Filipina health care professionals: immigration, work and family relations', *Asian and Pacific Migration Journal* 11: 47–65.

Faier, L. (2007) 'Filipina migrants in rural Japan and their professions of love', *American Ethnologist* 34: 148–162.

Foucault, M. (1988) 'Technologies of the self', in L. H. Martin, H. Gutman and P. H. Hutton (eds), *Technologies of the Self: a seminar with Michel Foucault*, London: Tavistock.

Fresnoza-Flot, A. (2009) 'Migration status and transnational mothering: the case of Filipino migrants in France', *Global Networks* 9(2): 252–270.

Fulk, J. and Collins-Jarvis, L. (2001) 'Wired meetings: technological mediation and organisational gatherings', in F. M. Jablin and L. L. Putnam, *The New Handbook of Organisational Communication*, Thousand Oaks: Sage.

Gell, A. (1998) *Art and Agency*, London: Clarendon Press.

Gershon, I. (2010) *The Breakup 2.0*, Ithaca: Cornell University Press.

Giddens, A. (1991) *Modernity and Self-Identity: self and society in the late modern age*, Cambridge: Polity.

Gibson, J. J. (1979) *The Ecological Approach to Perception*, London: Houghton Mifflin.

Gillespie, M. *et al.* (2010) 'Mapping digital diasporas @ the BBC World Service: users and uses of the Persian and Arabic websites', *Middle East Journal of Culture and Communication* 3(2): 256–278.

Glenn, N. E. (1994) 'Social constructions of mothering: a thematic overview', in N. E. Glenn, G. Chang and L. R. Forcey (eds), *Mothering: Ideology, Experience, Agency*, New York: Routledge.

Glenn, N. E., G. Chang and L. R. Forcey (eds) (1994) *Mothering: Ideology, Experience, Agency*, New York: Routledge.

Glick Schiller, N., Basch., L. and Blanc Szanton, C. (1992) 'Towards a definition of transnationalism', in L. Basch, N. Glick Schiller and C. Blanc Szanton (eds), *Towards a Transnational Perspective on Migration: race, class, ethnicity and nationalism reconsidered*, New York: New York Academy of Sciences, pp. ix–xiv.

Go, S. (1993) *The Filipino Family in the Eighties*, Social Development Research Centre. Manila: De La Salle University.

Goody, J. (ed.) (1968) *Literacy in Traditional Societies*, Cambridge: Cambridge University Press.

Golombok, S. (2000) *Parenting: what really counts?* New York: Routledge.

Grint, K. and Woolgar, S. (1997) *The Machine at Work; technology, work and organisation*, Cambridge: Polity.

Guardian (2006) 'Filipinos in Cambridge', 23 January 2006, www.guardian.co.uk/uk/2006/jan/23/britishidentity.features114?INTCMP=SRCH, accessed 1 July 2011.

Hargittai, E. (2002) 'Second level digital divide: differences in people's online skills', *First Monday* 7(4), http://firstmonday.org/htbin/cgiwrap/bin/ojs/index.php/fm/article/view/942/864, accessed.

Hargittai, E. and Hinnant, A. (2008) 'Digital inequality: differences in young adults' use of the internet', *Communication Research* 35(5): 602–621.

Hargittai, E. and Welejko, G. (2007) 'The participation divide: content creation and sharing in the digital age', *Information, Communication and Society* 11(2): 239–256.

Hays, S. (1997) *The Cultural Contradictions of Motherhood*, New Haven: Yale University Press.

Haythornthwaite, C. (2005) 'Social networks and internet connectivity effects', *Information, Communication & Society* 8(2): 125–147.

Hepp, A. (2009). 'Differentiation: Mediatization and Cultural Change', in K. Lundby (ed.), *Mediatization: Concept, Changes, Consequences*, New York: Peter Lang, pp. 135–154.

Hjarvard, S. (2008) 'The mediatization of society: a theory of media as agents of social and cultural change', *Nordicom Review* 29(2): 105–134.

Hochschild, A. (2000) 'Global care chains and emotional surplus value', in W. Hutton and A. Giddens (eds), *On The Edge: living with global capitalism*, London: Jonathan Cape.

Hollway, W. (2001) 'From motherhood to maternal subjectivity', *International Journal of Critical Psychology* 2: 13–38.

Hollway, W. and Featherstone, B. (1997) *Mothering and Ambivalence*, London: Routledge.

Hondagneu-Sotelo, P. and Avila, E. (1997) ' "I'm here, but I'm there": the meanings of Latina transnational motherhood', *Gender and Society* 11(5): 538–571.

Horst, H. (2006) 'The blessings and burdens of communication: cell phones in Jamaican transnational social fields', *Global Networks* 6(2): 143–159.

Horst, H. A. and Miller, D. (2006) *The Cell Phone: an anthropology of communication*, Oxford: Berg.

Hutchby, I. (2001) 'Technologies, texts and affordances', *Sociology* 35: 441–456.

Ilano, A. (2005) 'The Philippines telecoms sector', in R. Rodriguez and J. Albarracin, *Analysis of Selected Philippine Industries Vol 1*, Quezon City: UP Press.

ILO (2007) *Labour and Social Trends in ASEAN 2007*, Bangkok: International Labour Organisation Regional Office for Asia and the Pacific.

Iyer, A., Devasahayam, T. and Yeoh, B. (2004) 'A clean bill of health: Filipina as domestic workers in Singapore', *Asian and Pacific Migration Journal* 13(1): 11–38.

Jackson, R. (1994) *Mothers Who Leave: beyond the myth of women without their children*, London: Harper Collins.

Jaffe, A. (1999) 'Packaged sentiments: the social meanings of greeting cards', *Journal of Material Culture* 4(2): 115–141.

Jenkins, H. (2006) *Convergence Culture. Where old and new media collide*, New York: New York University Press.

Jha, S., Sugiyarto, G. and Vargas Silva, C. (2009) *The Global Crisis and the Impact on Remittances to Developing Asia*, Economics Working Paper Series, no. 185, Manila: Asian Development Bank.

Jocano, F. L. (2001) *Filipino World View: ethnography of local knowledge*, Quezon City: Punlad Research House.

Johnson, M. (1997) *Beauty and Power. Transgendering and cultural transformations in the southern Philippines*, Oxford: Berg.

Johnson, M. (1998) 'At home and abroad: inalienable wealth, personal consumption and the formulations of femininity in the southern Philippines', in D. Miller (ed.), *Material Cultures*, Chicago: University of Chicago Press.

Komito, L. (2011 in press) 'Social media and migration: virtual community 2.0', *Journal of the American Society for Information Science and Technology*.

Krotz, F. (2009) 'Mediatization: a concept with which to grasp media and societal change', in K. Lundby (ed.), *Mediatization: Concept, Changes, Consequences*, New York: Peter Lang.

Lamvik, G. (2002) 'The Filipino Seafarer: A Life between Sacrifice and Shopping', Unpublished Dr. Art., Trondheim, Norwegian University of Science and Technology.

Lauby, J. and Stark, O. (1988) 'Individual migration as family strategy: young women in the Philippines', Cambridge, MA: Harvard University Migration and Development Program.

Latour, B. (1993) *We have never been modern*, Cambridge, MA: Harvard University Press.

Levi-Strauss, C. (1963) *Structural Anthropology*, New York: Basic Books.

Licoppe, C. (2004) ' "Connected" presence: the emergence of a new repertoire for managing social relationships in a changing communication technoscape', *Environment and Planning D: Society and Space* 22: 135–156.

Little, L., Sillence, E., Sellen, A. and Taylor, A. (2009) 'The family and communication technologies', *International Journal of Human Computer Studies* 67(2): 125–127.

Livingstone, S. (2002) *Young People and New Media: childhood and the changing media environment*, London: Sage.

Livingstone, S. (2004) 'Media literacy and the challenge of new information and communication technologies', *Communication Review* 7: 3–14.

Livingstone, S. (2009a) *Children and the Internet*, Cambridge: Polity.

Livingstone, S. (2009b) 'On the mediation of everything', *Journal of Communication* 59(1): 1–18.

Lofgren, O. (1993) 'The great Christmas quarrel and other Swedish traditions', in D. Miller (ed.), *Unwrapping Christmas*, Oxford: Oxford University Press.

Lynch, F. and Guzman, A. (1974) *Four Readings on Philippine Values*, 4th edn, Quezon City: Ateneo de Manila Press.

Maas, M. (2003) 'Harnessing transnational linkages for development: the case of Dutch-Filipino connections', *Asian and Pacific Migration Journal* 12(4): 501–514.

MacKenzie, D. and Wajcman, J. (1999) 'Introductory essay', in D. MacKenzie and J. Wajcman (eds), *The Social Shaping of Technology*, 2nd edn, Buckingham: Open University Press.

Madianou, M. (2005) *Mediating the Nation: news, audiences and the politics of identity*, London: UCL Press/Routledge.

Madianou, M. (2011) 'Beyond the presumption of identity? Ethnicities, cultures and transnational audiences', in V. Nightingale (ed.), *Handbook of Media Audiences*, Cambridge, MA: Blackwell, pp. 444–458.

Madianou, M. (2012a) 'Migration and the accentuated ambivalence of motherhood', *Global Networks* (accepted, scheduled for July 2012).

Madianou, M. (2012b) 'News as a looking glass: shame and the symbolic power of mediation', *International Journal of Cultural Studies* 15(2) first published on August 11, 2011 as doi: 10.1177/1367877911411795.

Madianou, M. and Miller, D. (2011a) 'Mobile phone parenting: reconfiguring relationships between migrant Filipina mothers and their left-behind children', *New Media and Society* 12(3): 457–470.

Madianou, M., and Miller, D. (2011b) 'Crafting love: letters and cassette tapes in transnational Filipino communication', *South East Asia Research* 19(2): 249–272.

Madianou, M. and Miller, D. (in preparation) 'Polymedia, communication and long distance relationships'.

Malinowski, B. (1923) 'The problem of meaning in primitive languages', in C. K. Ogden and I. A. Richards (eds), *The Meaning of Meaning*, London: Routledge, pp. 146–152.

Manuel, P. (1993) *Cassette Culture: popular music and technology in north India*, Chicago: University of Chicago Press.

Marcus, G. (1995) 'Ethnography in/of the world system: the emergence of multi-sited ethnography', *Annual Review of Anthropology* 24: 95–117.

Marvin, C. (1988) *When Old Technologies Were New*, New York: Oxford University Press.

Massey, D. (1990) 'Social structure, household strategies, and cumulative causation of migration', *Population Index* 56: 3–26.

Massey, D., Arrango, J., Hugo, G., Kouaouci, A., Pellegrino, A. and Taylor, E. (1993) 'Theories of migration: a review and appraisal', *Population and Development Review* 19(3): 431–466.

Mauss, M. (1954) *The Gift*, London: Cohen and West.

McKay, D. (2007) '"Sending dollars shows feeling": emotions and economies in Filipino migration', *Mobilities* 2(2): 175–194.

McKay, D. (2008) 'Ghosts of futures present: photographs in the Filipino migrant archive', *Visual Anthropology* 21: 381–392.

McKay, D. (2011) 'On the face of Facebook: historical images and personhood in Filipino social networking', *History and Anthropology* (in press).

McLuhan, M. (2001) *Understanding Media*, 2nd edn, London: Routledge.

Medina, B. (2001) *The Filipino Family*, Manila: The University of the Philippines Press.

Merla, L. and Baldassar, L. (2008) 'Capabilities, wellness and social class', paper presented at COST-34 Symposium on Gender and Wellbeing, Barcelona, www.ub.es/tig/GWBNet/MadridPapers/Merla%20&%20Baldassar.pdf, accessed 30 July 2010.

Miller, D. (1987) *Material Culture and Mass Consumption*, Oxford: Blackwell.

Miller, D. (1997) 'How infants grow mothers in North London', *Theory, Culture and Society* 14(4): 67–88.

Miller, D. (2006) 'The unpredictable mobile phone', *BT Technology Journal* 24(3): 41–48.

Miller, D. (2007) 'What is a relationship? Kinship as negotiated experience', *Ethnos* 72(4): 535–554.

Miller, D. (2008a) *The Comfort of Things*, Cambridge: Polity.

Miller, D. (2008b) 'The uses of value', *Geoforum* 39: 1122–1132.

Miller, D. (2011) *Tales from Facebook*, Cambridge: Polity.

Miller, D. (in press) 'The digital and the human', in H. Horst and D. Miller (eds), *Digital Anthropology*, Oxford: Berg.

Miller, D. and Slater, D. (2000) *The Internet: an ethnographic approach*, Oxford: Berg.

Minges, M., Magpantay, E., Firth, L. and Kelly, T. (2002) *Pinoy Internet*, Geneva: International Telecommunication Union.

Mozere, L. (2005) 'Filipina women as domestic workers in Paris: a transnational labour-market enabling the fulfilment of life projects?', in E. Spaan, F. Hillman and T. van Naersen (eds), *Asian Migrants and European Labour Markets: patterns and processes of immigrant labour market insertion in Europe*, London: Routledge.

National Statistical Coordination Board (2007) *Philippine Statistical Yearbook*, Manila: NSO.

National Telecommunications Commission (NTC) (2006) Annual Report, http://portal.ntc.gov.ph/wps/html/ntc/reports/2006/Industry.pdf, accessed 6 April 2010.

Ong, J. and Cabanes, J. (2011) 'Engaged but not immersed: tracking the mediated public connection of Filipino elite migrants in London', *South East Asia Research* 19(2): 197–224.

Ong, W. (1982) *Orality and Literacy: the technologizing of the word*, London: Methuen.

Orwell, G. (1968) *The Collected Essays, Journalism, and Letters of George Orwell*, New York: Harcourt, Brace & World.

Paragas, F. (2009) Migrant workers and mobile phones: technological, temporal, and spatial simultaneity', in R. Ling and S. Campbell (eds), *The Reconstruction of Space and Time: mobile communication practices*, New Bruswick: Transaction Publishers, pp. 39–65.

Parker, R. (2005) *Torn in Two: the experience of maternal ambivalence*, London: Virago.

Parreñas, R. (2001) *Servants of Globalization, Women, Migration and Domestic Work*, Palo Alto: Stanford University Press.

Parreñas, R. (2005a) *Children of Global Migration: transnational families and gendered woes*, Palo Alto: Stanford University Press.

Parreñas, R. (2005b) 'Long distance intimacy: class, gender and intergenerational relations between mothers and children in Filipino transnational families', *Global Networks* 5(4): 317–336.

Parreñas, R. (2008) *The Force of Domesticity*, New York: New York University Press.

Pertierra, R. (2006) *Transforming Technologies, Altered Selves*, Manila: De La Salle University Press.

Pertierra, R. (2010) *The Anthropology of New Media in the Philippines*, Manila: Ateneo de Manila University Press.

Pertierra, R., Ugarte, E., Pingol, A., Hernandez, J. and Dacanay, N. (2002) *TXT-ING Selves: cellphones and Philippine modernity*, Manila: De La Salle University Press.

Pessar, P. (1999) 'The gole of gender, households, and social networks in the migration process: a review and appraisal', in C. Hirschman, P. Kasinitz and J. DeWind (eds), *The Handbook of International Migration: the American experience*, New York: Russell Sage Foundation, pp. 53–70.

Pingol, A. (2001) *Remaking Masculinities*, Diliman, Quezon City: University of the Philippines Press.

POEA (2008) and (2009) 2008 Overseas Employment Statistics, www.poea.gov.ph/stats/stats2007.pdf, accessed 19 March 2010.

Portes, A. (1995) 'Economic sociology and the sociology of immigration: a conceptual overview', in A. Portes (ed.), *The Economic Sociology of Immigration: essays on networks, ethnicity and entrepreneurship*, New York: Russell Sage Foundation.

Portes, A. and Rumbaut, R. (2006) *Immigrant America, a Portrait*, 3rd edn, Berkeley: University of California Press.

Rafael, V. (1993) *Contracting Colonialism: translation and Christian conversion in Tagalog society under early Spanish rule*, Durham: Duke University Press.

Rafael, V. (1995) 'Taglish or the phantom power of the lingua franca', *Public Culture* 8(1): 101–126.

Rafael, V. (1997) '"Your grief is our gossip": overseas Filipinos and other spectral presences', *Public Culture* 9(2): 267–291.

Rafael, V. (2003) 'The cell phone and the crowd: messianic politics in the contemporary Philippines', *Public Culture* 15(3): 399–425.

Rakow, L. F. and Navarro, V. (1993) 'Remote mothering and the parallel shift: women meet the cellular telephone', *Critical Studies in Mass Communication* 10(2): 144–157.

Reuters (2008) www.reuters.com/article/idUS94568+09-Jan-2008+PRN20080109, accessed 19 December 2010.

Reyes, M. (2008) *Migration and Filipino Children Left Behind: a literature review*, Manila: Unicef.

Rheingold, H. (2003) *Smartmobs: the next social revolution*, Cambridge, MA: Perseus.

Richman, K. (2005) *Migration and Vodou*, Gainsville: University of Florida Press.

Riley, D. (1983) *War in the Nursery. Theories of the child and mother*, London: Virago.

Rosaldo, M. Z. (1980) *Knowledge and Passion: Ilongot notions of self and social life*, Cambridge: Cambridge University Press.

Rosario, T. (2005) 'Bridal diaspora: migration and marriage among Filipino women', *Indian Journal of Gender Studies* 12(2–3): 253.

Rose, G. (2004) '"Everyone's cuddled up and it just looks really nice": an emotional geography of some mums and their family photos', *Social and Cultural Geography* 5(4): 549–564.

Rutter, M. (1981) *Maternal Deprivation Reassessed*, London: Penguin.

Salazar, L. (2007) *Getting a Dial Tone Telecommunication: liberalisation in Malaysia and the Philippines*, Singapore: Institute for SE Asian Studies.

Sampson, H. (2003) 'Transnational drifters or hyperspace dwellers: an exploration of the lives of Filipino seafarers aboard and ashore', *Ethnic and Racial Studies* 26: 253–277.

Sassen, S. (1988) *The Mobility of Labour and Capital*, Cambridge: Cambridge University Press.

Scheper-Hughes, N. (1993) *Death without Weeping: the violence of everyday life in Brazil*, Berkeley: University of California Press.

Siapera, E. (2010) *Cultural Diversity and Global Media*, Boston, MA: Blackwell.

Silverstone, R. (2005) 'Mediation and communication', in C. Calhoun, C. Rojek and B. Turner (eds), *Handbook of Sociology*, London: Sage, pp. 188–207.

Silverstone, R. and Hirsch, E. (1992) *Consuming Technologies*, London: Routledge.

Silvey, R. (2006) 'Consuming the transnational family: Indonesian migrant domestic workers to Saudi Arabia', *Global Networks* 6(1): 23–40.

Slater, D. and Tacchi, J. (2004) *Research: ICT innovations for poverty reduction*, New Delhi: Unesco.

Smart, C. and Neale, B. (1999) *Family Fragments?* Cambridge: Polity.

Sreberny-Mohammadi, A. and Mohammadi, A. (1994) *Small Media, Big Revolution*, London: Minnesota University Press.

Stafford, C. (2000) *Separation and Reunion in Modern China*, Cambridge: Cambridge University Press.

Stills, S. and Chowthis, N. (2008) 'Becoming an OFW: renegotiations in self-concept amongst Filipino factory workers in Taiwan', *Asian and Pacific Migration Journal* 17: 189–220.

Strathern, M. (1996) 'Cutting the network', *JRAI* (NS) 2: 517–535.

Suzuki, N. (2002) 'Women imagined, women imaging: representations of Filipina in Japan since the 1980's', in F. Aguilar (ed.), *At Home in the World?: Filipinos in Global Migrations*, pp. 176–206.

Swift, O. (2010) 'A model union village: Filipino international seafaring', Ph.D. thesis, Department of Anthropology, Goldsmiths College, London.

Szanton, B. (1996) 'Balikbayan: a Filipino extension of the national imaginary and of state boundaries', *Philippine Sociological Review* 44: 178–193.

Tacoli, C. (1996) 'Migrating "for the sake of the family"? Gender, life course and intra-household relations amongst Filipino migrants in Rome', *Philippine Sociological Review* 44: 12–36.

Tacchi, J., Slater, D. and Hearn, G. (2003) *Ethnographic Action Research*, New Delhi: Unesco.

Tadiar, N. (1997) 'Domestic bodies of the Philippines', *Sojourn: Journal of Social Issues in Southeast Asia*, special issue on Southeast Asian Diasporas, V. L. Rafael and I. Abraham (eds), 12(2): 153–191.

Tan, E. (2001) 'Labor market adjustments to large scale emigration: the Philippine case', *Asian and Pacific Migration Journal* 10: 379–400.

Thomas, W. I. and Znaniecki, F. (1996) *The Polish Peasant in Europe and America. A classic work in immigration history*, ed. E. Zaretsky, Urbana: University of Illinois Press.

Thompson, E. (2009) 'Mobile phones, communities and networks among foreign workers in Singapore', *Global Networks* 9(3): 359–380.

Thompson, J. B. (1995) *The Media and Modernity*, Cambridge: Polity.

Tilly, C. (1990) 'Transplanted networks', in V. Yans-MacLoughlin (ed.), *Immigration Reconsidered*, New York and Oxford: Oxford University Press, pp. 79–95.

Todd, J. (ed.) (2003) *The Collected Letters of Mary Wollstonecraft*, London: Allan Lane.

Turkle, S. (2011) *Alone Together*, New York: Basic Books.

Tyner, J. (2000) 'Global cities and circuits of global labor', *Professional Geographer* 52: 61–74.

Tyner, J. (2002) 'The globalization of transnational labor migration and the Filipino family: a narrative', *Asian and Pacific Migration Journal* 11(1): 95–116.

Uy-Tioco, C. (2007) 'Overseas Filipino workers and text messaging: reinventing transnational mothering', *Continuum* 21(2): 253–265.

Vertovec, S. (2004) 'Cheap calls: the social glue of migrant transnationalism', *Global Networks* 4(2): 219–224.

Vertovec, S. (2009) *Transnationalism*, London and New York: Routledge.

Wajcman, J. (2002) 'Addressing technological change: the challenge to social theory', *Current Sociology* 50(3): 347–363.

Wajcman, J., Bittman, M. and Brown, J. (2008) 'Intimate connections: the impact of the mobile phone on work/life boundaries', in G. Goggin and L. Hjorth (eds), *Mobile Technologies: from telecommunications to media*, New York: Routledge, pp. 9–22.

Widding Isaksen, L., Uma Devi, S. and Hochschild, A. (2008) 'Global care crisis: a problem of capital, care chain, or commons?', *American Behavioral Scientist* 52: 405–425.

Wikan, U. (1990) *Managing Turbulent Hearts: a Balinese formula for living*, Chicago: University of Chicago Press.

Wilding, R. (2006) '"Virtual" intimacies? Families communicating across transnational contexts', *Global Networks* 6(2): 125–142.

Williams, R. (1977) *Keywords*, London: Fontana.

Williams, R. (1984) *Television: technology and cultural form*, London: Routledge.

Wimmer, A. and Glick-Schiller, N. (2002) 'Methodological nationalism and beyond: nation-state building, migration and the social sciences', *Global Networks* 2: 301–334.

Winnicott, D. (1971) *Playing and Reality*, London: Tavistock.

Winnicott, D. H. (1975) 'Hate in the countertransference', in *Collected Essays: from paediatrics to psychoanalysis*, London: Karnac.

Wolf, D. (1997) 'Family secrets: transnational struggles amongst children of Filipino immigrants', *Sociological Perspectives* 40(3): 457–482.

Yeates, N. (2004) 'Global care chains', *International Feminist Journal of Politics* 6(3): 369–391.

Zelizer, V. (1994) *Pricing the Priceless Child. The changing social value of children*, Princeton: Princeton University Press.

Zialcita, F. (2005) *Authentic though not Exotic*, Manila: Ateneo de Manila Press.

INDEX

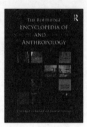